Excellence in Advertising

The Institute of Practitioners in Advertising is the trade association and professional body for UK advertising agencies. Its mission is to serve, promote and anticipate the collective interests of advertising agencies; and in particular to define, develop and help maintain the highest standards of professional practice within the advertising business.

The IPA's Seven Stages training programme, from which these contributions are drawn, provides continuous professional development for agency people from trainee to chief executive. Each course and workshop has been developed to provide the learning and support required at a particular stage in development, to encourage excellence at every level. This book and the Seven Stages programme are examples of the IPA mission in action.

Butterworth-Heinemann also publishes The Marketing Series, one of the most comprehensive collections of books in marketing and sales available from the UK today.

Produced in association with The Chartered Institute of Marketing, the series is divided into three distinct groups: *Student* (fulfilling the needs of those taking the Institute's certificate and diploma qualifications; *Professional Development* (for those on formal or self-study vocational training programmes); and *Practitioner* (presented in a more informal, motivating and highly practical manner for personal use).

Formed in 1911, The Chartered Institute of Marketing is now the largest professional marketing management body in Europe with over 60,000 members located worldwide. Its primary objectives are focused on the development of awareness and understanding of marketing throughout UK industry and commerce and on the raising of standards of professionalism in the education, training and practice of this key business discipline.

Excellence in Advertising
The IPA guide to best practice

Edited by
Leslie Butterfield

Butterworth-Heinemann
Linacre House, Jordan Hill, Oxford OX2 8DP
225 Wildwood Avenue, Woburn, MA 01801-2041
A division of Reed Educational and Professional Publishing Ltd

A member of the Reed Elsevier plc group

OXFORD   BOSTON   JOHANNESBURG
MELBOURNE   NEW DELHI   SINGAPORE

First published 1997
Reprinted 1997 (twice), 1998

British Library Cataloguing in Publication Data
Excellence in Advertising
  1. Advertising
  I. Butterfield, Leslie
  659.1

ISBN 0 7506 3129 5

Composition by Genesis Typesetting, Rochester, Kent
Printed and bound in Great Britain by MPG Books Ltd, Bodmin, Cornwall

This book is dedicated to the late Charles Channon, author of the original Seven Stages programme and inspiration to many of the contributors to this book

Contents

Contributors

John Bartle (*Joint Chief Executive, Bartle Bogle Hegarty*)
John Bartle began his career in 1965 with Cadbury's (later Cadbury Schweppes) as a marketing graduate trainee and worked there for eight years, latterly as Marketing Services Manager for the company's Foods Group. He left Cadbury Schweppes in 1973 to become a co-founder of the London office of the advertising agency TBWA. Initially TBWA's Planning Director, he became Joint Managing Director, with Nigel Bogle, in 1979, a position he held until leaving to start Bartle Bogle Hegarty in 1982. He is the current (1995–1997) President of the IPA (Institute of Practitioners in Advertising), is on the Council of the Advertising Association and is a Visiting Professor of Marketing at the University of Strathclyde.

Leslie Butterfield (*Chairman, BDDH*)
Leslie Butterfield was born in 1952, and graduated in 1975 with a First Class Honours degree in Business Studies from North East London Polytechnic and an MA in Marketing from Lancaster University. He joined Boase Massimi Pollitt (now BMP DDB) in the same year as an Account Planner, and was promoted to Associate Director in 1979. His accounts included Johnson & Johnson, CPC UK, Courage, Toyota and the Central Office of Information. In 1980 he joined the fledgling Abbott Mead Vickers as Planning Director and main Board member, with the brief of setting up an 'Account Planning' function within the agency. Over his seven years, AMV was one of UK's fastest-growing agencies and went public in 1985. It also developed one of London's most highly regarded planning departments. Leslie's account involvement at AMV included Sainsbury's, Volvo, Nabisco, Seagram, British Telecom, Carnation Foods and Yellow Pages. In 1987, Leslie left to set up his own agency, Butterfield Day Devito Hockney, the first of what came to be known as the 'Third Wave' of UK agencies. BDDH has gone from strength to strength over its independent ten-year history, and counts among its clients BT, Motorola, The Co-operative Bank, Sainsbury's Savacentre, Emirates Airline, Mercedes-Benz, Clerical Medical and Christian Aid. He has been Planning Director and

Chairman of the agency since its inception. Leslie is a frequent contributor to industry publications and often speaks at conferences and seminars. He was Chairman of the Account Planning Group from 1987 to 1989, and Chairman of the IPA's Training and Development Committee from 1989 to 1997. He was made a Fellow of the IPA in 1988.

Peter Doyle (*Professor, University of Warwick Business School*)
Peter Doyle has acted as consultant to many top international businesses and has run executive programmes for senior managers throughout Europe, the United States and the Far East. He has been voted 'Outstanding Teacher' on numerous university and corporate courses. In addition, he has published five books and over 100 articles in professional journals. He has a First Class Honours degree from the University of Manchester and an MBA and a PhD from Carnegie-Mellon University, United States.

Gary Duckworth (*Chairman, Duckworth Finn Grubb Waters*)
Gary Duckworth joined the advertising business in 1976 with a degree from Oxford University in philosophy, politics and economics, and has worked at BMP, Abbott Mead Vickers BBDO and Horner Collis and Kirvan. He set up Duckworth Finn Grubb Waters in 1989 and clients include Daewoo cars, Toshiba computers, the Independent Television Commission, Abbey National, the COI, HEA drugs education and Lyons coffee. DFGW has won creative awards in all the major festivals in the last two years including D&AD, Cannes, British Television and Creative Circle. He has written and spoken extensively on advertising topics, and authored the chapter on Brands and the Role of Advertising in *Understanding Brands* published in 1990. He was Convenor of Judges for the 1996 IPA Advertising Effectiveness awards.

Paul Feldwick (*Executive Planning Director, BMP DDB*)
Paul Feldwick was born in 1952. He took a First Class Honours degree in English Literature at Trinity College, Oxford, and in 1974 joined Boase Massimi Pollitt (now BMP DDB) as an account planner. He was head of Account Planning at BMP from 1988 to 1992 and is now Executive Planning Director. He was Convenor of Judges for the IPA Advertising Effectiveness Awards in 1988 and 1990, and editor of *Advertising Works 5* and *Advertising Works 6*. Paul has been Chairman of AQRP and APG and Chair of the IPA Research Working Party. He is a member of the Advertising Association's Economics Committee, preparing a report of advertising effects on category size. He was winner of the MRS 'Best Paper at Conference' 1990 and 1996 and is a Fellow of the IPA.

Chris Forrest (*Planning Director, Duckworth Finn Grubb Waters*)
Chris Forrest started his career in 1982 at the Qualitative Research Centre. In 1985 he moved with Barry Ross and Roddy Glen to set up the Strategic Research Group which grew to be one of the biggest qualitative research companies in the country. In 1986 he joined Ogilvy & Mather's planning department and was promoted to the board of Ogilvy & Mather in 1989, making him their youngest board director. In 1991 he joined Duckworth Finn Grubb Waters where he is Planning Director. He lectures regularly on IPA and MRS training courses. Chris has spoken about advertising on both LBC and Radio 4 and has contributed several articles to the marketing trade press. He has recently been elected Vice Chairman of the Account Planning Group. Chris lives in Wimbledon and is married to a qualitative researcher. They have three young respondents.

Roddy Glen (*Qualitative Researcher*)
Born in Glasgow in 1949, Roddy graduated from Strathclyde University in 1972 with a BA(Hons) in Marketing and Administration. He started his career in advertising in 1973 at CDP where he worked as an Account Executive on Whitbread, Heineken and Coty. In 1976 he left to travel the world. On returning to the UK, he joined Schlackman Surveys as a qualitative and quantitative researcher. After two years, he joined BMP as a qualitative researcher and remained in charge of the Research Department there until 1982 when he left to set up as a freelance researcher. In April 1985 he and Barry Ross founded the Strategic Research Group, one of the UK's most respected qualitative marketing research companies. Roddy teaches regularly on courses run by the Market Research Society, the IPA and the Association of Qualitative Research Practitioners, of which he was Chairman from 1987 to 1989. He lives in Rutland with his wife Maggie, an author and illustrator of children's books and his son, Calum, born in 1991. He now works as a freelance qualitative researcher and consultant.

Bruce Haines (*Chief Executive Officer, Leagas Delaney*)
Bruce Haines began his advertising career at Garland Compton in 1972, working as New Business Coordinator and on the national launch of Head & Shoulders shampoo for Procter & Gamble. After a couple of years, Bruce moved to the Kirkwood Company, and in 1977 to Young & Rubicam, where he was promoted to Account Director on Smirnoff, Croft Sherry, Rank Xerox, Kodak and, for the second time, Procter & Gamble. In 1983 he moved to Abbott Mead Vickers with account responsibilities for Smith's Foods, Britvic, Cow & Gate and Beecham and Northern Foods. He was appointed Client Services Director in 1984. Bruce was asked to become Managing Director at Leagas Delaney in 1986. The partnership with Creative Director Tim Delaney proved highly successful with twenty new accounts being gained and a highly creative reputation won for the agency.

In 1992, Bruce joined KHBB as CEO where he restructured the agency. Two years later he left, having been invited back to Leagas Delaney as CEO. He is Chairman of NABS, and Honorary Secretary of the IPA.

Steve Henry (*Creative Director, HHCL*)
Steve Henry was born in Hong Kong in September 1955 during a hurricane! He took a First in English Literature, Oxford University, 1978, and from 1981 to 1985 was a Copywriter at GGT where he worked on London Docklands, London Weekend Television, Holsten Pils and *Time Out*. From 1985 to 1987 he was a Group Creative Director at WCRS and worked on Carling Black Label, Midland Bank, Prudential and Tennents Extra. He set up Howell Henry Chaldecott Lury in 1987 and his 'favourite' clients since then include Molson lager, First Direct bank, Fuji Film, Danepak Bacon, Britvic Soft Drinks (including Tango), Mercury Communications, Martini, the Automobile Association and Mazda cars. HHCL was voted Campaign Agency of the Year in 1989 and 1994, Fuji was voted Advertiser of the Year 1990, and Tango was voted Campaign of the Year 1992. Steve has won many major creative awards, including a Gold pencil at D&AD, the Grand Prix at Cannes, the Grand Prix at British Television and the President's Award at Creative Circle. Steve is married with two daughters and lives in Wandsworth in south London.

Iain Jacob (*Director, Motive*)
Iain graduated from Nottingham University in 1982 with a degree in Chemistry. In 1983 he joined BMP as a media trainee, specializing in television and in 1987 became a founder member of the then newly formed media department at Bartle Bogle Hegarty. He was promoted to head of media buying in 1992 on the board of BBH, and in 1993 took over responsibility for BBH international clients. In July 1995 he was part of the management team who set up Motive, the media communications division of BBH. Iain remains a director of both BBH and Motive. Iain's client experience includes Audi, Levi's, Sony, Heineken, Girobank and Häagen-Dazs, among others. As well as teaching on IPA courses, Iain carries out various lecturing assignments for the Media Circle and has been Chairman of the media committee of the International Advertising Association.

Jim Kelly (*Managing Partner, Rainey Kelly Campbell Roalfe*)
Jim Kelly graduated in 1976 from Christ Church, Oxford where he read PPE. After a short spell at Wasey Campbell Ewald he joined Saatchi & Saatchi in 1978 and became an Account Director before moving to Gold Greenlees Trott in 1982. He worked on many of that agency's most famous accounts and was Managing Director from 1987 onwards. In 1993 he was reunited with his former colleague and planner M. T. Rainey to start up RKCR. In three years the agency has won clients such as *The*

Times, Virgin Atlantic, Miller Pilsner and Tia Maria (all in competitive pitches). Miller Pilsner was voted Campaign of the Year 1995. Jim is married with three daughters.

Michael J. Sommers (*Director, Paradigm Agency Ltd*)
Mike Sommers has worked in marketing for 25 years, although his career began as an Account Executive at JWT. From 1975 to 1983 he was at CPC (UK) Ltd moving from Senior Product Manager to Head of Marketing. From 1985 to 1991 he was at Woolworths plc, first as Marketing Director, then Business Director Entertainment and finally Commercial Director. After two years as Marketing and Premises Director, TSB Bank plc, he joined MGM Cinemas Ltd as Managing Director. Following the sale of MGM to the Virgin Group he set up his own marketing and management consultancy – the Paradigm Agency Ltd – in February 1996.

Foreword

The IPA Seven Stages programme provides continual professional development for advertising agency people from trainee to chief executive level. Each course and workshop is delivered by people who have achieved excellence in their field, whether they are advertising practitioners, business academics, marketeers or professional trainers. Over the years the reputation of the programme has continued to grow, not just in the UK but worldwide, despite the fact that courses are open only to IPA member agencies. Now, thanks to the vision and determination of Leslie Butterfield, the editor of this book, some of the more tangible evidence of this excellence is available to a wider audience.

The Institute of Practitioners in Advertising is dedicated to promoting the highest standards of professional practice within the advertising business. Advertising at its very best is a collaborative and cooperative process and this book, which shares wisdom from many sources and suggests best practice in many areas of advertising, is thus a highly relevant expression of what the IPA seeks to achieve.

Miranda Kennett
Director of Training & Development, IPA

Preface

This book was born of an idea. From 1989 to 1997, in addition to my full-time job as Chairman of one of the UK's top 30 advertising agencies, I have been Chairman of the IPA's Training and Development Committee – the body that designs, supervises and organizes the majority of the educational initiatives and courses for the UK's advertising agencies. The backbone of these courses is still the IPA's Seven Stages programme – designed to parallel the seven stages of development of a career in advertising, from graduate entrant to Chief Executive. This concept was originally conceived and designed by the late Charles Channon, to whom this book is dedicated.

Over the seven years, and still today, some of the finest talents in the UK advertising industry deliver some outstanding individual contributions on the courses on which they are speaking. What struck me, though – and was the idea behind this book – was that each of those individually excellent papers was reaching an annual audience of only a few dozen people! My aim in putting together this compilation of papers therefore is simple: to try to capture and record the very best of those contributions and make them available to a much wider audience in the future.

The authors of the individual chapters are themselves at the very top of their disciplines and, at the time of writing at least, will be known to most readers from the industry. For the reader from outside advertising, though, their profiles are described briefly in the List of Contributors. To each I owe a particular word of thanks, since writing a chapter for a book such as this is a much tougher task than producing speaking notes for an often quite informally delivered presentation to a small audience. Their efforts I hope are rewarded by the quality of this, the finished article!

It is also worth saying a word or two about the context in which this book has been produced. The first half of the 1990s has been undoubtedly the toughest period in the advertising industry's history. There have been casualties, and fundamental rethinks about the structure and purpose of the industry. Yet it is still an industry that is admired around the world. Despite the strictures of the last five years, the quality of the people in the industry and of its creative product is just as strong as it was before the recession. Usually, it is the creative output of the industry that is most admired internationally – and most fêted within. But none I think would argue with the contention that it is because of the *composite* skills of an advertising agency that such work is forthcoming.

This book is consciously not a celebration of the creative output – there are many other sources for that. Rather it seeks to highlight excellence in all the other, less visible disciplines that contribute to outstanding advertising: planning, account management, media and so on. It also puts the spotlight on those parts of the process that the casual observer of the industry might never see: research, 'pitching', the development of strategy, the client's perspective, etc. All these areas are opportunities for excellence – and one of the pleasures (still) of this industry is the teamwork between talented people in these areas. If one could assemble all the authors of the chapters in this book into a single agency . . . well, who knows what they might achieve!

Yet, as the title of the book suggests, this is not just a book about excellence, it is also about practice. I challenge the reader to open it at any chapter and *not* find something that can help improve some aspect of their day-to-day career in advertising, or their understanding of the depth and richness of advertising as an industry. It is a celebration therefore of excellence in both process and practice. Some of the views are highly personal, some controversial, but all are enthusiastically expressed and written with a verve that is a characteristic of the spirit of the industry. I hope you learn from it. Above all, I hope you enjoy it.

Leslie Butterfield

Acknowledgements

First and foremost, my thanks go to Miranda Kennett, Director of Training & Development at the IPA, and her colleagues, Veronica Wheatley and Kerry Walsh, for all the help they have given me in assembling the various original papers included in this book, and for helping manage the process to completion. Thanks also to my colleagues on the IPA Training and Development Committee for their support, and those at my agency, Butterfield Day Devito Hockney, for putting up with my occasional absence. Apart from the contributors to this book (whom I will thank separately), there are also many other speakers, tutors and, of course, delegates who make the IPA's programme the success it is. To them too I owe a special debt of gratitude. Finally, thanks to my wife, Judy, for her forbearance over my not-too-occasional weekend working, and to my secretary, Carla Webb, for assembling all the various elements for publication. Without her computer skills all, quite literally, would have been lost!

Overview: Chapter 1

Peter Doyle and Stage 5 of the IPA's Seven Stages training programme have become almost synonymous over the last decade. In fact Peter ran the first course on Advertising and Business Effectiveness in 1979, and has done so in every subsequent year. Ratings of the course never stray far from excellent and many agencies have become regular and loyal users.

While the structure of the course has evolved, its core purpose is unchanged: to enhance the strategic understanding of people in advertising of current business management and marketing techniques. As such it aims to place advertising in its proper context: one tool among many (albeit an important one) in the businessperson's armoury.

The chapter included here was never presented in its entirety on the course. It does, however, do justice to the 'spirit' of the course, in particular by examining the issue of brands and branding, and by painting an honest picture of how advertising can contribute to these. Specifically, it covers:

- The value of successful brands
- The role of quality, service and communications in creating such brands
- The case for building as against acquiring brands
- Brand-extension strategies.

In its coverage, it sets a kind of framework for all that is to follow. Great advertising does not exist in a vacuum, it is there to serve a commercial goal. Enhancing the value of a brand is its greatest prize.

1 Building successful brands

Peter Doyle

Introduction

The role and valuation of brands has recently become a controversial issue. Not only is the importance of successful brands emphasized by marketing managers, some financial executives have developed a new enthusiasm for brands, having seen that their inclusion in the balance sheet enhances shareholder funds, reduces company gearing, and so facilitates further growth by acquisition. This chapter explores five key questions about brands: (1) What is a successful brand? (2) What is the value of a brand? (3) How are successful brands built? (4) What are the comparative advantages of buying brands versus building and developing them internally? and (5) What are the logic and economics behind brand-extension strategies?

The successful brand

Before defining a brand it is first necessary to define a *product*. The concept of a product is not straightforward. First, products and brands are mistakenly often associated only with fast-moving consumer goods. But today, the most rapidly growing and profitable products are in services – financial, retail and management. Also, besides products and services, people, places and ideas can be thought of as 'products'. Politicians, movie-stars and privatization schemes are now marketed in much the same way as Coca-Cola or Crest toothpaste.

Second, products mean different things to people *inside* the business than they do to people *outside*. Inside, to the firm's managers and accountants; a product is something produced in the factory or the office. It is about materials, components, labour costs, quality and output specifications. But outside, to the consumer, a product is something different – it is a means of meeting his or her needs or solving their problems. These needs and problems are as likely to be emotional and psychological as functional and economic. It is a product's ability to meet these needs and aspirations which creates its value. The value of a product is not what the producer puts in but what the consumer gets out. As the chief executive of Black & Decker put it, 'Our job is not to make quarter-inch drills, but to make quarter-inch holes'. Or the chairman of Revlon Cosmetics, 'In the factory we make cosmetics, but in the store we sell hope'. Similarly, IBM has always maintained it 'doesn't sell products. It sells solutions to customers' problems' (Rodgers, 1986).

A *product* then is *anything which meets the needs of customers*. When several companies are offering rival products, they will want to identify and distinguish their particular offering. This is called 'branding', so there is a Black & Decker brand, a Revlon brand and an IBM brand. But the focus here is not on brands *per se* but on successful brands. Just because people are aware of a specific brand does not mean that it is successful. People recognized brands like the Sinclair C5, the Ford Edsel, the Co-Op, or Wimpy restaurants, but they did not develop preferences for them. The recent Landor Survey found, for example, that British Telecom was in the UK's top ten brands for awareness, but in terms of esteem it was rated number 300. BT has been referred to as a strong *negative* brand. It was known for all the wrong reasons.

A positive or successful brand can be defined as follows. *A successful brand is a name, symbol, design, or some combination, which identifies the 'product' of a particular organization as having a sustainable differential advantage.*

'Differential advantage' means simply that customers have a reason for preferring that brand to competitors' brands. 'Sustainable' means an advantage that is not easily copied by competitors. That is, the business creates barriers to entry, for example by developing an outstanding reputation or image for quality, service or reliability. Brands like IBM, Coca-Cola, Sony and Marks & Spencer are successful brands because they have such sustainable differential advantages, which, as shown below, invariably result in superior profit and market performance. Successful brands are *always* brand leaders in their segments.

Two implications of this definition can be noted. First, brands are only assets if they have sustainable differential advantages. If they are negative or neutral brands like BT, Woolworth's, or the Austin Maestro, they should not appear on the balance sheet, however much is spent on advertising. Any profit these brands achieve is through their property or distribution investments rather than through the brand's differential advantage.

Similarly, if the differential advantage is not sustainable, it should not appear on the balance sheet. In some markets such as games or children's toys, a successful brand often has a life expectancy of only six months and thereafter has no value.

Second, like most other assets, brands depreciate without further investment. If management fails to reinvest in enhancing quality, service and brand image then the brand will decline. Hoover, Singer, Frigidaire, and MG are examples of brands which were once so successful as to be almost generic names for the product, but which have since declined or disappeared due to lack of investment.

This is often underestimated. Most models suggest that brands tend to decay logarithmically (e.g. Parsons and Schultz, 1984). This means that in the short term managers can increase profits without damaging the brand's market share by cutting back brand support. However, the mistake is in thinking that brand disinvestment can be continued. Without adequate support, typically after around a year (Clarke, 1976), the brand enters a period of spiralling decline.

How brands work

Brands work by facilitating and making more effective the consumer's choice process. Every day an individual makes hundreds of decisions. He or she is besieged by countless products and messages competing for attention. To make life bearable and to simplify this decision-making process, the individual looks for short-cuts. The most important of these short-cuts is to rely on *habit* – buy brands that have proved satisfactory in the past. This is particularly the case for low-involvement purchases, which make up most of the things people buy. This does not mean that people are totally brand loyal, of course, since most of them know that many brands will satisfy their needs. Most people ask for Coca-Cola but they are not too disappointed when they are offered Pepsi.

But this habit rule is not just based upon experience of use, it can also be based upon long-standing *perceptions*. People can have quite strong brand preferences even though they have never bought the product. This is especially true for aspirational products. My son has had a long preference for a Porsche, even though he has still to wait another five years before he is old enough for a driving licence. Such preferences or brand images are based upon cultural, social and personality factors, as well as commercial stimuli like advertising, public relations and prominence of distribution.

Even with non-routine, supposedly highly rational purchasing situations in the industrial sector, where decisions are taken by technical personnel, it is remarkable how important brand image is in the choice process. Even industrial buyers tend to rely on experience and long-held attitudes about the brand, rather than undertake a zero-based approach to the wide range of alternative options (see Levitt, 1983a). As the cynical IBM salesman is supposed to have said to a purchasing manager, 'Nobody's ever been fired for buying IBM'.

Successful brands are those which create this image or 'personality'. They do it by encouraging customers to perceive the attributes they aspire to as being strongly associated with the brand. These attributes may be real and objective (e.g. quality, value for money) or abstract and emotional (e.g. status, youthfulness). The personality of the brand is a function of its rational characteristics but is has to be augmented and communicated to consumers through advertising, design, packaging and effective distribution and display. These position the brand's personality in the consumer's mind, generate confidence, and create the purchasing environment.

The value of a successful brand

Successful brands are valuable because they can create a stream of future earnings. It is useful to dissect the mechanisms by which brands generate these income streams.

Brands, market share and profits

A successful brand is one which customers want to buy and retailers want to stock – it achieves a high market share. Brands with a high market share are much more profitable. The well-known PIMS findings

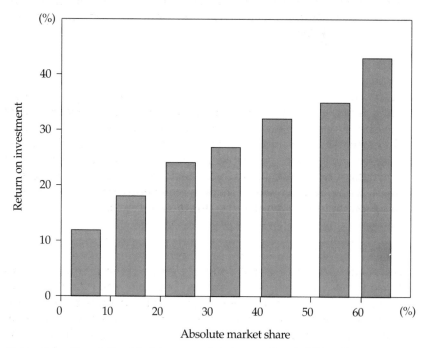

Figure 1.1   *The relationship between market share and profitability. (Source: Buzzell and Gale, 1987)*

Table 1.1 *Market share and average net margins for UK grocery brands*

Rank	Net margin (%)
1	17.9
2	2.8
3	−0.9
4	−5.9

(Buzzell and Gale, 1987), based on detailed studies of 2600 businesses, showed that, on average, products with a market share of 40 per cent generate three times the return on investment of those with a market share of only 10 per cent (Figure 1.1). Weak brands mean weak profits. A UK study shows that for grocery brands the relationship is even stronger. The number one brand generates over six times the return on sales of the number two brand, while the number three and four brands are totally unprofitable (Table 1.1). The pattern is similar in the United States, where a recent survey of American consumer goods showed that the number one brand earned 20 per cent return, the number two around 5 per cent and the rest lost money (*The Economist*, 1988).

The value of niche brands

The above findings do not mean that the brand has to be large in absolute terms. It is normally much more profitable to be number one in a small niche market than to be number three in a huge market. It is market share which is the key to performance, not absolute sales. In fact, Clifford and Cavanagh (1985) provide convincing evidence that a strong brand in a niche market earns a higher percentage return than a strong brand in a big market (Figure 1.2). In large markets, competitive threats and retailer pressure can hold back profits even for the top brand.

Brand values and prices

Because successful brands have differential advantages, they are normally able to obtain higher prices than less successful brands. Sometimes this occurs at the customer level but more frequently it is earned at the retailer level. Strong brands can resist pressure from the trade for discounts. This, in turn, generates superior earnings. Clifford and Cavanagh (1985) found that, on average, premium price products earned 20 per cent more than discount brands (Figure 1.3).

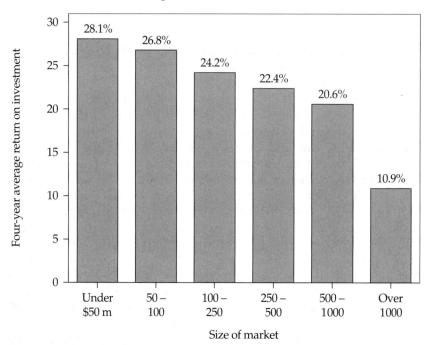

Figure 1.2   *Size of market and business performance. (Source*: Clifford and Cavanagh, 1985)

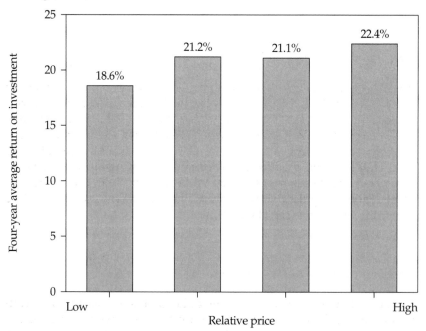

Figure 1.3   *Relative price of products and business performance. (Source*: Clifford and Cavanagh, 1985)

Brand loyalty and beliefs

Successful brands achieve higher customer loyalty. Unsuccessful brands or new brands have to attract customers. This hits the net margin because it is much more expensive in advertising, promotion and selling to win new customers than to hold existing satisfied ones. One study has suggested that it cost six times as much to win new customers as to retain current users (quoted in Peters, 1988).

Strong brands can also override the occasional hitches and even disasters which can destroy weaker brands. After terrorists poisoned samples of the leading analgesic, Tylenol, in 1987, US retailers had to remove entirely the brand from their shelves for several months. Once the scare was over, however, customers went back to the brand they trusted, leading to a remarkably complete recovery for Tylenol. Tom Peters tells a revealing story about Federal Express, which has a superb reputation for service. He telephoned FEX twenty-seven times over a six-month period to request service. Twenty-six times a FEX employee answered immediately after the first ring of the telephone. On the twenty-seventh time the telephone rang repeatedly without any response. After repeated rings, he put the phone down because he assumed that *he* had made the mistake of calling the wrong number! Of course, if this had been a neutral or negative brand it would have simply reinforced one's current image of the brand.

Common products, unique brands

Today, competition can quickly emulate advances in technology or product formulation. Competitors can quickly copy a cigarette, a soft-drink formula or PC specification. But what cannot be copied is the Silk Cut, Coca-Cola or IBM brand personalities. Studies show overwhelmingly that the best feasible strategy is to focus on brand differentiation, rather than cost and price, as a way of building profitability and growth (Figure 1.4). While the best strategy in theory is both low cost and high differentiation, in practice it is worth paying some cost penalty to achieve strong differentiation (see Hall, 1980).

The brand growth direction matrix

The product life-cycle is a well-known phenomenon. The product peaks and eventually dies as its markets mature and new technologies replace it. But this life-cycle refers to products, not to brands. There is no reason why a brand cannot adapt to new technologies and move from mature

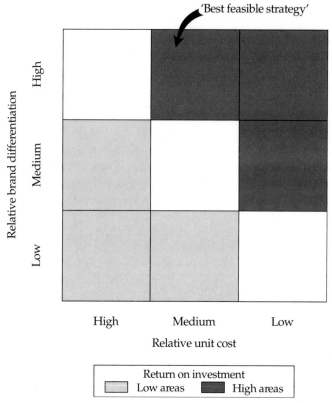

Figure 1.4   *Brand differentiation, unit cost and business performance. (Adapted by author from Hall, 1980)*

into new growth markets. The brand growth direction matrix (Figure 1.5) indicates the main growth opportunities available. Initially brand share is the strategic focus. But most of the successful brands which have lasted the decades have shifted to incorporate *new technology,* ingredients and packaging developments to circumvent the product life-cycle. Similarly, Johnson & Johnson's Baby Shampoo is only one of the many examples of brands which have moved into *new market segments* to continue growth. The fourth growth direction is towards *global branding,* which appears to offer increasing opportunities to today's multinationals (Levitt, 1983b). Growth based upon continuously developing successful brands appears to provide a securer foundation than that based upon unrelated acquisitions or new untried products where failure rates are as high as 95 per cent (Booz, Allen and Hamilton, 1982).

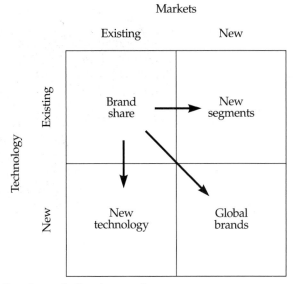

Figure 1.5   *Brand growth direction matrix*

Competitive depositioning

The brand leader is in an enormously strong position to fend off attacks. First, it has financial strength – almost invariably it will have the highest market share and the highest profit margins. This should enable it to outgun competitors in terms of aggressive promotion and innovation. Second, the trade is always reluctant to add new brands if the existing brand leader satisfies the customers and themselves. Third, the brand leader can exploit its superiority, as Coca-Cola does with its 'real thing' advertising. Without a major strategic window (Abell, 1978), only a substantial under-investment in quality and brand support is likely to dethrone a successful brand.

Motivates stakeholders

Companies with strong brands find recruitment easier. People want to work with companies that exhibit success. Strong brands also widen share ownership by increasing awareness and understanding of the company. Finally, successful brands elicit local authority and governmental support. Western countries, for example, compete with inducements to attract the better-known Japanese companies to build their brands with them.

The creation of successful brands

Brands are rarely created by advertising. This is often misunderstood because the advertising is generally much more visible than the factor which creates the differential advantage. For example, Singapore Airlines is a strong brand and does some attractive advertising. But the advertising is not the basis of the brand – rather, the advertising communicates and positions it. The basis of the brand is the superior customer service provided by the cabin staff. This, in turn, is largely achieved by Singapore Airlines putting in more cabin staff per plane than other airlines. Equally striking is the fact that Britain's strongest brand – Marks & Spencer – has historically done little or no advertising at all. There is little correlation between the amount spent on advertising and the strength of the brand.

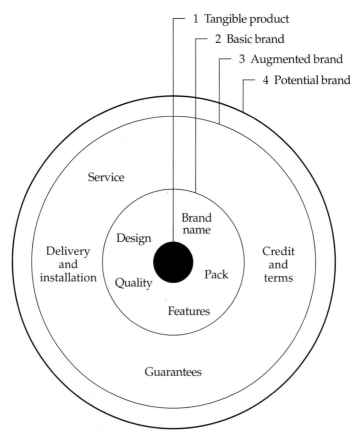

Figure 1.6   *What is a brand? (Adapted by author from Levitt, 1983a)*

The other common mistake is to think that brand loyalty is irrational. A recent survey on branding by *The Economist* (1988) reflected this view: 'people all over the world form irrational attachments to different products. Humans like to take sides ... By most "tangible" measures, BMW cars and IBM computers are not significantly better than rivals, but customers will pay significantly more for them.' Levitt (1983) provides a framework for understanding how successful brands are created and why customers are not 'irrational' to choose them (Figure 1.6).

At the core of every brand there is a *tangible* product – the commodity which meets the basic customer need. For the thirsty customer, there is water. For the production manager with a data storage problem, there is the computer. This tangible product is what economists believe rational consumers should base their choices on.

But to generate sales in a competitive environment, this tangible core has to be put in the form of a *basic* brand. It has to be packaged conveniently, the customer needs to know the features of the product and its quality. It should be designed to facilitate ease of use. But there are further ways to *augment* the brand to enhance its value by guaranteeing its performance, providing credit, delivery, and effective after-sales service. Finally, there is the *potential* brand, which consists of anything that conceivably could be done to build customer preference and loyalty. Which of these dimensions appear to be most important in practice?

1 *Quality is number one.* Overwhelmingly the most important determinant of brand strength is its perceived quality. Britain's top ten brands (Table 1.2) are all quality brands. The PIMS analysis showed that brands with high perceived quality earned double the return on investment and return on sales of low-quality brands (Figure 1.7). Quality generates higher margins in either or both of two ways. First, quality boosts market share, which results in lower unit costs through economies of scale. Second, by creating a differential advantage, quality permits higher relative price.

2 *Build superior service.* Service is perhaps the most sustainable differential advantage. While products are easily copied by competitors,

Table 1.2 *Britain's top ten brands*

1 Marks & Spencer	6 Boots
2 Cadbury	7 Nescafé
3 Kellogg	8 BBC
4 Heinz	9 Rowntree
5 Rolls-Royce	10 Sainsbury

Source: Landor Imagepower Survey, 1989

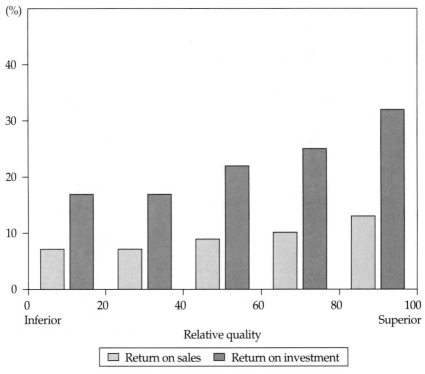

Figure 1.7 *Quality and profitability. (Source*: Buzzell and Gale, 1987)

service, because it depends on the culture of the organization and the training and attitudes of its employees, is much more difficult. McDonald's, IBM, Singapore Airlines and Federal Express are all brands built on service. A study by Albrecht and Zemke (1985) showed the importance of service: In their sample survey, 67 per cent of customers changed brands because of poor service. Of those customers who did feel unhappy with the service provided by the bank, hotel or supplier, only 4 per cent bothered to complain – they just did not expect any satisfaction. Of those that did complain, 91 per cent dropped the brand permanently. But, interestingly, suppliers who dealt with complaints fast and generously held on to the vast majority of dissatisfied customers. In fact, there was some evidence that really effective responses to complaints actually increased brand loyalty.

3 *Get there first.* Perhaps the most common means of building an outstanding brand is being first into a market. This does not mean being technologically first, but rather being first into the mind of the consumer. IBM, Kleenex, Casio and McDonald's did not invent their respective products, but they were first to build major brands out of them and bring them into the mass market. It is much easier to build a

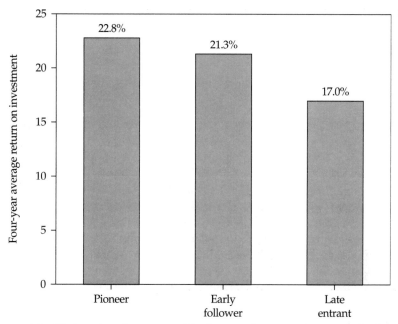

Figure 1.8 *Timing of market entry and business performance. (Source*: Clifford and Cavanagh, 1985)

strong brand in the customer's mind and in the market when the brand has no established competitors. This is why Clifford and Cavanagh found that pioneering brands earned on average more than one third higher returns on investment than late entrants (Figure 1.8). There are five ways of 'getting there first': (1) exploiting new technology (e.g. Xerox, IBM); (2) new positioning concepts (The Body Shop, Foster's lager); (3) new distribution channels (e.g. Argos); (4) new market segments (e.g. Amstrad); and (5) exploiting gaps created by sudden environmental changes (e.g. egg substitutes).

4 *Look for differentiation.* In building brands the principle is to invest in markets which are highly differentiated or where such differentiation can be created, as, for example, The Body Shop or Levi's jeans have done in recent years. Where markets are strongly differentiated – i.e. different segments are looking for different bundles of attributes – then both niche brands and big power brands can potentially earn very high return on investment. Power brands like IBM, Marks & Spencer and Coca-Cola can earn high returns because they are perceived of as high-quality brands in most of the segments. Niche brands like Top Shop or Iron Brew can earn high profits by being preferred in one segment even though their overall rating in the broad market is not great. In markets which are undifferentiated, however – i.e. where customers do not see much

difference between the brands – none typically earns exceptional returns.

To summarize, building successful brands is about quality, service, innovation and differentiation. What, then, is the role of advertising? Advertising has two functions in building successful brands. First, successful advertising accelerates the communications process. Marks & Spencer built a great brand without advertising. They relied primarily on their high street presence, customer experience with the brand, and word of mouth. But it took them thirty years to build the strong brand of today. Now, one cannot wait that long – competition would pre-empt the brand before it had positioned itself in the customer's mind. Advertising speeds up the process of generating awareness and interest in the brand. The second function of advertising is to position the brand's values in a manner which appeals to the target customers and increases confidence in the choice process. The creative messages of the Levi's or the Nescafé advertisements, for example, present the brand as having a set of values which match the aspirations of target customers.

Buying brands versus building brands

Today there are two routes a company can follow to obtain brands – it can build and develop them or it can acquire them, or rather acquire companies which possess them. The former is obviously a high-risk, slow and expensive route. Studies have shown clearly that a very high proportion of new brands tested and introduced into the market fail (e.g. Booz, Allen and Hamilton, 1982). It takes time and investment to build a brand and position it in the minds of consumers. In contrast, acquisitions are a deceptively quick route to obtaining a brand portfolio and it is a route which is increasingly followed today, especially by British companies. It also appears a cheap alternative, especially if the acquirer is exchanging high-valued shares in buying a company operating on a lower price–earnings ratio. Unfortunately, there is comprehensive evidence that most such acquisitions fail to generate long-term value for the acquirer's shareholders or build lasting brand portfolios (e.g. Porter, 1987). How can this dilemma be explained and resolved?

Previous studies (Doyle, 1987; Doyle *et al.*, 1986) suggest the approach companies adopt depends upon what their primary objectives are. Some companies have objectives which are primarily about marketing and market share. Others are primarily orientated to return on investment and financial objectives (Figure 1.9). Generally, companies which have objectives that are mainly marketing ones ('right-hand companies') choose to build brands. Companies whose objectives are primarily financial ('left-hand companies') are orientated towards buying brands or companies with brands.

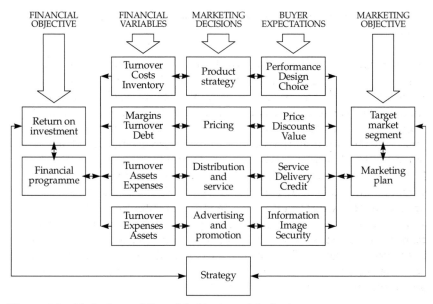

| FINANCIAL OBJECTIVE | FINANCIAL VARIABLES | MARKETING DECISIONS | BUYER EXPECTATIONS | MARKETING OBJECTIVE |

Figure 1.9 *Marketing and financial objectives of the business*

Japanese companies, for example, tend to be overwhelmingly right-hand orientated. The objective is market share. They believe that the most appropriate way to achieve market share is the development of strong brands which offer customers differential advantages. So they adopt a classical marketing approach – understand the expectations of customers in the target market segments and seek to match them. They seek to build brands that provide the customers with value and which beat the competition. Japanese companies rarely acquire because they believe that they have the skills to do it better. It is not surprising that most of the great new global brands in the last decade have been Japanese – Sony, Toyota, National Panasonic, Honda, Canon, Casio, etc.

British companies, on the other hand, have been more left-hand or financially orientated. Stock market pressures have made return on investment the primary goal and financial budgets rather than marketing plans the main planning mechanism. In these companies, products, pricing and promotional decisions are dictated mainly by financial constraints rather than marketing requirements. One result is that while there have been very few major global brands developed by British companies in the last ten years, they have led the world in acquisitions. British companies are much more aggressive in making acquisitions than companies from Japan, the United States or the rest of Europe.

The recent debate about brands in the balance sheet in Britain is essentially about acquisition strategy rather than about building customer value. Acquisition-orientated managers have observed that if brands are put in the balance sheet, then balance sheet gearing can be reduced, retained earning enhanced and so further acquisitions are facilitated. Paradoxically, companies that put brands in the balance sheet are likely to put *less* emphasis on brand building and brand development than those that do not follow this practice.

Of course, acquiring brands sometimes makes sense. The problems with acquisitions are, first, that in the long run the evidence suggests they rarely work. Second, they do not create coherent brand strategies, especially at the international level. In general, the company ends up with a rag-bag of brands with different brand names in different countries, different positioning strategies and no synergy with the existing business. Table 1.3 suggests a checklist which appraises those conditions when acquiring companies with brands makes sense.

If it is a low-growth unattractive market, building a brand costs too much. It is generally cheaper to buy competition and competitors' retail space than to beat out well-entrenched brands. This is why companies

Table 1.3   *Building versus buying brands*

	Build	Buy
Market attractiveness		
Market growth	High	Low
Strength of competitors	Weak	Strong
Retailer power	Weak	Strong
Relative cost of acquisitions		
Industry attractiveness	High	Low
Valuation of company	Full	Undervalued
Restructuring potential	Low	High
Brand's potential	Realized	Unrealized
Acquisition's potential synergy		
Cost reduction potential	Low	High
Marketing competence	Unchanged	Increased
Complementarity	Low	High
Relevant management expertise	Low	Transfers
Brand's strategic opportunity		
Product performance	Breakthrough	Me-too
Positioning concept	New	Mature
Market opportunity	High	Low
Corporate situation		
Growth potential	High	Low
Cash situation	Average	Abundant
Marketing/R&D capability	Strong	Weak

like Hanson and BTR have focused their acquisition strategies on these dull mature markets. The other advantage of these types of markets is that the relative cost of acquisitions may be low. Often the stock market undervalues these apparently dull companies and there is substantial restructuring potential in selling off parts after the acquisition.

Acquisitions work when there is real potential synergy – when the acquirer can reduce joint costs or improve marketing competence by coming together. Finally, the strategic opportunities offered by the acquirer's existing brand portfolio and its corporate cash situation play a major role. If the company's current products are me-too, if it has limited skills but abundant cash spun-off from its portfolio of mature products, then acquisitions appear attractive. By contrast, it is generally better to develop and build on the company's own brands if these are operating in growth markets, if the company possesses potentially strong brands and if inside the company there are strong marketing and development skills. These five sets of factors are the key criteria in making judgements about the balance between building and purchasing brands.

Brand-extension strategies

Brand-extension strategies are another controversial area in branding. Brand extension means transferring the name of a successful brand to additional products possessed by the company. The advantages of such extensions may be three: (1) it encourages customer confidence in a new product; (2) it may create scale economies in advertising and promotion; (3) it opens up distribution and retail channels. The dangers are that it confuses the brand identity and can degrade the reputation of a successful brand.

What are the principles in striking a balance? The right approach depends on the similarity of the positioning strategies of the brands. Four brand-extension options can be identified (Table 1.4):

1 If the brands appeal to the same target market segment and have the same differential advantage, then they can safely share the same company name or range name. Here, there is consistency in the positioning strategies. Examples of this type of extension would include IBM, Timotei (from Unilever), Dunhill and Sony – the same name applied to different products.
2 If the differential advantage is the same but the target market differs, then the company name can be extended because the benefit is similar. However, it is important to identify the 'grade'. For example, both the Mercedes-Benz 200 and 500 series offer differential advantages based upon quality, but the more expensive 500 series appeals to a much more

Table 1.4   *Brand-extension strategies*

BRAND POSITIONING GRID

| | Differential advantage | |
	Similar	Different
Similar	COMPANY OR RANGE NAME (IBM, Timotei)	COMPANY PLUS BRANDS (Kellogg's Cornflakes, Kellogg's Rice Krispies)
Target market segment		
Different	COMPANY PLUS GRADE ID (Mercedes 200, Mercedes 500)	UNIQUE BRAND NAMES (P&G: Tide, Bold, Dreft, Ariel, ...)

prestige segment of the market. The supplemental number acts to preserve the prestige positioning of the latter marque.

3 If a company has different differential advantages, then it should use separate brand names. It can find some synergy if the brands are appealing to the same target market, by using the same company name with separate brand names. For example, different brands of Kellogg's may well be selected within the same family unit.

4 But if both the target customers and the differential advantages are different then using unique brand names is logically the most appropriate strategy. So Procter & Gamble believe that it is worth losing out on the advantages of a common corporate name in order to separately position the brands in the market – to give each brand a distinct positioning appeal to a separate benefit segment. Similarly, Honda has recently separately positioned its Acura brand because it wishes uniquely to position it away from its existing models.

Summary

Successful brands are built upon the principle of seeking to build sustainable differential advantages for the customer. The levers for developing such brands are four: quality, service, innovation and differentiation. Strategies based upon acquiring brands generally fail to work because they are more usually geared to satisfying the interests of the stock market rather than the long-term interests of customers. The danger of the 'brand in the balance sheet' argument is that it leads to weaker rather than stronger branding strategies. Finally, on brand-extension strategies, there are real advantages in brands sharing a corporate logo, but care is required in not eroding a successful brand's unique positioning.

References

Abell, D.F. (1978), 'Strategic windows', *Journal of Marketing*, **42**, No. 3 (May).

Albrecht, K. and Zenke, R. (1985), *Service America*, Homewood, IL: IEE/Dow Jones/Irwin.

Bettman, J.R. (1979), *An Information Processing Theory of Consumer Choice*, Reading, MA: Addison-Wesley.

Booz, Allen and Hamilton (1982), *New Products Management for the 1980s*, New York.

Buzzell, R.D. and Gale, B.T. (1987), *The PIMS Principles: Linking Strategy to Performance*, London: Collier-Macmillan.

Clarke, D.G. (1976), 'Econometric measurement of the duration of advertising effect on sales', *Journal of Marketing Research*, **13**, No. 3 (Fall).

Clifford, D.K. and Cavanagh, R.E. (1985), *The Winning Performance: How America's High Growth Midsize Companies Succeed*, London: Sidgwick and Jackson.

Day, G.S. and Wensley, R. (1988), 'Assessing advantage: a framework for diagnosing competitive superiority', *Journal of Marketing*, **52**, No. 1 (April).

Doyle, P. (1987), 'Marketing and the British chief executive', *Journal of Marketing Management*, **3**, No. 2 (Winter).

Doyle, P., Saunders, J. and Wong, V. (1986), 'A comparative study of Japanese marketing strategies in the British market', *Journal of International Business Studies* (Spring).

The Economist (1988), 'The year of the brand', 24 December, p. 93.

Engel, J.F. Blackwell, R.D. and Kollat, D.T. (1978), *Consumer Behavior*, New York: Holt, Rinehart and Winston.

Hall, W.K. (1980), 'Survival strategies in a hostile environment', *Harvard Business Review*, **58**, No. 5 (September).

Howard, J.A. and Sheth, J.M. (1969), *The Theory of Consumer Behavior*, New York: Wiley.

Landor Associates (1989), *The World's Leading Brands: A Survey*, London.

Levitt, T. (1983a), *The Marketing Imagination*, London: Collier-Macmillan.

Levitt, T. (1983b), 'The globalization of markets', *Harvard Business Review*, **83**, No. 3 (May).

Parsons, L.J. and Schultz, R.L. (1984), *Marketing Models and Econometric Research*, Amsterdam: North-Holland.

Peters, T. (1988), *Thriving on Chaos*, London: Macmillan.

Porter, M.E. (1987), 'From competitive advantage to corporate strategy', *Harvard Business Review*, **65**, No. 3 (May).

Rodgers, B. (1986), *The IBM Way*, New York: Harper & Row.

Overview: Chapter 2

At the time of publication, John Bartle will be coming towards the end of his two-year term as President of the IPA. His tenure has been a busy but rewarding one – and few former presidents have been as committed to training and development as he. This commitment has been evidenced too by John's speaking role on the IPA's Stage 3 course: 'How to get the most out of your clients.' This course aims to enhance agency–client relationships through promoting better understanding of the context for advertising in client organizations.

John is a passionate advocate of the value of good advertising, and some of this zeal comes across in the chapter. Like many others in this book it started life as a speech (first delivered on Stage 3 in 1994), but I think the reader will sense its power even in the written word. Specifically, it covers:

- The difference between a product and a brand
- The transformation from one to the other, and the role that creativity can play in this
- The concept of head and heart in developing effective advertising
- The 'magic' that can occur when both are in play and are supported by substantial media presence.

Some of the examples used are famous across the industry, and even the non-specialist reader will get a feel for the enduring effect of great creative communication.

2 The advertising contribution

John Bartle

Introduction

This talk – which is what this chapter originally was – made its first 'public appearance' at an IPA Stage 3 training course. One of the IPA's Seven Stages training programme, Stage 3 has particular significance in being the first stage to provide comprehensive *client* input for people in the advertising industry.

Three to four days' exposure to a number of eminent client speakers outlining the issues, stresses and strains of what they do for a living is not only a very important eye-opener but also a particularly effective way of setting advertising into its proper business context. Potentially almost too effective!

At the end of these intensive days it could be possible to lose sight of advertising's particular contribution, its particular qualities and those things it can do particularly well.

Hence this talk, at the tail-end of the course. A reminder to all, hopefully, and a little bit of counterbalance for some, should that have been necessary.

Contribution to what?

Advertising does not 'float free'.

We all know that, don't we? It's just one marketing tool, one business tool. It operates in conjunction with a whole host of other things. We all know that but, so often, we behave as though we do not, as though advertising operates in complete isolation and is an end in itself rather than a means, and just one means at that.

A means to what? My title begs that question. A contribution to what?

Let us be in no doubt about what the answer has to be; it is the contribution to positive business performance. It is clear. It is that hard-nosed. It is not about creative accolades or agency success. Advertising stands or falls by its contribution to positive business performance.

I deliberately do not say that it is about contributing to business success – you may be trying to stop failure. That is also why I do not say that it is all about increasing sales; it may be about halting or slowing decline. Or about holding what you have got in the face of increasing competitive pressure. Or about supporting a price premium, or building one, or enhancing one.

In all these circumstances the contribution is about improving the commercial position, in a given time frame, against what would have happened without advertising at all or without the particular advertising in question.

The particular contribution

Advertising can make its contribution in a number of ways, of course, against a variety of target audiences.

It can make short-term announcements – a sale, a promotion, the latest prices. It can be used to help boost a share price or City standing. It can be used almost as PR against opinion leaders. It can be used to instil pride and confidence in a workforce. It can be used to encourage a positive trade response, to deliver shelf-space and prominent featuring as a consequence. It can simply provide information, like much government advertising does, for example.

Advertising is nothing if not versatile but, primarily, its particular contribution is in *helping to build and sustain brands* which, over long periods of time, provide the bedrock of so many consumer businesses and deliver positive business performance.

So, to understand fully the advertising contribution we need, most of all, to understand brands and, then, where and how advertising plays its part.

From product to brand

Over thirty years ago, in the very earliest days of my career, I believe now that I learned the most important lesson of all. I suspect that the last thirty years have really largely been about relearning the lesson in a whole variety of circumstances in an increasingly complex environment.

The lesson was learned when I started working, at Cadbury (before it became Cadbury Schweppes). My 'teacher' was the extensive product testing that the company carried out. Underlying that product testing programme was a belief in the vital importance of understanding basic product performance, and in assessing any product improvements, against the main competitors in the marketplace. To this end most of the tests were conducted 'blind', i.e. brand identity was completely masked.

But, sometimes, this was not the case. Then brand identity was revealed and, when undertaken in the same project with matched samples of recipients, one sample receiving the products 'blind', the other branded, the results were markedly different.

There is published evidence of this phenomenon, showing a number of different outcomes.

In the first example (Figure 2.1) a parity performance on taste when two food products are tested 'blind' becomes a clear taste preference for one (brand B) when the two brands are identified.

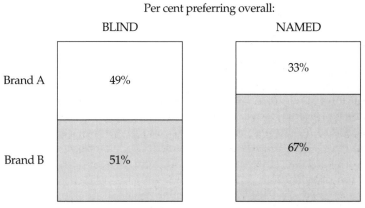

Figure 2.1 *Blind versus named product test: food product (excludes don't knows). (Source*: King, 1971)

In Figure 2.2, for a household product, a clear performance deficiency is removed when brand identities are revealed.

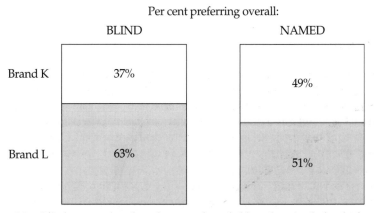

Figure 2.2 *Blind versus named product test: household product (excludes don't knows). (Source*: King, 1971)

And, in the final example (Figure 2.3), where the brands are helpfully identified, there is a turn-round in taste preference without and then with disclosure.

	Blind	Branded
Prefer Diet Pepsi	51	23
Prefer Diet Coke	44	65
Equal/don't know	5	12

Figure 2.3   *Blind versus named product test: diet colas (%). (Source*: De Chernatony and Knox, 1990)

(It is important to understand that these results are from identical questions on actual *product* performance, whether presented blind or branded, and not buying intention or brand preference questions though that, of course, is precisely what they reflect. Consumers *are* saying that the products taste different, work differently when they know what brand the product is.)

None of this is meant to suggest that basic product performance, as evaluated when the products are presented 'blind', is unimportant when building a strong brand. On the contrary, brand K in Figure 2.2 above, for example, might well have problems sustaining its brand values over time without some attention to its basic product. Indeed, what an opportunity it must surely have if the product can be improved. Alternatively, find those 'preferrers', segment the user base and concentrate activity accordingly. All is not gloom in such circumstances but some action is certainly indicated.

What is very clear, however, is that pure product performance can and will be transformed when all the aspects of identity are brought to bear, when consumers bring their preconceptions and beliefs to the product experience. *Performance is transformed when all aspects of communications are added to the basic product.* Things can taste better, perform better (or worse). A product's value to the consumer can and will change.

This is what brands are – product plus communications in all its forms. (These communications include both direct ones like brand name, company name and reputation, packaging format and design and less direct ones like advertising and PR.)

A lesson learned over thirty years ago. A simple one you may think. Certainly derived from the simplest kind of research. I wish I had appreciated then just what a profound lesson it actually was. I have spent the last thirty years discovering just that!

(As an aside, one wonders whether this simplest of all research, the side-by-side blind and branded product test, is conducted anything like as frequently as it might be. As a simple barometer of relative brand strength it has so much to commend it.)

The brand difference

The difference illustrated in those product tests is nicely and simply described by Jeremy Bullmore:

> *A product is an object or service that's available. A brand is a complex set of satisfactions delivered.*

It was famously expressed by Charles Revson, Revlon's founder:

> *In the factory we make cosmetics but in the store we sell hope*

and, again, in a more recent quote by the President of Black & Decker:

> *Last year one million quarter-inch drills were sold. Not because people wanted quarter-inch drills but because they wanted quarter-inch holes.*

All three quotes are making some vital distinctions; between what is made and what is delivered, between production and consumption and between features (of limited consumer interest) and benefits (of, potentially, much greater interest).

A brand is not only different from a product, it is much more than a product. It is much more than its functional performance. Brands are much more complex and multi-faceted than that.

The complexity of brands

The chart which follows (Figure 2.4), derived by combining several different sources, attempts to illustrate the totality of the brand as I view it.

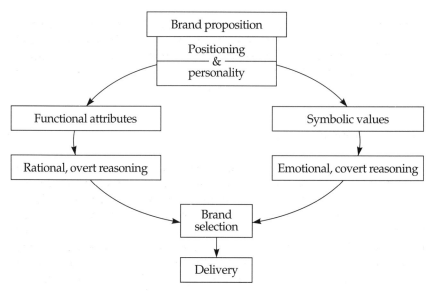

Figure 2.4   *The totality of the brand. (Sources*: De Chernatony, 1992; Hankinson and Cowling, 1995)

This illustrates the two broad areas, short-handed as the rational and the emotional, which combine to make up the brand. On the one side the functional attributes which feature in those 'blind' product tests, on the other all the communication aspects which surround the products. When these two are *taken together* we produce the total brand picture (and those branded product test results).

At our agency (Bartle Bogle Hegarty) we talk about the two sides of this chart as 'head' appeal and 'heart' appeal and we believe strongly that successful advertising requires *both* to be present, in a unique combination, although the particular contribution of advertising more often nowadays lies in its ability to bring 'magic' to the emotional side, a point we will return to. Nevertheless, in our view, one 'appeal' without the other is never enough.

The top part of this diagram, used by Hankinson and Cowling, is described by them as:

> *A brand is a product or service made distinctive by its positioning, relative to the competition, and by its personality ... Positioning defines the brand's point of reference either by price or usage. Personality consists of a unique combination of functional attributes and symbolic values with which the target audience identifies.*

This reinforces the importance of functional attributes and symbolic values in combination, acknowledges that brands require both consumer perception and consumer response (which is why I have added 'delivery' without which, against expectations, no brand can be complete) and identifies the paramount importance of distinctiveness for successful brands. This, again, is an area where good advertising makes a significant contribution, to which we will return later.

Emotion about emotion

Everyone involved in brands, in marketing and advertising, will recognize that brands are constructed in the quite complex way I have just described. When dealing with brands we must never forget this.

Rationalization, and post-rationalization, tend to dominate in our measurement – rational responses to rational questions – and in our deliberations if we are not careful. But careful we have to be because it is in getting that correct rational/emotional balance, no matter how difficult, that the key to continuing brand success lies. That is why care in research methodology, analysis and interpretation are so important.

Our critics would have a field day, would they not, dismissing as nonsense all this emotional stuff. They would see the blind/branded difference as indicative of either consumer stupidity or, at best (or should it be at worst?) evidence of how easily we can manipulate.

They would be completely wrong, of course, demonstrating only their lack of understanding of consumers and of the role that brands play, and not acknowledging that, as consumers themselves, they would behave in exactly the same way.

In fact, consumers are being both human and actually rather sensible. Human in their individuality, unpredictability and, above all, their complexity. Human also in demonstrating an acceptance, indeed a desire, for 'emotion' to add interest and variety to their lives. Sensible in taking advantage of the short-cuts and, indeed, the satisfactions that brands can deliver. Eschew these, behave rationally at all times, and inaction, 'paralysis through analysis', really would occur.

Treat your customers as stupid, underestimate their ability to evaluate your brand in all its complexity or abuse your brands by failing to sustain them or to deliver against the promises made and, as we know, you will soon learn who is really in control and how fast brand strengths can disappear. This is what the marketing challenge is all about.

The extra values for brands

We have established by now, I hope, that brands are different from products and that what makes them different is that they have extra values attached. They are products plus. If no extra values are attached then there is no brand. So, *while every brand has a product or service within it, not every product, by a long way, is really a brand.*

These extra values are in many ways 'intangible' values. They are feelings, images, associations, the statement that something makes about you. And they are not to be taken lightly or invented with no reference to consumers. Rather they are to be valued and respected since they are fundamental to our nature as social human beings. As such, we all use goods and services, in part to define ourselves, our values, our natures, our wealth, and to express these things to others.

Often we talk about 'added value' in this context. I deliberately have not, since *brands can have extra values that subtract value.*

Our product tests earlier may well illustrate this. They certainly do in relative terms and I am sure we all have examples where the extra values actually undermine the product, where the plus bit in 'products plus' is actually a minus.

In my view 'brand' is far too often used as a synonym for 'successful' when clearly this is far from always the case. There is a hierarchy of brands from the clearly unsuccessful, whose days are numbered unless remedial action is taken, all the way through to what are sometimes called the 'power brands', those which have adapted particularly well, over time, to their environment and to changing market conditions, thriving strongly as a result.

The vital ingredient – differentiation

There are many shades of grey and there is much fluidity between these two extremes, with large areas occupied by too many 'me-too' copy-cat brands. The culprits here are often research not looking beyond the tendency of consumers to respond to the familiar, and the need for security and risk aversion on the part of manufacturers or service providers. These brands may have limited success for a time, though sacrificing much if not all of any price premium in the process, but they are not likely to survive into the longer term unless action is taken to really differentiate them from the competition.

The absolute key to brand success is *motivating differentiation*. Differentiation which creates what Stephen King has described as 'a bit of a monopoly in the mind of the consumer'. Only from this can the value of the brand be fully derived and its full value reflected in the price which its consumers are prepared to pay.

As George Bull of Grand Met has said:

People pay more for brands because they offer more, satisfy more, work better, look better, feel better – in short, give better value.

Truly successful brands, as well as providing consumers with a believable 'guarantee' via their identity, also provide a melange of values – physical, aesthetic, rational and emotional – that is seen by consumers as, in combination, *particularly* appropriate, worth paying for and, with the promise met (or exceeded), worth paying for again.

Peter Doyle summarizes this as:

> *The specific characteristic of a successful brand is that in addition to having a product that meets the functional requirements of consumers it also has the added values that meet certain of their psychological needs.*

(Note, again, this talk of additional values. These extra values are never, for any length of time, a compensation for functional inadequacy. They must enhance the functional or your brand is built on rapidly shifting sand.)

The importance of brands

There has been a presumption thoughout this that brands, successful ones, are 'a good thing'. And, of course, they are.

Much has been written and many words spoken about the importance of brands to consumer businesses and there are a number of examples (Nestlé's purchase of Rowntree for one) of the value that can be placed on them.

Their importance to companies is well described by Sir Michael Perry of Unilever:

> *The major assets of a consumer business, overwhelmingly, are its brands. They are of incalculable value. They represent both its heritage and its future. To succeed as a consumer products business there is no alternative but to invent, nurture and invest in brands.*

Successful brands provide better security and stability, better protection, in an unpredictable world, for all involved in and with the company; shareholders, managers, the salesforce, the production line, whoever.

Brands have great value from the demand end too, of course, from the consumer perspective. Again greater reassurance and certainty are derived. Brands offer an easier and much more time-efficient purchasing life. As such, brands are needed by consumers. It is an irony that something as complex as a brand is needed to make life simpler!

But they are also *wanted* by consumers. It is not overstating to say that brands enrich their consumers' lives adding a host of possible inner- and outer-directed satisfactions, adding fun, enjoyment, self-expression, self-reward, etc.

Essentially it is the durability of successful brands that makes them so important and valuable to both companies and consumers. *If brands are nurtured, developed and evolved the life-cycle theory becomes completely redundant*, something for products but not for brands, as the longevity of so many of the great brands – Coca-Cola, Kodak, Goodyear, Gillette,

Sony, Levi's – testifies. They need constant attention, complacency is the enemy and evolution a necessity but the prizes for success are huge.

Summary so far

Let me summarize where we have got to so far:

- Products and brands are different.
- Brands combine non-functional values with the functional ones to provide differentiation.
- Successful brands are differentiated brands.
- The non-functional, intangible values are crucial to successful brand differentiation.
- For successful brands these extra values represent added value.
- Successful brands are of great value and importance to companies and to consumers.

...And so to advertising

Thus far, and this is called 'The Advertising Contribution', and little mention of advertising. Not really, of course. *All of what has gone before is, or could be, about advertising.* Advertising can be, and is, used in a variety of different ways but *its prime contribution is in helping to build and sustain brands for commercial benefit, often leading this process.*

Much discussion in recent times has revolved around media fragmentation and the growth in importance of non-advertising methods of communication. While these are all developments of which we must be mindful, and which we should all know a lot more about, the continuing pre-eminent position of consumer advertising is illustrated by a 1994 survey among 131 clients (see Table 2.1).

Table 2.1   *Relative importance of different communications techniques to business (total sample: 131 respondents)*

(%)	Very	Quite	Neither	Not very	Not at all	D/K	Mean
Consumer advertising	76	9	4	3	5	2	4.52
Public relations	36	38	15	6	2	3	4.04
Sales promotions	31	36	13	11	5	5	3.80
Direct marketing	27	23	13	16	16	5	3.31
Trade advertising	17	23	21	18	16	6	3.07
Sponsorship	11	19	18	29	18	5	2.77

Source: *IPA Survey* (March 1994)

The advertising contribution

In its brand-building role the major contribution that consumer advertising can make lies in its ability to communicate the totality, that crucial combination of the rational and emotional, the 'head appeal' and 'heart appeal' that I mentioned earlier. In particular, advertising can add emotional values in a way, in my view, that no other element of the marketing mix can. Its multi-facetedness and its potential subtlety mean that it can appeal to the senses and affect the emotions in ways that nothing else can with the same permanence, not least because we live in such a visually literate age with increasingly advertising-sophisticated consumers.

In a world of increasing complexity I would argue that the ability to add the emotional, more intangible value (the right-hand side of Figure 2.4) is becoming more rather than less important. The crucial requirement of differentiation is less and less readily delivered on a functional level. The days of the unique selling point, certainly of the enduring USP, are very largely gone. Competitors are smarter and faster than ever and, in some cases, with research and development alliances, technical leads disappear by definition.

It has been reported that just one year after the introduction of the Apple PC it had eleven competitors, eight years later over 500. Sony has said that any technical lead it might have enjoyed in the past, with Walkman for example, would now be six months only. And we can all see how rapidly FMCG successes are followed by own-label competitors.

If the USP is fast disappearing then what becomes correspondingly more important is what we call the ESP (the emotional selling point) and this is pre-eminently the business of advertising and advertising agencies.

Let me say again, though, that this is not to argue that the functional is of no importance. It is important *in combination* with 'heart appeal' and all the strongest brand propositions are rooted in a product truth, even if that truth is not unique. What is added on the emotional side then creates the uniqueness. Emotional appeal alone, in my view, will result in emptiness which, however glossily presented, stays superficial and will be found wanting in time.

... In practice

These beliefs about advertising and brands inform the whole of the creative process at our agency. Indeed we 'enshrine' it in all our creative briefs, each of which asks for two descriptions; what 'the product is' and what 'the brand is' (Figure 2.5).

Bartle Bogle Hegarty **Creative Brief**	CLIENT _____ BRAND _____

THE PRODUCT IS:

THE BRAND IS:

Figure 2.5   *The creative brief*

There, on every job, is a reminder that the two are different and that advertising's task is to contribute to the journey, the transformation, from one to the other. The task for the rest of the brief is to identify the role of advertising in effecting that transformation and providing support – functional and non-functional – on which to build the piece of communication under development. Thus the Häagen-Dazs 'journey' (see Figure 2.6) derived largely from consumer response to the consump-

Product	Super-premium, fresh cream ice cream
Brand	The ultimate sensual, intimate pleasure

Figure 2.6   *Häagen-Dazs ice cream*

tion experience rather than simply from the contents of the pot, high quality though it and its ingredients are. This has lifted this brand beyond simply a very high-quality ice cream to something altogether bigger (with, interestingly and importantly I think, no mention at all of ice cream in the brand statement) (see Figures 2.7 and 2.8).

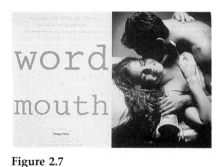

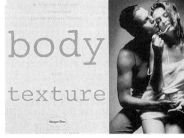

Figure 2.7   **Figure 2.8**

The contribution of advertising, specifically the initial burst, was considered and quantified in the IPA Effectiveness Awards paper (published in *Advertising Works 7*) from which Figure 2.9 is extracted.

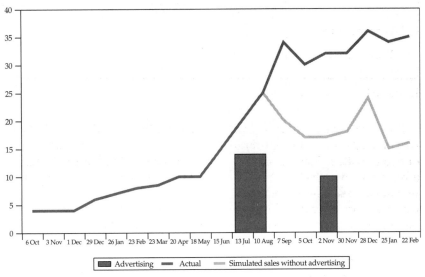

Advertising ▬ Actual ▬ Simulated sales without advertising

Figure 2.9 *Häagen-Dazs sales as a result of increased demand. (Source*: Kendall, 1993)

Boddington's similarly moves, from a fine product, but one of several in a highly competitive market, to a highly distinctive entity (Figure 2.10)

Product	Cask conditioned ale from Manchester
Brand	The smoothest drinking bitter – with a Mancunian point of view

Figure 2.10 *Boddington's beer*

using press (and, later, television) executions on the Cream theme. The Cream analogies have allowed us to take a clear product characteristic and ally it with strong personality characteristics – humour, directness, unpretentiousness, urbanness and Mancunian qualities – to produce something proud to be Mancunian and of which Manchester can be proud; truly the 'Cream of Manchester' (Figures 2.11 and 2.12).

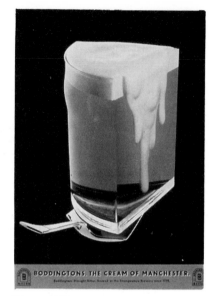

Figure 2.11   **Figure 2.12**

The advertising contribution is, again, covered in *Advertising Works*, in this case Volume 8. Figure 2.13 illustrates the advertising effect for the canned variant of the brand, as an example.

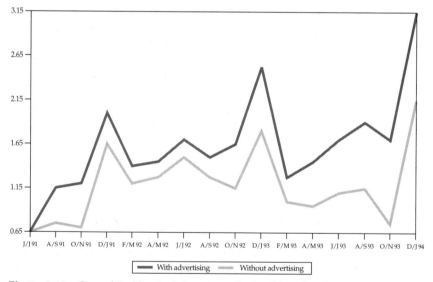

Figure 2.13   *Canned Boddington's beer: rate of sale with and without advertising.* (*Source*: Murphy, 1995)

Applying this same discipline to Phileas Fogg (Figure 2.14) led to the 'Medomsley Road, Consett' television campaign and, in the case of

Product	A range of adult snacks from around the world
Brand	An original and 'authentic' snack experience, eccentric through where it's made (Consett, County Durham)

Figure 2.14 *Phileas Fogg snacks*

Levi's, to a memorable series of commercials for 501s, supported by press advertising, starting in 1985 and continuing today (Figure 2.15).

Product	Five-pocket western heavyweight denim jeans
Brand	The original and definitive jeans. The embodiment of jeans values (freedom, individuality, rebellion, sex, masculinity, originality and youth)

Figure 2.15 *Levi's jeans*

I talk about the product/brand journey as a transformation and I would argue that advertising is the best way to effect this in a successful and *enduring* way. It can be done relatively quickly and, certainly, to a large audience, in a very public way. And, contrary to what one might be led to believe, it can be done relatively cheaply when viewed in cost per person terms, if not in terms of absolute cost.

I do not think it is too fanciful to talk of the best of advertising, with the greatest powers of transformation, as almost performing *magic*, turning the familiar and similar into the very special and unique.

The advertising challenge – breakthrough

This chapter and the transformation to differentiation that I have just talked about are all about the *content* of advertising. This is not the whole story, of course. Presence is the other factor in the advertising equation.

The crucial challenge for advertising, equally obviously, is to achieve breakthrough with the designated target audience. Without it we have nothing. If enough can be spent then presence, sheer advertising weight, regardless of content, can achieve that breakthrough of itself; conquest via attrition.

This cannot be denied (and it may well explain the success of some apparently average advertising). But fewer and fewer advertisers have the funds available to do this, certainly when faced with the increasing proliferation, clutter and complexity of today's media environment. Greater and greater onus, therefore, is placed upon the content of what we present.

Real creativity here (in which media creativity also has a significant role to play) must be measured by the ability to make your expenditure go further, do more, than the equivalent spent by your competitors. That is real creativity. The result is advertising which captures both the attention and the imagination, and the prize is brand and business success.

Then, the more you have to spend, the more you can look towards a real 'win–win' situation, when potent content meets the luxury of substantial presence.

In addition, of course, at its best, advertising can achieve a further dimension again, growing well beyond the confines of paid-for media altogether. A Häagen-Dazs, a Levi's, a Wonderbra or a Gold Blend would all illustrate this. When you really capture the imagination you can and do get unexpected and very considerable extra benefits, not least the benefits of fame, as identified by Jeremy Bullmore:

> *Just about the only thing that successful brands have in common is a kind of fame...Fame lends a curious value to things – and to people. Famous things can be shared, referred to, laughed about. Famous things are, literally, a talking point.*

In conclusion

Successful brand building needs time and sustained effort as well as faith, money and consistency. And it needs to transcend the countervailing short-term pressures.

The strongest brands endure and advertising, in my view, is the best way of building endurance into brands. At its best it can produce magic.

But it cannot work miracles. Without a good product it is impossible to create a successful brand – it was Bill Bernbach, I think, who said something like 'nothing kills a bad product faster than good advertising' – but, given the product, *advertising can best provide the awareness, the breakthrough, the emotional resonance and the differentiation which will endure and without which even the best product does not leave the factory in any real volume.*

References

Bull, G. (1994), *Brands – A Load of Bull*, D&AD Festival.

Bullmore, J. (1991), *Behind the Scenes in Advertising*, NTC Publications.

Bullmore, J. (1994), *Advertising Costs Half As Much As You Think It Does. But Do You Know When Half?*, IPA.

De Chernatony, L. (1992), *Creating Powerful Brands*, Butterworth-Heinemann, Oxford.

Doyle, P. (1994), *Marketing Management and Strategy*, Prentice Hall.

Hankinson, G. and Cowking, P. (1995), 'What do you really mean by a brand?', *Journal of Brand Management*, August, Henry Stewart Publications.

IPA Survey, (1994), March.

Kendall, N. (1993), 'Haagen-Dazs: dedicated to pleasure – dedicated to advertising, *Advertising Works 7*, NTC Publications.

King, S. (1971), *What is a brand?*, JWT.

Murphy, G. (1995), 'Boddingtons: "By 'eck"', *Advertising Works 8*, NTC Publications.

Perry, Sir M. (1993), *Advertising Association Annual Luncheon*, Advertising Association.

Overview: Chapter 3

It's no accident that this chapter by Mike Sommers follows John Bartle's. Mike, too, is a passionate speaker and writer. He too has spoken on the IPA's Stage 3 course ('How to get the most out of your clients'). But his advocacy is from the position of the often misunderstood and occasionally maligned client.

This chapter (originally presented in 1992) seeks to show that while the ends of marketing endeavour have remained the same for the last quarter century or so, the means of implementation have changed radically in line with changes in marketing media, increased competitive innovation, but most importantly a bias among new marketing clients toward the retail and service industries.

Using the example of a real-life strategy audit (Woolworths) it shows how the day-to-day pressures on clients spring from their changing strategic focus. This is followed by a discussion of how advertising agencies might adapt better to their clients, first by placing the advertising consultancy in the hierarchy of outside advice used by clients, then by contrasting the attitudes of agencies and clients to the job in hand and finally suggesting the establishment of wholly new 'client-adapted' agency models.

3 An overview of the pressures on the client

Michael J. Sommers

Introduction

In order to get to know each other better, or to put it more formally, to calibrate our terms, I would like to ask you – dear reader – to consider your response to the following question:

1 *Question* You're a client. It's 9.30 a.m. on a Friday morning. You've been called out of a board meeting which convened at 7.30 to discuss the extremely poor sales position of the last several weeks. On your way to the phone your secretary uses the opportunity to tell you that the corrective promotion you had hoped to run has been declared illegal, and that the two key executives you needed to see later that morning in order to share the panic are on a buying trip to the Far East. Behind your back your colleagues – you are sure – are using your absence from the room as an opportunity to stress to the Managing Director how much the sales situation is down to your indecisive management style. You pick up the phone, it's the Creative Director of your agency who says 'Look, I know you were pretty definite with Jeremy, but I just wanted to check if we were right down to the wire on the price issue. We really *don't* want to put a price flash on tomorrow's ad – we think it's much better if it's left to the reader's imagination. If you could come over and let the creatives explain then we've got the *Mirror* to delay its deadline on the copy – you'll only miss the Northern Ireland edition and the position will be virtually as good as the original negotiation.'
2 *Do you*
   (a) Suggest the board meeting is postponed due to an important development at the agency?
   (b) Ring your Account Director suggesting he run the ad as you agreed and stop the Creative Director bothering you?
   (c) Give everybody at the agency both barrels over the phone and then put a call into the Ad Agency Register?
   Here's a clue – the answer is not (a).

To many people on the agency side of the fence this scenario and others like it all featuring a harassed and somewhat dishevelled client as anti-hero sound suspiciously like the merely urgent driving out the important from the agenda. What's critical, however, for any agency offering consultancy support of whatever sort is to understand what a client thinks of as important and why. The tactical or day-to-day pressures exemplified above are, in reality, the result of the more strategic concerns which form the background to any client's approach to his work.

In order, therefore, to give an impression of why clients think the way they do, I want first to cover the way some clients at least think about their strategy, what their prime focus is, and only then go on to discuss the way their agency relationships fit into the picture.

The development of a business strategy

The prime objective of all client corporations is to make a good return on shareholders' funds and, wherever possible, a better return than that offered by other companies in the same sector in order to achieve a premium to the market. In that sense all the strategic pressures on a client are in some way financial. It is, of course, possible to achieve a short-term killing for the shareholder without doing end customers any favours at all, but in the longer term all clients, in some cases unconsciously, are driven by the need to achieve a closer proximity to customer needs than that offered by their competitors. All sustainable long-term earnings growth comes from this effort.

While all corporations start with the objective 'make more money' the processes they use to analyse the corporate competitive situation which will (or will not) permit them to reach this admirable goal are manifold. For our purposes we can lump them all under the general heading of 'strategic auditing'.

The strategy audit

The best way for me to talk about this process is to be specific. As an example I'll describe the situation confronting F. W. Woolworth back in 1986, the analytical techniques used to survey their strategic environment and the conclusions they drew.

As I've already implied, the principal drivers of the strategy audit are (1) what customers want and (2) the corporation's *distinctive* ability to supply these needs. Having said that, any analysis of potential future strategy based on these two criteria will still leave a list of strategic options which cannot all be pursued within available budgets. Some form of priority evaluation needs to be overlaid to establish which are the most attractive options for the company to pursue.

In the case of Woolworths two principal appraisals were conducted to fulfil the needs of the strategy audit. The first was a qualified assessment of the company's strengths and weaknesses compared to the opportunities and threats posed by the market environment (what is commonly referred to as a SWOT analysis). The second was a more quantified assessment of the potential offered by the various product markets in which Woolies operated. There are several forms of 'portfolio appraisal' which would have satisfied this need, but in this case the 'Boston' matrix (named after its inventors, the Boston Consultancy Group) was used.

SWOT Analysis

Commercial management at Woolworths sat down and generated lengthy lists of company attributes and trends in the marketplace. These were then ruthlessly pruned to leave only the most important factors, according to consensus.

When conducting this sort of analysis the participants have to be rigorous in cutting out the irrelevant. For instance, when considering the company's internal strengths and weaknesses only those factors which are *distinctive* elements, specific to the client in question, should be included.

So while the temptation was for Woolworths to write down '800 stores' as a strength, they didn't, since Boots had over 1000 and most other competitors (like W.H. Smith) had enough outlets to be available to the vast majority of the population. After lengthy argument the critical 'strengths' were refined down to three:

1 'Leading market positions' – Woolworths was market leader in toys, confectionery and recorded music.
2 'Prime high street locations' – Despite a programme of property sales the company still owned a significant number of landmark stores which were on the best pitch in town – typically adjacent to Marks & Spencer. It was recognized that a large number of the stores did not fall into this category.
3 'Brand heritage' – The Woolworths brand, while weak in some areas (see below) had excellent components with regard to *price* and being *traditional* – they had been around a long time, not potential fly-by-nights.

Similarly, the 'weaknesses' were summarized under three headings which were in many ways the opposite face of the same coin as the strengths. They were:

1 'Store size mix' – The largest unit, at 60 000 square feet in Wolverhampton and the smallest 2000 square feet in Ashby-de-la-Zouch were not radically different in terms of the product markets they attempted to

cover! Most of Woolworths' competitors had a much narrower range of store sizes to manage and therefore a significantly less complex product range management task.

2 'Major town exits' – As mentioned above, previous management had closed and sold many units leaving the company with no major store in Manchester, Birmingham, Bristol, Norwich, Leicester, and many more similarly significant towns.

3 'Brand heritage' – The downside of Woolworths' inheritance was that they were increasingly regarded as *incompetent* – out of stocks proliferated and it was difficult to tell customers when new merchandise might fill the gaps – and *old-fashioned*, the variety concept which had flourished during austerity was now faded, downmarket and lacking in taste.

So following huge consumption of flipcharts, marker pens and Blu-Tack in smoke-filled rooms Woolworths had sifted out three critical internal strengths and three critical internal weaknesses. It's noticeable that advertising was seen neither as a weakness nor a strength. Retailer appeal is principally driven by rational attributes: range, price and location. Until these are right, advertising cannot be of critical importance. 'The Wonder of Woolies', remembered by all, ran for only three years in the 1970s, and had no meaning beyond a memorable jingle. Notice also that the only 'brand' properties which concerned management were the price reputation and the positive nostalgic aspects of the heritage. Again retail 'branding' in general is, in the main, the sum of its product delivery attributes rather than a discrete ethos.

When Woolworths moved on to look at the upside and downside of the future trading environment they would face, they were similarly vigorous. 'Opportunities' and 'Threats' are the significant changes you expect to see in the company's environment going forward. When people do this sort of appraisal there's a tendency to write down the strategy you want to pursue, like 'open a chain of video stores' as an opportunity – which I suppose it is, but in this context an opportunity is intended to be something significant changing outside the company which seems potentially beneficial and might prompt a change of resource allocation.

After a similarly vigorous process Woolworths identified four critical *threats*:

1 'Rent/rate inflation' – Back in 1986 property values and changes to business rates meant one of any retailer's prime costs was likely to inflate far faster than prices over the five year term.

2 'Labour costs' – Again, due to the falling number of school leavers retailers were beginning to make substantial pay awards in order to

attract scarce salesfloor staff (of course, the recession fixed this one as it turned out!).

3 'No real price inflation' – By earlier standards general levels of inflation were falling and competition was increasing. For a retailer with relatively high stockholding costs this was a significant problem.

4 'Out-of-town erosion' – Woolworths had already lost much of its 1960s specialism to out-of-town sheds, notably DIY. In 1986 the arrival of Toys 'R' Us, massive electrical stores and forecasts of other big developments like Warehouse Clubs meant that the high street would continue to lose out.

Compensating for this Woolworths' management could foresee three major areas representing *opportunities*:

1 'Demographics' – After many years of decline, the birthrate had turned round in about 1980. By the mid-1980s therefore there was a relative boom in pre-school children and young families. The primary school population was set to grow and – shortly – the pre-teen market with their heavy consumption of pop music. At the other end of the spectrum healthy 'empty nesters' with a wide range of leisure interests and time to indulge them were foreseen.

2 'Kingfisher portfolio' – The immediate business environment for Woolworths was its membership of the Kingfisher Group. No matter how attractive or unattractive its own business potential was it had to be compared with the demands and potential of the other companies, principally B & Q and Comet (Superdrug hadn't yet been acquired). In 1986 B & Q's expansion programme could be foreseen as slowing down and electrical goods were going into one of their periodic downcycles. Woolworths' management could see themselves becoming more able to attract investment from its parent company.

3 'Less cyclical/steady trends' – Which was a reinforcement of the previous point. Woolworths operated in relatively low-ticket regularly purchased markets which were not subject to the more pronounced business cycles of B & Q and Comet. (It isn't really a separate opportunity, but since it was my fault that it made the final list I should include it out of honesty if nothing else.)

The beauty of being as exclusive as possible in making up the four topic lists involved in a SWOT analysis now becomes clear since all four can be summarized in Figure 3.1 which makes it easy for those involved to 'eyeball' the whole picture, and also easy to communicate to others.

Now good strategy, at its simplest, is exploiting those opportunities which your strengths permit. Simply from looking at Figure 3.1 and without all the background of customer research and the like that went on we can see emerging some of the reasons for Woolworths seeking to

STRENGTHS	WEAKNESSES
• Leading market positions	• Store size mix
• Prime high street locations	• Major town exits
• Brand heritage + price + Traditional	• Brand heritage + incompetence + Old-fashioned
OPPORTUNITIES	THREATS
• Demographics	• Rent/Rate inflation
• Kingfisher portfolio	• Labour costs
• Less cyclical/steady trends	• No real price inflation
	• Out-of-town erosion

Figure 3.1   *Woolworths SWOT analysis (1986/1987)*

exploit young family markets, particularly in its existing product strength areas.

Far too many clients, it has to be said, pursue strategies which seek to cure weaknesses rather than build on strengths. In general terms this is fatal. It would have been possible to include the fact that various major markets were expected to grow – compact discs and videos, for example – as 'opportunities', but Woolworths chose to leave product market analysis to the portfolio appraisal stage of the strategy audit.

The Boston Matrix

As I commented earlier, any corporation needs some sort of priority evaluation of its product market options to overlay on its view of the strategic environment. Portfolio appraisal, as this is known, comes in many forms, the most common of which is the 'nine-box' or market attractiveness grid. At Woolworths the Boston Matrix was used.

Without going into the theory too much, this plots products on two dimensions, the vertical axis being 'market growth' – either historical or prospective – and the horizontal is 'relative market share' which much research proved to Boston's satisfaction was an adequate measure of 'earnings potential'. Relative market share is calculated by dividing your own share by that of the largest competitor. So if you have, say, a 10 per cent market share and the next biggest competitor has 5 per cent the relative share would be 2.0. It stands to reason, therefore, that if you're biggest you'll have a score of more than 1.0, which is the point placed at the centre of the x-axis. This axis is on a log scale, since obviously it's possible to have very high relative shares – as when you have 90 per cent of a market where the next best is 2 per cent, i.e. a relative share of 45.

I was convinced of the virtues of 'relative brand share' as a measure when working at CPC (United Kingdom) in the late 1970s. Table 3.1 is a comparison of six major products in their portfolio at that time in descending order of their relative share with the percentage gross profit they were achieving.

Table 3.1 *Comparison of six major products*

Product	Relative share	Gross profit (%)
A	20.0	64
B	7.0	51
C	5.0	42
D	1.7	15
E	1.3	39
F	0.7	29

The one anomaly is obviously product D which was Mazola Corn Oil. While it was the biggest brand in its market at the time (and therefore had a score greater than 1.0) it should probably have been measured against *total* own-label oils – which was more like the real purchasing situation. In that case its relative share would have fallen to 0.3 and its position in the relative share league would have matched its profitability. Apart from convincing me of the efficiency of the measurement system, this anomaly is also an object lesson in how important it is to get the market definition right when making such calculations.

When Woolworths came to put their product market on this matrix the results (grossly simplified for the purpose of this chapter) looked like Figure 3.2. Now, generalizing about experience of the matrix, products falling in the high-share high-growth quadrant (top left) are referred to as

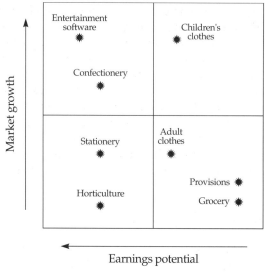

Figure 3.2   *Relative brand share (extract from Woolworths Product Portfolio 1986)*

stars. Typically they should attract investment to sustain their position. Products in the bottom left – high share, but low growth – are referred to as *cash cows* which should throw off funds to apply to stars. The trickiest area is the top right – growth markets in which you have a weak share. These are referred to in the literature as *wild cards* or *question marks*. Here you must make a choice to either exploit the growing market and by investment turn your product into a star or recognize that as market growth slows your product will fall into the bottom-right quadrant. These are low-growth low-share no-hopers referred to as *dogs*.

The focus strategy

Taken together, and with volumes of other detail, these elements of the Woolworths strategy audit led the company to something of an about-turn. Adult clothing, grocery and provisions (all DOGS on the matrix) were eliminated from the chain, despite the fact that they represented nearly a quarter of turnover! The space and management resources released were then applied to providing more comprehensive and coherent ranges for young family entertainment and leisure. Obviously the strategy audit provided only the pointers for a more thorough appraisal of the implications of such massive change, but these techniques at least had the advantage of being easy to present and communicate to the thousands of people who were to become involved in the ensuing implementation.

Only after this 'high-level' analysis of what customers might want and how Woolworths might satisfy them was consideration given to the 'low-level' marketing and advertising implications. While the changes in media and product focus and in the tone of voice and personality of our advertising became important to the strategy's implementation, they were not our initial prime focus. Retail 'branding' tends to be the sum of a company's product-delivery attributes – 'they have what I want from them when and where I want it' – rather than an ethos which is regarded as almost separate from the product itself, as is often the case in FMCG. I will return to this, but any advertising agent working on a retail or service business should always bear in mind that to such clients marketing activity is often purely a matter of publicizing and incentivizing trial of demonstrable product attributes and benefits.

The impact of strategic change

Over the last twenty years all clients have been faced with strategic overhauls at least comparable to that which Woolworths underwent. The pace of change in consumer wealth and aspiration, in available technology, in globalization and in competition has continued to accelerate. Steady-state markets are now virtually non-existent and corporate management's principal focus has perforce become strategic adaptation.

Elsewhere in this book, Leslie Butterfield will refer to the hierarchy of objectives and consequent strategy running down from 'corporate' through 'marketing' and only then reaching 'advertising'. With clients' focus shifting upstream to radical adaptation of their corporate strategies we should expect not only seismic consequent change downstream to the goals set for advertising but also a growing impatience with the detail of implementation. As Kevin Morley said when he took over the integrated marketing for Rover, 'Agencies must realize that Chief Executives have more important things to worry about than approving marketing expenditure'.

These changes should cause advertising agencies to adapt to the new concerns of potential clients; without adaptation, the pressures being felt by clients will be vented as frustration with their ill-equipped marketing services consultants.

How agencies can adapt to client pressures

Before being prescriptive about necessary changes, it's worthwhile to remember that advertising agents are only one of several external consultants used by clients. In the strategic hierarchy many levels of consultancy are possible and several distinctive consultancy forms have evolved.

The hierarchy of consultancy

The development of a business strategy may well involve the use of management consultants, as well as some of the strategic issues which flow out of the initial appraisal – such as seeking acquisition targets, or the need to replace a factory. Both the annual overhaul of the business strategy and such projects are highly suited to the classic management consultancy method of operation which is relatively short term, *ad hoc* and discontinuous in its nature.

The norm is an intermittent, project-based relationship. As a result, management consultancies have little guaranteed income beyond the short term, their consultants are frequently underutilized and consequently their daily charge-out rates are probably the highest of all the 'outsiders' bought in by the firm. Of course, to justify these price tags they must deliver work clients feel they couldn't possibly have accomplished themselves, in terms of either time or scope. In consequence, management consultants compete to employ the most intelligent workaholics they can find.

But the next big step down from the business strategy in the client's hierarchy of concerns is the marketing strategy. Marketing strategy differs from the more project-based strategies which trickle down from the chosen business direction in that it is subject to a more continuous appraisal, and a more continuous feedback from customers. While changes in organization and methods within the firm are assessed and then implemented, sometimes over a long period, changes in marketing strategy tend to have immediate results often calling for a rethink or adaptation in real time. In my experience, marketing strategy development is not the forte of management consultants both because its nature doesn't suit *ad hoc*, once-off assessment and also because it involves consumer behaviour, fashion, predicted needs, etc., none of which are readily reduced to the kind of digital input on which the typical MBA seems to flourish.

There are three principal competitors for external consultancy input to the development of the corporation's marketing strategy: management consultants (doing it badly in my book), marketing consultancies and the more thoughtful advertising agencies. Now in this competitive market the people with the advantage should be those with a *continuous* relationship with the issues as opposed to the traditional *ad hoc* consultants' approach because, as I've said, of the nature of marketing strategy itself. The advertising agency is at least continually associated due to the nature of ad agency contracts and their day-to-day dealing with the client department that tends to handle both the advertising and the marketing strategies.

Assuming we've got the marketing strategy right, we then move on to its component executions: advertising, promotions, direct marketing, public relations. As far as the advertising strategy is concerned, then, of course, clients' number-one consultancy is the ad agency. It's a shame, however, that more clients, and in particular more ad agencies, don't think about 'communication' as a strategy. Advertising as an activity has only taken historical precedence because of the relative scale of resources allocated to it, *not* out of a divine right of seniority in terms of effectiveness in communicating with potential customers. The fact that the biggest and most powerful marketing services companies – ad agencies – and their clients have tended to confuse the advertising strategy with what should be a total communication strategy means that we have confused one executional approach with the whole idea – we thus select our means before we've properly defined our ends. This tends to hobble all other forms of communication – point-of-sale, promotions, PR – and relegate them to a 'tactical' role, where tactical equals inferior. This is probably because way back with our mother's milk we were fed the belief that advertising is the only 'strategic' area of communication since it's capable of supporting and building brands. But the nature of available promotion has shifted, and, as I'll return to later, the nature and role of branding has changed radically as well.

So the client is involved in a hierarchy of strategic concerns each with relevant outside consultancy support available. At the critical level of marketing strategy formulation clients seem to be turning increasingly to the newer marketing consultancies and management consultants for help while ad agencies seem to be quitting the field. Rather than pushing upstream, I have the feeling that agencies are sinking below even advertising strategy and are down to the strategy of creative execution as their key concern. Clients feel they are increasingly detecting unsupported advertising chauvinism from their ad agencies, and therefore turning to sources they regard as more dispassionate. Given advertising agencies' inheritance and their regular contact with the client's marketing team, this shouldn't have happened; and it wouldn't have if agencies had concentrated on customer service and moved with their customers' changing needs.

Clients and ad agencies: an increasing mismatch

In April 1993 when Chris Powell took over at the helm of the IPA, he commented thus:

> *The double squeeze of reduced advertising spends and negotiated remuneration levels has left agencies severely weakened. Unable to cut deep into the 'do it' creative and media functions, account teams in London shed over a fifth of their staff last year [i.e. 1992] alone.*

This process was an acceleration of a trend developing since the mid-1980s, albeit it was masked in the early days by the transient once-off government-inspired advertising boom of privatizations.

And the process has carried on. As I put it at the 1995 ISBA Conference, 'In the complex balloon game of staying afloat, many suits and in some cases all the planners, have been thrown overboard, and those remaining can't find the necessary time and focus to develop the close relationship with a client and his product necessary to stimulate original thinking'. So at a time when understanding your client should be at a premium, ad agencies have felt it necessary to cut back most on the traditional channel of agency/client communication. This sort of cutback would be risky at the best of times, but at a time when clients themselves were radically evolving and their implicit demands on their demand-side consultancies were changing rapidly, it was suicidal.

'New' clients and their needs

All in all, the key difference in the 1990s clients from, say, their 1960s and 1970s counterparts, is that they have completely different strategic priorities. In exasperation in 1995 Andrew Seth (former Unilever marketing chief) said of ad agencies 'their real job is brand building which is what they used to be bloody marvellous at, and what we really paid them for, and what they deserved huge money for – which now takes second place to clever advertising, making jokes, high impact, getting awareness'. What Andrew was doing here is, however, making the same mistake as those he criticizes. He is harking back to the late 1960s when the vast majority of advertising spend was poured into fast-moving consumer goods – food, drink and tobacco.

In those days 'client' was largely synonymous with 'manufacturer'. Mega-clients built up their products' sales volumes in order to gain more economic production runs in their factories; they employed large salesforces and substantial distribution fleets to ship their products everywhere ... and then they sought to distinguish very similar product performances by 'branding' them. 'Branding', generically, means providing customers with reassurance prior to product purchase or experience; at its simplest, seeking the response 'it must be all right if it's from Heinz' or at its most complex, unconscious and almost subversive 'my family will appreciate me more if I use Heinz'.

In that golden age of FMCG 'branding' the advertising process was the highest form of marketing. It was the most important aspect of the job. What the client did that wasn't advertising was basically accountancy – running the brand budgets – and salesmanship – administering the promotional or below-the-line discounts. But are today's clients as focused on 'branding'? More importantly, if they were would they look to advertising to develop their brand?

A full answer to these two questions would occupy the majority of this book instead of a part of one of its chapters, but I will try to use some examples (from which I will generalize later) to demonstrate the different approach of 'new' clients.

Food manufacturing compared to food retailing

If my advertising for, say, Hellmann's mayonnaise tells you that it is 'yummy' stuff and a bottle you can put on the table without losing self-respect, then the product you obediently purchase – be it in Aberdeen or Plymouth – is identical. The base on which the branding is to build is sound and consistent.

But whatever I tell you about shopping at Tesco, your response is almost wholly governed by how good or bad *relatively* your local Tesco is. And the nature of retailing means the delivery can *never* be consistent, due to the different vintage, and therefore facilities, offered by each store unit. For example, whatever the attributes of the brand MGM in *cinema* retailing, however good their customer services at their traditional cinema in Cambridge, the opening of an eight-screen multiplex a mile away led to an immediate loss of 85 per cent of its business. The new *product* was technically superior and no amount of emotional overlay could rescue the old outmoded cinema.

Or take the case of Japanese cars. Until the recent Nissan Micra advertising I can't recall any Japanese car advertising which was highly regarded; or for that matter any real focus on what we short-hand as branding. While we Europeans worry about the allusive context of BMW, Rover, Citroen – what precise positioning each of them should have – the Japanese merrily bang on bringing out Charades, Stanzas and Preludes (what rotten brand names!). Their focus is on product enhancement, product reliability and all-round quality. And in every market in which they're allowed to, or where chauvinism isn't institutionalized, they walk all over their beautifully branded but performance-inferior competition. It's no use talking about purchase decisions never just being rational, because ultimately they always are.

The pace of product innovation in retailing, be it grocery or cinema, and the global car market is so fast now that there are *always* real rational product differences with which to motivate customers to consider product trial. In these circumstances a large part of advertising's role should simply be to inform, to bring to people's attention these product benefits. There's little need or use for careful long-term brand building.

Advertising is not synonymous with marketing

For many of today's advertisers, advertising is not synonymous with branding or even marketing as it used to seem in those far-off 15 per cent commission days. If marketing means the better adaptation of the corporation's assets to customer needs then that can include radical product redesign; re-engineering of the supply chain; loyalty rewards and even radical cost reduction. In fact, if you simply lift traditional 'branding' methods from the days of FMCG dominance and apply them to the newer service industry clients then the results can backfire.

Financial services have been the prime example of this mistaken 'expertise transplant'. Midland Bank attempted to come up with branded and segmented current accounts each with their own targeted advertising. Where are Orchard and Vector now? Or take the lengthy attempt by NatWest in recent years to invest in a branding campaign making generalized reassuring noises at a time when all banks' customers were demonstrating disaffection and all tabloid editors were actively seeking service exceptions to undermine such claims. A campaign that set out to 'provide customers with reassurance prior to product purchase' wound up looking like arrogance.

The IPA's view?

The situation I've described is one in which ad agencies have been cutting back to stay afloat, and clients are increasingly going elsewhere for their marketing advice – not merely *because* the agency has cut back but because the focus of their marketing concern is elsewhere.

Chris Powell, in the inaugural address I've already mentioned, set out the terms of the ad industry's crusade as he (and presumably the IPA) saw it in 1993:

> *The task we face is to convince those clients – perhaps for whom marketing is less central, or who are newer to it – that don't share their conviction in the business value of well-thought-out advertising, that they would be better served by making it possible for their agencies to deliver the quality of advice and work that builds brands and profits.*

Fine, but as I've already implied, *advertising* is less central to newer marketing companies but the advertising industry is being myopic if it assumes therefore that such clients' focus isn't just as concentrated on the *larger* issue of *marketing*.

No-one, for example, would deny that Rover is a better company with better products than it was ten years ago – it *is* better marketed in terms of its adaptation to available demand. And yet few would believe that its advertising and promotion have been improved. How much better might Rover be if it had had great advertising, I'm sure Chris would counter. I'd answer – probably not much, in all honesty; and if in getting that marginal improvement Rover had deflected management attention and resource from the quality-enhancement focus which has so dramatically improved the marketability of their models, then it would quickly have become self-defeating.

The client's view?

My main point is that the evolution of consumer expenditure has, for a large proportion of goods and service suppliers, outmoded the traditional advertising agency model. For many clients agencies have either too little marketing understanding to provide them with dispassionate guidance or, looked at the other way, too much advertising infrastructure for their needs.

Jeremy Bullmore spoke at an IPA breakfast address timed to celebrate the launch of *Advertising Works 8*. In commenting on the most successful papers he noted a common thread:

> *'Long before a single ad had been written, let alone run, that client company had gained insights and the confidence to change direction, modify product, restructure recruitment policy and rearrange priorities – sometimes to quite extraordinary commercial and financial advantage.'*

And Jeremy rightly commented that where this worked, the process of running all the way up the hierarchy to corporate strategy and back down again to the matter in hand of developing advertisements was particularly suited to the traditional agency – client relationship, for three key reasons. First, the process had an end objective; it was focused by the need to make advertising, and this deadline forced practical conclusions on what could otherwise become an arid, never-ending analysis. Second, he noted that the process had no common name and was a mixture of planning, research and serendipity, largely based round relatively long-term personal acquaintance. Third, as he pointed out, it comes free with the ads.

This is all true, but as I've been arguing, a lot of today's clients don't find advertising central to the task of adapting their company to the customer. I was a retail client for twelve years with four very different organizations. The final one, MGM Cinemas, was the most extreme example of what I'm talking about. Producing an ad for MGM mainly involved sticking something like Figure 3.3 in the classifieds. Producing this (with wit and originality of course) was hardly likely to admit the agency responsible to the innermost sanctum of MGM's marketing strategy. Advertising for any cinema operator will never be as central to their marketing as it is for some other clients.

MGM Uxbridge Road

Screen 1 :   Toy Story 3.0, 5.0

7.0, 9.0

Screen 2 :   Goldeneye, etc. etc.

Figure 3.3   *An ad for MGM*

There is no doubt that the higher up the strategic hierarchy of a client's consultancy needs you go, then the more value the service has for the client. The business results of the examples Jeremy Bullmore highlighted were incalculable in their positive benefit to the respective clients. Those clients, I'm sure, will therefore be less prone to argue about the percentage commission or retainer fees they are paying. In other words, the more an agency relationship can extend up into marketing *direction* rather than allowing itself to be reduced to marketing *implementation*, then the more it will be worth to its clients (the more of those pressures it will alleviate) and the more it can charge them. But for an increasing number of clients the development of an ad or even a campaign does not provide the opportunity for the total business reappraisal evidenced in Jeremy's examples, even though such clients still desperately need such an insightful reappraisal of their operation.

New agency models

There's a desperate need for a new form of marketing services agency which shares some characteristics with traditional advertising agencies – particularly relatively long-term and close day-to-day client association – but which succeeds in building marketing partnerships with its clients without the need to produce important advertising. Somehow Jeremy's identified benefit 'it came free with the ads' needs to be adapted to 'it came free with the marketing spend'.

Various attempts are being made at 'integration' or 'unbundling' and the like but they mostly seem to be repackaged approaches to the production of creative advertising as opposed to recognizing, from the beginning, that advertising might not be the critical element for some clients in their continuous process of marketing reappraisal.

What is needed is a return to the 'lead agency' concept in which the agency's management, account direction and planning functions are qualified to consult with the client at the level of marketing strategy and are then equally able to propose and manage all forms of resultant marketing expenditure. Since it is unlikely that such an agency could sustain the overhead involved in being equally excellent in creative advertising, promotional work, public relations and database marketing it seems to be that some or preferably all of these would be bought in – as *à la carte* as media has already become. The 'lead agency' would maintain two key distinctions in-house – the ability to think deeply and dispassionately about the management of consumer demand and the ability to coordinate all the resulting expenditures to best effect on the client's behalf. Indeed, by letting go of the traditionally in-house creative department such an agency type would *qualify* itself better as a dispassionate marketing services partner, and find it easier to avoid suspicion as an advertising chauvinist.

Until such a new 'lead agency' concept emerges which can operate as the true 'agency of record' for the sort of clients I've been referring to they will continue to be forced to rely on their internal resources and intermittent corrective visits to expensive management consultancies. For these clients at least, the current model advertising agency does nothing to relieve the pressures strategic adaptation has created. All too often they simply add to it.

Conclusion

I have argued that the ends clients look to from the marketing profession and its agency services have not changed over the last thirty years. But the required strategies for achieving those ends have changed considerably as continually developing consumer sophistication renders the previously esoteric commonplace and brings new products and services into the spotlight – all requiring explanation and connection with latent demand.

In the face of this change marketeers, and especially their agents, seem to have been singularly unable to adapt the tools of their trade and, more importantly, their thinking to the new reality. The principal characteristic of the marketing 'market' of the 1960s and early 1970s was its homogeneity. An awful lot of products required similar marketing answers. Advertising, promotion, design and research needs were very similar and led, I think, to institutionalization and ossification in our thinking. Here was a product needing 'marketing'. We asked ourselves 'what sort of advertising does it need?' rather than 'does it need advertising?' Indeed, marketing in many places became synonymous with advertising and promotional spend rather than the strategic adaptation of the company's offer. With the benefit of hindsight, this period of homogeneity was freakish. It is in the nature of things that different product and service categories will need very different approaches to their marketing to customers. The best sort of marketing goes back every time to first principles and tries to understand what business the company's in before adapting the offer itself to make it most readily saleable – and only then considers what means of selling to use.

Today's advertising agencies face a much wider spectrum of advertisers from those who need to be told 'Don't!' through those whose requirement is for a simple, rational explanation to be broadcast, and then on to those requiring their advertising to build branded distinction.

An agency can only be judged by how well it serves its customers, how well it shoulders the pressures on them. Too many of today's agencies are still chasing all forms of income and stretching their credibility by trying to be all things to all people. My concern is that by failing to adapt and focus to the changing client market, agencies are losing market share most rapidly in the highest value-added areas – the level at which clients describe their agency relationship as a marketing partnership. We need more initiatives to reverse that trend if we're to have happier, less pressurized clients.

Overview: Chapter 4

This chapter began life in 1986, at the inception of the IPA's Stage 4 course on 'Better account direction'. That course in turn was designed by myself, David Cowan (my former boss at BMP) and the late Charles Channon.

It had been Charles who had conceived the original 'Seven Stages' programme of IPA courses and to whom I owe a debt of gratitude both for his professional contribution to this chapter and for his personal contribution to my career. Charles really was a pursuer of all things excellent!

This chapter retains pretty much intact the structure of the speech as it was first given, although a number of the examples have, of course, been updated. It seeks to give a conceptual as well as a practical framework for developing strategy, summarized in the now-infamous (!) 'diamond' illustration. Along the way, though, it touches on a number of the key issues faced by advertising and marketing strategists daily:

- Defining business problems
- Utilizing the concept of the marketing mix
- The three-way relationship between consumer, brand and advertising
- The difference between objectives and strategies, and the hierarchy of these and finally
- The elusive 'Eureka' moment!

It uses as an analogy the concept of the strategist as 'brand doctor' – which was not part of the original paper, but is a parallel that I have grown increasingly to respect and enjoy.

Sadly, the owners of the copyright to the *New Yorker* cartoon mentioned in the opening paragraph would not allow it to be reproduced here. I have attempted a narrative description, but those readers who know the original will realize how far short this falls of replicating the wit and insight of Steinberg's classic illustration!

4 Strategy development

Leslie Butterfield

Introduction: a question of perspective

There is a famous cartoon from the cover of the *New Yorker* magazine that shows a New Yorker's view of the world in the form of a mental map. The foreground is dominated by 9th and 10th Avenues and the apartment blocks and car lots between them. Beyond, across the Hudson River, lies New Jersey and, in the distance, 'remoter' parts of the United States: Kansas City, Nebraska and the California Coast. Beyond that are specks in the distance representing China, Japan and Russia.

As a cartoon, it's both amusing and pointed. People do tend to focus on, and hence enlarge in importance, that which is closest to them. But it's also inaccurate, and potentially misleading. The same phenomenon is true even now in the advertising industry. Here also, too many people have a 'mental map' of the position, and hence importance, of advertising relative to the rest of the business world that is distorted, and similarly misleading.

Clearing this first hurdle of perspective is the starting point for anyone who wants to take the job of advertising strategy development seriously. It is one thing to be proud of the contribution that advertising can make to a business; another to assume that it is a kind of panacea for all business problems. Yet very often that is precisely the assumption that is made. To make matters worse, many agencies persist in training people to be advertising specialists, while at the same time protesting that too few clients treat them as 'business partners' (and pay them accordingly!). Frequently these advertising specialists start their thinking process from where advertising can have an effect, rather than from where the process actually begins, which is at the beginning.

The brand doctors

The experience of working with and observing many talented strategic thinkers (mostly, but not always, account planners) has led me to the conclusion that there is, in the best ones, a highly developed sense of curiosity. I hesitate to call it innate, since I do believe it can be honed and sharpened as a skill, though I suspect the kernel must be there at the outset.

And it is not an aimless curiosity that sets such thinkers apart; the best ones are able to pursue parallel thought processes, both imaginative and analytical. The approach is characterized by a number of traits. First and foremost is curiosity of the most basic sort – the desire to know why, and to keep asking the question 'Why?' after all others have given up or got bored with the quest. In tandem with this goes persistence: literally, not taking 'no' for an answer. This because very often answers are there to be found, if one digs deep enough. Too often, though, the guardians of such information can't or won't search their memories or their files for the answers.

The rigour of this process continues even when these 'secondary' sources are exhausted. That is the point at which the unanswered questions can be addressed directly, usually through research, and where the strategist's skill as designer of such research comes into its own.

Paralleling this is the imaginative skill; the ability to make intuitive leaps from experience or just a hunch, to put oneself in the other person's shoes, and see a problem from a new perspective, to frame hypotheses that suggest a different path through the information or the data. When asked to distil all of this down to a single word that defines what makes a good strategist, the word that is often used is 'detective'.

But while the detective analogy is one that suits the *sequence* of strategic development well, the *breadth* of approach that is required, the value of experience and the ability to marry analytical with imaginative skills all suggest that in fact the strategist's role is more akin to that of a doctor, with the client as his or her 'patient'.

Consider the parallel for a moment. The doctor enters the patient's life at the point of consultation, usually at the patient's request. The patient is reporting one or more symptoms, and possibly volunteering explanations or even causes. But doctors draw a distinction between symptoms (as reported subjectively by the patient) and signs, i.e. things noted objectively by the doctor. The former may be misleading, the latter are indications of the true nature of the ailment. So, while listening carefully to the patient's reported symptoms, the doctor is also assessing the context of what is being reported: the patient's medical history, his or her demeanour in the consultation, the apparently irrelevant asides that may hold clues to causes (weight loss, dietary change and so on).

The doctor's task at this stage is simply to listen. Only after having done so fully does he or she move into proactive mode: probing for the presence of other symptoms that might give a clearer picture, looking for connections with other reported illnesses historically, constantly trying to narrow the field *retrospectively*, discarding the irrelevant, seeking to identify the key sign of the current reported condition; the 'problem' in other words. Only when this is defined does the doctor move *forward* to consider possible causes: cross-referencing combinations of symptoms and signs, running tests as an aid to diagnosis. Having arrived at an identified ailment or disease, the next step is to consider possible treatments and the likely effect of these (the prognosis). Here too, though, the doctor is checking for any intolerances, allergies or indications of resistance from the patient, a clue perhaps to rejection of the diagnosis or a lack of preparedness to collaborate in the treatment!

The good strategist works along similar lines; listening carefully to his or her client, noting the unsaid as well as the spoken report, looking for the clues, then probing for other explanations, clarification, more information, personal views.

The point of this analogy is that, just as with the investigation of an illness or ailment, the exploratory nature of the strategic process begins and ends at a very definite point. While the strategist (like the doctor) may enter the process some way down the line, his or her first task is to go back to the beginning and define the problem in the clearest possible terms. Only then can he or she start to broaden out the investigation of possible causes – possibly casting the net very wide. And then at some point comes the need for distillation as the strategist moves into a more prescriptive mode: identifying and evaluating possible treatments as he or she starts to move towards a solution.

The framework for strategic analysis is now beginning to take shape and I have characterized it for the purpose of this chapter as being in the shape of a diamond (Figure 4.1).

Diamonds are forever

The diamond shape as a framework for strategic analysis is quite deliberate. The vertical 'dimension' approximates to the sequence of steps involved in the process (from top to bottom). The horizontal 'dimension' – the width of the diamond at various points – represents the breadth of consideration, analysis and research implicit in those steps. It does, as described above, start and finish as a point. But it does also 'cast the net wide' towards the middle of the process. It moves from the specific to the general, and then back to the specific again.

The larger part of this chapter will be given over to an exploration of the sequence outlined in this framework, with attention being paid to the appropriate actions at each step.

1 Defining the business problem

From all that has gone before it should be clear that while every advertising problem starts life as a business problem, not every business

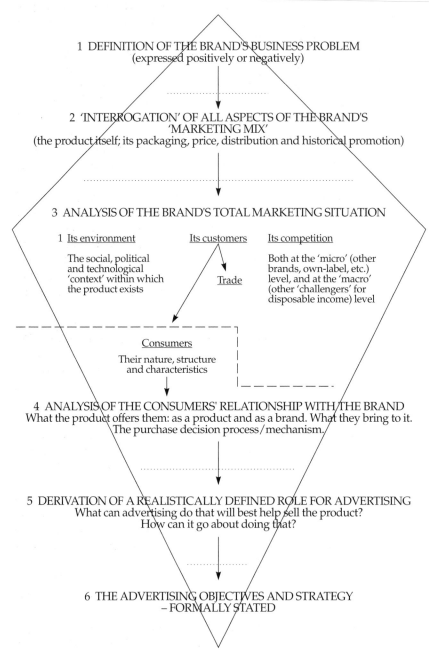

1 DEFINITION OF THE BRAND'S BUSINESS PROBLEM
(expressed positively or negatively)

2 'INTERROGATION' OF ALL ASPECTS OF THE BRAND'S
'MARKETING MIX'
(the product itself; its packaging, price, distribution and historical promotion)

3 ANALYSIS OF THE BRAND'S TOTAL MARKETING SITUATION

1 Its environment   Its customers   Its competition

The social, political   Both at the 'micro' (other
and technological   brands, own-label, etc.)
'context' within which   Trade   level, and at the 'macro'
the product exists   (other 'challengers' for
                                             disposable income) level

Consumers

Their nature, structure
and characteristics

4 ANALYSIS OF THE CONSUMERS' RELATIONSHIP WITH THE BRAND
What the product offers them: as a product and as a brand. What they bring to it.
The purchase decision process/mechanism.

5 DERIVATION OF A REALISTICALLY DEFINED ROLE FOR ADVERTISING
What can advertising do that will best help sell the product?
How can it go about doing that?

6 THE ADVERTISING OBJECTIVES AND STRATEGY
– FORMALLY STATED

Figure 4.1 *A conceptual framework for strategic analysis*

problem ends up with an advertising solution. To understand whether advertising has a role to play and what that role is depends on clarity of definition at this early stage. Indeed it is generally true to say that the better defined the business problem, the quicker and more accurate the solution. And let's also be clear that we're talking about the brand's *business* problem, usually expressed in commercial terms, not just an attitudinal or 'image' issue. There must be a business reason why the client is talking to the agency. It is your job as strategist to find it.

It may be clearly stated in the brief or apparent by reading between the lines. It may emerge in conversation or simply through observing some basic fact about the market. More usually, it will be shrouded: reported in the form of symptoms or observations, some accurate, some misleading, some perhaps irrelevant.

So the problem will need searching for: in available (secondary) research sources, among industry or audit data or as a result of primary research of your own. Just as importantly it may be defined either negatively ('true' problems) or positively ('opportunity' problems). But however you arrive at it, arrive there you must, because without being able accurately to define the business problem you won't even be able to begin to set off down the road to an advertising solution, if that is indeed the outcome.

Let's take an example, one that we will use to illustrate this process. Some years ago within the portfolio of branded spirits of Seagram (UK) Ltd (one of the world's biggest drinks companies), one profitable brand (White Satin Gin) was underperforming in sales terms relative to others in the Seagram portfolio and the gin category in total. In discussion with its recently appointed advertising agency, Seagram presented the problem exactly in this way, and suggested advertising as a possible solution. Resisting the temptation to 'just do it', the agency planner began to probe a bit further. Why was White Satin underperforming? Why did it use to perform better? What had changed about the brand? Or in the market?

After much investigation it became clear that the problem was not a general 'underperformance' one but something much more precise. While the spirits market had generally been static, the gin category had actually experienced some growth in previous years, largely because of its popularity at Christmas. White Satin, however, had consistently lost out in the important pre-Christmas period – *its otherwise healthy year-round brand share pattern declining markedly in the last quarter of the year.*

It should be apparent that this redefinition of the problem was a major step forward. Rather than a general observation of sales performance versus other brands in the client's portfolio or against the category in total we now had a much more precise understanding of when the White Satin brand was 'underperforming'. This, then, was our start point.

2 Interrogating the marketing mix

The concept of the marketing mix is one of the most basic marketing concepts of all – but still one of the most useful – if only because it stops us thinking that 'advertising is all', because in fact advertising is only *one quarter of one quarter* of the total mix.

Before we can define what role advertising can play we have to understand all the other components of the mix for our brand – and how they interrelate – hence the notion of 'interrogation'. Let's take a look now at each element in turn.

Distribution

- What are the existing distribution channels for the brand?
- How much control do we have over them?
- What other opportunities exist?
- What constraints are there: shelf life, perishability etc.?
- What are the costs associated with developing *new* channels?
- What rub-off effects do the outlets themselves have on our brand?

The key question here is: what role can distribution play in solving our 'business problem'? If we take our earlier example: it may be the case that our brand might not be well enough represented in those outlets used by occasional category buyers who only enter the market in the pre-Christmas period (grocery multiples, for instance). Curing that problem might of itself be enough to solve the share problem.

Pricing

Thinking back again to our White Satin problem, it might be the case that some sort of pre-Christmas price promotion would be beneficial, perhaps tied in with our attempt to open up new distribution channels. Or might this sort of activity simply aggravate the very problem that we have?

Perhaps it is *because* the product is thought too cheap for a Christmas gift that it suffers at this time of year. So should we *increase* the price, and if we do, what will be the effect in the other nine months of the year?

To answer these kind of questions, we need to know how the brand has performed historically:

- What happened when the price went up last time?
- What were the price relativities to other brands before and after?
- What effect did it have on sales? How 'elastic' is demand?
- Can we analyse audit data by price band or relativities?
- Do we *mind* if sales go down given the margin we're making?
- How far could they drop before we *did* mind?
- Should we be proposing some kind of pricing research?

Again, answering these questions may help us define whether advertising has a role to play, and indeed whether we can afford to advertise given a price promotion strategy.

Product

Maybe there's something about the product itself that is aggravating our 'problem':

- Are the values or images that the product itself conveys somehow less appropriate to Christmas or 'gift-giving' than other brands?
- If so, is *that* something advertising can address, or is it the case that these are harder to resolve and therefore we should be looking for a second (more seasonal) brand in this category?
- Or is it just that the packaging is letting us down? Should our drinks product, for instance, have come in a special Christmas gift pack, or a larger size, or smaller?

Would any of these be enough to solve the problem? Or is it that our competitors' brands just seem to have some attribute that makes them *more* appropriate. If so, what is it? How do we find out? Can we get some of it for our brand? Or does that affect our performance in the other nine months of the year too?

Promotion

I've already mentioned price promotion, but is there some other way we can use one of the other below-the-line tools to advantage in this period?

- Could we offer some additional incentive related to our product?
- Does the product need *merchandising* better? Perhaps linked to some other *category* of product altogether?
- What do we know about how promotions work in this market?
- What is the historical evidence?
- What are our competitors doing?
- Are promotions likely to be more or less cost-effective than advertising – how do we know?

The list is extensive, but the point is that there are many, many more ways to address a business problem than simply to say 'Let's advertise'. Too often that is precisely the kneejerk response that clients do get from agencies – and too often it's wrong. What I am trying to illustrate at this stage is that, as a strategist, your perspective has to be broader than this if you are to gain your client's confidence – and indeed perform professionally yourselves. The 'mix' concept has to work as an attitude too: the strategist needs to balance the various elements and opportunities that present themselves before moving on to a prognosis. So take a step back the next time you are in this situation: interrogate the product, and take a long hard look at all those other aspects of the marketing mix that just might do the job better than a 30-second commercial!

3 Analysing the product's total marketing situation

Our analysis of the marketing mix, while valuable, has the potential downside of leading to a somewhat static view. So now there is a need to broaden the perspective further, to look over the horizon to the bringers of change, the sources of threat or opportunity at both the 'environmental' and 'competitive' levels.

The environmental level is external to the product field in which we are involved. It embraces all those factors of technological, social or legal/political change which can dramatically alter the shape and character of a market and our ability to survive in it. The competitive level is within the product field, taking a longer view of the four 'P's' and the way they are likely to change and develop, particularly as these trends might affect our competitive edge and positioning and that of the competition.

At the environmental level of technological, social or political/legal change, the contemporary marketplace furnishes a number of examples of astonishing range and power. I just want to take one illustration of each:

1 In technology, that of the development of mobile telephony
2 In social trends, that of the seemingly unstoppable concern with health, fitness and environmental protection
3 And in political/legal developments, that of the destabilizing effects of deregulation in once-conservative and protected markets like personal financial services.

Technological change

In 1987 mobile phones were a rarity and a luxury. They weighed as much as a bag of sugar and were almost as bulky. Discreet usage was well-nigh impossible, hence the conspicuous 'yuppie' image that they developed. Ten years later, weight, size and price have all reduced dramatically – and penetration has increased correspondingly. There is now a strong repeat purchase market – and most first-time buyers are now social rather than business users. Four networks currently compete for airtime sales, and soon the products will be the size of a matchbox, and only slightly heavier. Today you can wear a phone, not carry one. The effect of this development on the domestic phone is only just beginning. Soon, consumers will be choosing between conventional landlines for the home and, on the other hand, digital personal communications networks as their primary means of communication. The effect of this blurring between the edges of conventional and mobile telephony will be to increase the importance of brands, as increasingly bewildered consumers look to this very traditional form of reassurance in an uncertain marketplace. This is the challenge that a brand like Motorola, for example, faces. The task of advertising will become polarized between short-term launch support for products that will lose their competitive advantage very quickly, or long-term corporate support which is designed to underpin the masterbrand and the company's reputation in its prime markets. This polarization in the roles for advertising is something we shall be seeing a lot more of in the future in other product fields (Figure 4.2).

Figure 4.2

Social trends

Social trends may be equally powerful in their effect on consumers, but without affecting the structure or economics of the marketplace in quite such a radical way. Healthy eating is a trend of this type. Health is not a new preoccupation, but today's health concerns have outpaced the 'subsistence' issues that concerned earlier generations. The increase in interest seems to be almost exponential and is rich in threats as well as opportunity. The rise of brown bread and stoneground flour was an early harbinger. Red meats now have more to fear than just the threat from chicken. Butter sales are still going down and dairy fat brands have had to extend their umbrella to half-fat products. We have all been long aware of these trends but threats and/or opportunities can still arise with what seems remarkable suddenness – witness the recent BSE controversy.

Social trends in health, fitness and environmental protection and so on have a number of characteristics which we can learn to recognize in our search for strategy. Most obviously they introduce new motivations which we can pick off with a new brand or sub-brand, or allow us to change the agenda for an old one. The many reincarnations of Lucozade are a classic example of this latter approach.

Political/legal change

Political or legal changes like those in technology can often affect the structure of markets. Witness the enormous extra power handed to the big retailers by the abolition (in 1995) of retail price maintenance on books. Something similar has been happening with the progressive deregulation of financial services offered by banks, building societies and life assurance companies. Now that companies are competing in each other's markets (and must indeed do so if they are to survive profitably) marketing has to mean more than training the counter staff to treat customers decently, and advertising has to mean more than giving a human face to institutions competing for unsophisticated first-time account holders. Life-stage marketing and relationship selling should be the name of the game, with a consequent change in the role and prime targets of media advertising, which in some cases quite rightly must now play second fiddle to direct marketing. But second fiddle does not mean unimportant. The enhancement effect of brand advertising on counter staff selling or on response levels from direct marketing or other promotional activities when there is a support campaign in the media is becoming increasingly important and increasingly well understood.

Mini-Case: The Co-operative Bank

In 1990, the Co-operative Bank was a little-known and even less well understood minority player in both the current account and credit card markets. It was also making losses.

My agency (BDDH) was appointed by the bank in that year, and has worked with them subsequently to develop a unique proposition: that of the 'ethical' bank.

This positioning did not appear from the ether. It was carefully honed from a study of the bank's history and working practices, its customer base and commercial ambitions, and above all from the desire to distinguish itself in a crowded market.

Over the years 1990–1996, the positioning has been refined and developed – and expressed consistently in advertising – to the point where the Co-operative Bank has now shrugged off its former dowdy, 'cloth-cap' image and emerged as a desirable alternative brand that today even has a degree of cache with some audiences.

The commercial implications of this transition have been equally profound. Not only has the bank significantly grown its share of current account business (specifically among younger, more upmarket customers) but it has also created for itself a platform for the successful launch of new products. Most notable among these has been the Gold Visa Card (a product that it would have been hard to imagine coming from the Co-operative Bank even five years previously), that is now the most successful and widely circulated Gold Visa card in Europe (see Figures 4.3 and 4.4).

Figure 4.3

The C(O)PERATIVE BANK

Guaranteed free for *life.*

The offer 1 million people couldn't refuse.

This is the most popular credit card offer ever, and it's easy to see why. You'll never be charged an annual fee for your Co-operative Bank Visa Card. Guaranteed. Think what that could save you over a lifetime. And you can transfer your existing balance from any other major credit card company at a special discount rate of just 1% per month

(12.6% APR variable). So, if you owe say £3,000 on a Barclays or NatWest Bank credit card you could save up to £290 over two years.* You don't even have to bank with us. We guarantee to match the credit limit you currently enjoy. (Our Gold Card carries a minimum £3,000 limit.) It's an unbeatable offer, so call us free now.

No annual fee. Ever.

0800 000 365

Pay off your existing balance at 12.6% APR variable.

Save up to £290 on your debt.*

Keep your credit limit.

Gold Card limit £3,000 minimum.

Call free quoting reference no. 57254 or post the coupon
....

Post to: Visa Card dept., Co-operative Bank p.l.c., FREEPOST (MR8192), Manchester M1 9AZ or phone 0800 000 365 (24 hours a day, 7 days a week). Please use block capitals.

Full name _____ Address _____

_____ Postcode _____ Phone number _____

Please tick card interested in ☐ Visa Card ☐ Gold Visa Card   57254

THE BANK MAY DECLINE ANY APPLICATION. CREDIT FACILITIES ARE SUBJECT TO STATUS AND NOT AVAILABLE TO MINORS. CUSTOMERS MUST USE THE CARD AT LEAST 10 TIMES PER YEAR. WRITTEN QUOTATIONS ARE AVAILABLE ON REQUEST CO-OPERATIVE BANK VISA CARDS AT 21.7% A.P.R. *TYPICAL EXAMPLE IS BASED ON A TRANSFER BALANCE OF £3,000, THE BALANCE IS REPAID IN FULL OVER A PERIOD OF 24 MONTHS AND PAYMENTS ARE MADE 25 DAYS AFTER STATEMENT DATE. BARCLAYS BANK VISA CARD @ 22.6% A.P.R. WOULD COST £695, NATWEST VISA CARD AT 23.4% A.P.R WOULD COST £714, CO-OPERATIVE BANK BALANCE TRANSFER AT 12.6% A.P.R. WOULD COST £416. ALL RATES CORRECT AS AT 11.3.96

Figure 4.4

The brand campaign has not only successfully underpinned launches such as this – it has also transformed the internal morale of the organization both at management and counter staff levels.

And in 1995, the Co-operative Bank made record pre-tax profits for the second consecutive year of £37 million.

At the competitive level, it is worth bearing in mind that marketing and advertising are essentially competitive businesses even when the competition is not someone else's brand or service but a state of mind like ignorance or apathy. That said, there is no doubt that the strategist has an easier task when the competition can be identified in specific behavioural terms like alternative brand usage. If you can answer the question *'What is who buying or doing instead? And why?'* you've got a head start in differentiating both the problem and its solution.

In pursuing the specifics of advantage it is often best to start not only with what you know of the consumer's perception of what the brand does in the marketplace but also with what the client thinks it is doing. How does the client see the marketing task? The client's and the consumer's view may or may not be the same, and if they are different there is a need to sell the problem before you sell the solution.

So what does the client think is its differential advantage? What does he think he is selling, precisely, that the others haven't got? At its simplest this can be represented as some basic permutation of price and quality such as:

- A better product at a parity price
- A parity product at a cheaper price
- A better product at a premium price
- A parity product at a parity price

Asking oneself these elementary questions about what the client really thinks he's doing can be a powerful simplifier of the search for specific differences even though the answers are not always as black and white as the questions. In practical terms, a lot turns on what 'better' in this context precisely means and here the list of possibilities is *not* mutually exclusive:

- Better functional performance
- Better social gratification
- Better identity/personality

The power of these simple distinctions gets blunted because clients and agencies have a tendency to believe, often without sufficient evidence, that what is supposed to be better is in fact perceived as such by the consumer! And, of course, there are some situations in which 'better' may simply mean 'different', that is, better for some people some of the time.

Many clients and agencies tend to see performance strategies and gratification strategies as alternatives. But this isn't strictly true, even though as far as communications are concerned it may be best to be single-minded about one or the other. Generally, a gratification strategy in advertising will presume or imply better performance as well; Nescafé

Figure 4.5

Gold Blend would be a classic case in point. Their use of a 'soap opera' based around the developing relationship between two 'beautiful people' (and, of course, numerous coffee-drinking occasions!) suggested not only vicarious pleasure from those occasions but was also laden with quality clues in the execution (Figure 4.5).

Many brands (like Gold Blend) offer an enhancement of the role or situation in which they are consumed. Indeed, social gratification strategies are one of the most elegant and useful ways of differentiating the product benefit. They also happen to be heavily dependent on packaging and advertising in the marketing mix. In effect, both the packaging and the advertising say that this brand not only 'works better' but also 'means more', perhaps segmenting the market (by user or by end use) and justifying a premium price in the process.

Where 'better' simply means 'different' we are in urgent need of another classic source of specific difference, namely, the identity or personality of a brand. To look at some formats for creative briefs used in agencies you might have difficulty in deducing that this dimension of differential advantage even existed. And yet it is vital in many marketplaces: perfumes and standard lagers being prime examples.

4 An analysis of the consumer's relationship with the brand

As we have investigated the sources of competitive difference, we have inevitably found ourselves talking more and more about the three-way

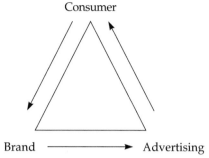

Figure 4.6 *The three-way relationship*

relationship between the consumer, the brand and the advertising (Figure 4.6). This three-way relationship lies at the heart of our search because the search for strategy has the same characteristics as the goal of strategy. And the goal of strategy is something like this:

> The choice of those consumer perceptions which advertising itself is able to create or influence
>
> ↓
>
> that fit the target market's needs to the satisfactions the brand can be seen to offer
>
> ↓
>
> in a way that maximizes the brand's differential advantage over competition
>
> ↓
>
> and, as far as possible, protects that competitive edge against erosion in the marketplace over time

And all this, of course, has to be achieved in a way that is compatible with the total marketing and corporate objectives for the brand.

Exploring and understanding consumers' relationships with brands is probably the most time-consuming but most rewarding part of the whole strategic development process. And because it is by definition different for each and every brand analysed, it is also the hardest part of the process to be prescriptive about.

This is where the strategist as researcher really comes into his or her own: designing and executing tailor-made research solutions aimed at gaining an in-depth understanding of the relationship. Qualitative research, in particular, has a key role to play here, and while it produces few genuine 'Eureka' moments, it is almost always rich in the learning it provides.

It goes almost without saying that this part of the process is best approached with two things held firmly in mind. First, a set of hypotheses. It is poor practice indeed, for example, to approach a qualitative exercise purely on a 'let's find out' basis. Rather the strategist, perhaps because of the process that precedes this point, should have in mind his or her own thoughts about what the key dynamics of the relationship might be. This does not imply any lack of objectivity in the process, it is simply an extension of the Natural Science model into this part of the quest.

Second, for each project (and probably therefore for each focus group conducted within the project), the strategist should have in mind 'the big question' that needs answering – which may be as simple as 'why do people who buy this brand do so' or 'why do those who don't, not'. It seems obvious, but too often researchers lose sight of this central ambition.

Finally, bear in mind that the issue here is *relationship*. For this reason verbal reportage may not suffice. Much has been written on the value of projective techniques as mechanisms to elicit non-verbal representations of brand relationships and the strategist most certainly admits these into evidence. Sometimes the truth of consumers' relationships with a brand is hard (or even embarrassing) to express consciously – and projective techniques provide a powerful cipher for emotional expression.

Mini-case: Savacentre

Retail brands are, in some respects, the most challenging brands of all from the point of view of strategy – because their physical realities at the local level are so varied. Supermarkets are something of an exception – all the major chains are now at some degree of parity, at least at the larger end of the scale.

Discrimination by consumers is increasingly based on the quality of the service offer and, of course, brand values. Tesco and Sainsbury's still have different identities, even though their larger stores are increasingly similar. My own client, Savacentre (part of Sainsbury's), is the UK's leading hypermarket brand, but its identity is underdeveloped.

In qualitative research we used projective techniques to tease out these perceptions in a way that didn't force consumers to take up artificial positions based on their own shopping behaviour. Instead we asked them to construct collages of photographic images of people and houses that represented their impressions of the competitive chains. From this exercise not only did we learn about the relative image strengths of brands like Waitrose, but also the extent to which Savacentre was described rationally rather than emotionally. Large houses, for example, were selected for both brands – but while in the case of Waitrose this reflected impressions of 'upmarketness', in the

Figure 4.7

Figure 4.8

case of Savacentre it was to do with family size and hence scale of weekly shop (see Figure 4.7).

Very significantly, while the Waitrose collage was full of stereotypically 'posh' families, the Savacentre collage contained almost no human references at all. A reflection of the lack of identity that the brand currently suffers from – and a significant challenge for BDDH in the future. (Watch this space!)

5 *Deriving a realistic role for advertising*

Perhaps this is a good moment to 'take stock' of what we have talked about thus far. We started out by looking at trying to define the business problem that the brand faced, and then examining or interrogating all aspects of the marketing mix in order to establish where advertising might fit in. We broadened that still further by examining both the environmental and competitive environments in which the brand exists – and then analysed all aspects of the consumers' relationship with the brand.

So what have we got? Well, one thing we've got is a real danger of being overloaded with masses of information. This is often referred to as 'analysis paralysis', yet at the end of the day we've got to rise above it all and walk a clear path back to the client with our view – and ultimately translate that into a brief.

The task now therefore is distillation or, if you like, synthesis. Out of all this knowledge and investigation we have got to pull out a direction, an intent and a way of getting there. But before we can even think about the niceties of objectives and strategies we must be crystal-clear as to what role we are expecting advertising to play at all.

We can begin to define this role if we think back to some of the things that have been said so far. We know that our role of advertising must be defined with reference to the other elements in the 'marketing mix'. This has to be our first stage of distillation or synthesis. There is no point in defining as a role for advertising some task that is more easily or cost effectively achieved through other means. (If the brand's entire business problem can be solved through improving its distribution base then that must be recognized, and the investment made towards that goal.) Hopefully, in addressing this first stage of synthesis it will have become clear that it is also not realistic to define the role of advertising as loosely as 'to increase sales'.

Our second stage of distillation lies in the concept of 'difference'. I have my own pet expressions in this area:

- 'Acceptable substitute' and
- 'Desirable alternative'

If what you think you can say about your brand only gets it as far as the former, then think again. To define the role of advertising as simply to make the brand 'acceptable' probably means you haven't gone far enough.

So here too is an opportunity for synthesis: does my strategy set me apart in any way from what others are doing, or could I easily substitute some other brand into my defined role?

Next comes the toughest part of all: distillation that springs uniquely out of the knowledge you have yourself gained in the course of your investigations and debate. I say it's the hardest because by definition each time it happens it is unique but often absolutely vital. It may be the little 'nugget' of information that doesn't quite 'fit' with everything else you've read; the irritating little piece of data that somehow contradicts everything else you know about the brand.

You try to get round it this way and that, and can't. And then you realize why, and it begins to change the way you look at all that has gone before. And suddenly out of the whole morass of data that you've been buried in there emerges a new direction that instantly allows you to discard 80 per cent of the rest of the knowledge you've gained because it's no longer relevant. When the 'blinding flash' hits you it suddenly clears up all the questions: the role of advertising, the objectives and strategy, even the target audience.

Mini-case: Clerical Medical

There are very few 'Eureka' moments in strategy development. This, though, was one.

Clerical Medical appointed BDDH in 1989 to help them develop an advertising campaign in the newly deregulated financial services market. The problems Clerical Medical faced were legion: small share, distributed indirectly (through IFAs) at a time when the market was increasingly moving towards direct contact, disparate product ranges (pensions, investments and life assurance), no clear brand positioning or history of advertising and a name that was not only dull but also misleading (they don't do medical insurance!). In fact Clerical Medical had been set up in 1824 to look after the financial needs of clerics (the clergy) and doctors – two of the leading professions of that era.

Early exploratory qualitative research (at the time of the pitch) had been undertaken by the agency to examine the general attributes of companies in the sector. One of the techniques used in the research was that most basic of all: an adjective card sort exercise. As the cards, bearing single words like 'upmarket', 'friendly', 'secure', 'modern', etc., were being spread around the floor of the venue, one respondent leant forward and plucked a card bearing the word 'professional' from the array.

'That's interesting,' he said, 'I've never thought of one of these companies catering for professionals.' (In fact, ironically, the card had originally been written to describe a company's *approach*, not its

Figure 4.9

audience.) Nevertheless, this was indeed the 'blinding flash' – the groups that followed merely served to confirm the power of a strategic and creative route based on the idea of 'professional'.

All the pieces suddenly slotted into place: 'Professional' explained Clerical Medical's name and origins, it flattered and motivated the professional IFA intermediaries, and it (accurately) reflected the more upmarket bias of the company's product range and current customer base. More important still, interpreted in an inclusive way, it formed the basis of an advertising campaign based on the line 'The Choice of the Professional' that in turn was powerful and effective in bringing in new customers – particularly from the wealthier ABC1 segment. Never in my experience has the power of a single word been so graphically demonstrated!

Often, though, the pursuit of the four elements

- Role
- Objectives
- Strategy
- Audience

is much more tortuous: a combination of scientific method, detective work, commonsense and intuition. But, once again, what all of them are about is distillation and synthesis.

So why bother with the discipline of objectives and strategy at all? One of the key reasons for setting advertising objectives is to define clearly the role which advertising can be expected to play within the total marketing context, and to ensure that this role for advertising is fully integrated with those for other marketing elements. Second, it ensures that clients and agencies are aware of any assumptions that may be being made and hence of the degrees of risk. By implication, therefore, it assists in determining advertising budgets. Third, it helps the agency prepare and evaluate creative briefs and creative executions as well as aiding the decision about how best to monitor or measure the effectiveness of that advertising.

Given, then, that there are sound reasons for setting objectives, how should these be constructed?

6 The advertising objectives and strategy

Simply stated, the difference between objectives and strategy is as follows:

An objective is the goal or aim or end result that one is seeking to achieve.

A strategy is the means by which it is intended to achieve that goal or aim or end result.

Thus one should be able to state an objective in the absolute, to preface it with the word 'to'. A strategy therefore becomes the conditional element, prefaced by the word 'by'. Hence a typical marketing objective might be:

'To increase market share for brand X.'

and the marketing strategy might be:

'By continuing to improve product quality on the dimensions of taste and colour.'

Similarly, a typical advertising objective might be:

'To demonstrate the versatility of brand X.'

and the advertising strategy:

'By giving examples of both in-home and out-of-home usage.'

So an objective is where you want to be, a strategy is how you intend to get there.

It should be clear from the example above and from the earlier discussion about setting advertising within a total marketing context that it is not appropriate to set objectives such as 'to increase market share' for advertising alone, since advertising alone is unlikely to achieve this. Advertising objectives should be set according to what advertising alone is capable of achieving and within the context of broader marketing objectives. Thus, advertising objectives fall into a number of categories, generally relating to awareness, trial, informing or educating, changing attitudes, reminding, addressing image or identity or conveying a specific message. From this it should be clear that objectives such as those relating to market share, penetration, sales, distribution or category growth are generally considered to be *marketing* rather than advertising objectives:

A hierarchy of objectives

It is generally recognized that the setting of objectives and strategy is both a logical and a sequential process, and this does have an interesting (and useful) result in terms of writing objectives. Starting from the top, the hierarchy runs as shown in Figure 4.10. It follows from this that very

Figure 4.10   *A hierarchy of objectives*

often, for example, the marketing objectives in effect represent the execution of the corporate strategy and the advertising objectives represent the execution of the marketing strategy. In other words, if you can write the marketing objectives and strategy, the advertising objectives will almost write themselves! They are likely, in effect, to represent part of the execution of the marketing strategy.

This hierarchical model – that effectively puts communications 'below' marketing – has served businesses well for many years. In this model, communications starts with the 'product brand', and its role is to be part of the 'delivery mechanism' for the marketing strategy. Today, though, I believe there is a case for re-examining that relationship, particularly in the following circumstances:

1 Where the *company* is the brand and bears the same name across many product sectors (e.g. Virgin)
2 Where the 'company brand' is more significant than its 'product brands' (e.g. BT, BMW)
3 Where the *values* of the company (often ethical) are a key competitive differentiator (e.g. The Body Shop).

In each of these examples, and perhaps more generally in the future, the hierarchy may be redefined from:

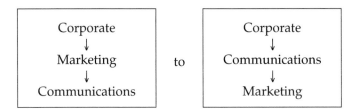

In this 'new' model, communications starts with the *company* and marketing becomes part of the 'delivery mechanism' for the communications strategy.

The marketing purist may protest that this is effectively elevating communications above other elements of the marketing mix – and in a sense it is. More accurately, it suggests a discrimination between *tactical* communications (still part of the marketing armoury) and *strategic* communications (those that emanate from the highest levels of the corporation).

What it also suggests is that perhaps the classic marketing functions of product, price and distribution are today increasingly 'hygiene factors' whereas communications is a higher-order tool. The preparedness of companies to 'outsource' manufacturing, physical distribution, service support, etc. would tend to support this view. By contrast, outsourcing the responsibility for strategic 'company brand' communications would be tantamount to outsourcing the brand itself.

Particularly in the growth areas of ethical or cause-relating marketing, it will be the board (rather than the marketing department) that will define the vision and values of the corporation, and this will provide the rationale for elevating communications to the highest levels, since those values must be seen to infuse *all* aspects of the company's activities. (This is only the communications equivalent of Total Quality Management and, like TQM, will require strategic vertical integration of communications within the organization.)

Communications will stand above other elements of the marketing mix in these companies because *it* will define what the company stands for (its vision) and *it* is tasked with expressing that on behalf of the corporation: whether that be directly to stakeholders (employees, shareholders, *et al.*), via PR, or through advertising etc. to customers. By contrast, marketing in those companies will be charged with physically delivering the corporate vision, via its products, to the end user.

In a speech at the IPA Effectiveness Awards in November 1996, Lord Sheppard (former Chairman of Grand Metropolitan) talked about how in the future 'customers will look *through* the brand at the company behind it and decide whether they like what they see'. Herein lies the rationale for communications in its elevated role: it has to present a seamless and honest top-to-bottom picture of the company.

Marketing departments have got used to the idea of the tactical integration of communications message *across* different media. Increasingly in the future they will have to embrace the idea of strategic *vertical* integration – speaking with one voice from the CEO's office right down to the supermarket shelf – even though such a realignment may eclipse their former pre-eminent role.

Overview and conclusions

If there is one big lesson from the process I've tried to outline in this chapter then it is this:

- *Don't* start thinking about advertising solutions first (the base of our diamond).
- *Do* go back to the beginning of the process, find out the essence of the business problem – and start from there.

Experience teaches good strategists that the best-defined business problems generally lead to the quickest and most appropriate advertising solutions. But this maxim of 'best defined, quickest solved' only works to the optimum if you know the right questions to ask, and have sufficient breadth of experience to interpret the answers accurately.

This is where the medical analogy that I mentioned at the outset is so pertinent. In many respects, as we saw, the strategist is like a doctor, and although the process is a great deal more time consuming than the average doctor's consultation, the task of the strategist is similar, and goes beyond simply what the 'patients' say of themselves.

Also as with modern medical practice, the strategist's role is constantly evolving. Just as with the doctor, the emphasis is shifting from cure to prevention (perhaps we shall soon see 'well-brand clinics' for clients!). Similarly again, just as the doctor seeks to build trust and iterative learning into the relationship with the patient, so too with the strategist. He or she seeks to add value to the relationship with the client by building a databank of information and knowledge that can inform future decisions, especially where there are predictable, cyclical issues to address or where cumulative long-term understanding is vital. Thus brand *care*, rather than just brand *share*, becomes the principal goal.

On this point of 'understanding' it is worth remembering that brands seldom exist in one dimension or have an immediately obvious 'truth' attached to them. That's why the good strategist takes time to explore the brand in all its facets. He or she is a seeker after truth, because the truth is the most powerful weapon in the communications armoury. Given the choice between an invented virtue that can be bolted-on to a product (commonly referred to as 'adding value') and a truth that already exists from which a powerful message can be derived (which can be likened to 'extracting value'), the choice should almost always be the latter. Building on this, the strategist seeks further to understand the identity of the brand, both actual and potential, considering the brand's personality, the clues to its 'soul', even its body language.

The aim of all this is to go beyond the (familiar) language of brand 'image' – which implies a rather shallow, two-dimensional picture of the entity in question – to a fully fleshed-out model of the brand's 'architecture'. I use the word 'architecture' because to really know and describe a brand does require the perspective that goes with operating in three dimensions:

- The product itself
- Its 'truth'
- Its identity

Only when all three of these are defined, not just descriptively but in terms of how consumers *relate* to each, can the brand truly be said to be understood.

There are many pitfalls on the way to that understanding. Common among these are the politics of the client (or even the agency) in terms of preconceptions about the brand. Then there are the 'myths' that build up around the brand that are often ill-informed or outdated (for example,

'70 per cent of our consumers are repeat buyers'). There is the classic trap of misleading research – that which may have been conducted among the wrong people and yet conclusions have been drawn which are then deemed to have general applicability. Finally, there is the problem that's 'just too big' – where all, it seems, have given up hope.

The strategist is not diverted by any of these! He or she does not take 'no' for an answer, but appraises each piece of research on its *own* merits, constructing hypotheses without fear or favour, seeking understanding against all these odds.

And when it is achieved, you can look back over the whole process with some considerable satisfaction, because your actions may have made a life-saving difference to the brand. But whilst you can feel rewarded, you can never feel complacent, because of one thing you can be assured: when the next problem comes along it's sure to be different!

Overview: Chapter 5

Chris Forrest's enactment of the 'planner as detective' on the IPA's Stage 2 course (Campaign Planning) is as memorable for its humour as for its purpose. But the serious point it makes is a fundamentally important one: that not only need quantitative data not be daunting, sometimes it can hold the key to unlocking some of the mysteries of a market.

This chapter seeks to cover the basics of quantitative research as used in the development of advertising strategy. It outlines how to look at quantitative data and touches on the principal sources of data which advertising agencies use.

It begins by discussing the importance of having the right approach before even looking at the data. A list of useful question areas is then set out as part of the recommended approach. Finally, the data sources are discussed individually in terms of what they are most useful for and how to use them.

What the written chapter cannot replicate is Chris's consummate style in delivering the paper – nor the delight with which his acting skills have been received in each year since 1992 by some of the brightest and best young talents in the industry!

5 Quantitative data and advertising strategy development

Chris Forrest

I've never liked maths. I passed maths O-level at 15 but then I failed additional maths O-level the following year, burnt my logarithm tables and switched to the arts stream. I thought I'd escaped.

One day in my early twenties, while working as a qualitative researcher, a busy client handed me a pile of computer tabulations and asked me to give her, within the next couple of days, a topline view of what the data was saying. My insides turned to water.

The tabs were on those scary rolls of computer print-out with the thin green lines and holes down both sides. You know, that stuff that spews unstoppably out of computer rooms in those films where the mainframe goes insane. Numbers swam before my eyes. I had to leave the building and walk around the block to control my rising panic.

So if you turned to this chapter with a sinking feeling, expecting not to like it, then you've come to the right place. If I can relax and learn to make numbers speak to me, anyone can.

The secret, which I eventually worked out the hard way, is to have an approach, a set of questions which can act as a route map through the statistics. In this sense quantitative research is very different from qualitative research. It's difficult to get badly lost in qualitative research. You can ask a group discussion which brands they buy and what they like about them and, generally, respondents will try to help you out and tell you useful things.

Numbers don't make any effort to help. They say things like '139.877' or '42 per cent' or '6' or even '0**' and then just sit there with their arms folded, waiting for you to ask another question.

Questions, questions, questions

From identifying the information need down to questionnaire design, quantitative research is all about asking questions. In fact if you're not careful you can generate such long lists of questions that it's not so much the numbers as the questions which start swimming before your eyes:

Where are the gaps in our knowledge?
Where are the unmet needs in the market?
What is the most appropriate role for advertising?
Which is more crucial, penetration or frequency?
What are the key demographics/psychographics?
What does our brand stand for?
Is the market going up or down?
When did you last see your father?
Why did the chicken...?
etc.

If quantitative research is all about asking questions then the hard part is *selecting the right questions*.

Other chapters in this book discuss advertising strategy. In this chapter my main objectives are;

1 To introduce the principal types of quantitative data you'll probably be working with.
2 (More importantly) to show how to approach quantitative data as part of your work to develop a strategy. I shall try to set out a framework for knowing which questions to ask when. If you can crack the approach then you have a context for the numbers and their relative importance. The specifics of each research technique also become less daunting. You won't have the time to become a Black Belt in every research methodology you encounter but you'll be able to work out what are the key things you need to understand about it.

Be a detective

The approach to adopt is that of a detective as opposed to a uniformed policemen. The uniformed police conduct house-to-house enquiries asking people where they were on the night of the twelfth. They are the research compilers. They follow up all leads to ensure they have interviewed everyone who might have seen anything (Figure 5.1). The detectives are the research users who are meant to cut through the mountains of paper and ask the incisive questions which ultimately solve the crime. These incisive questions are a mixture of knowing the correct procedures and relevant precedents off by heart and then adding a layer of commonsense, intuition and sheer genius.

It's all too easy to lapse into compiler mode when working with quantitative market data. You can spend a lot of time trying to find out something simply because you want to tick every box, only to discover that this particular box is empty and that, with hindsight, you could have foreseen that it was going to be empty. Back in 1980 a couple of my Leeds

Figure 5.1 *(Copyright Ladybird Books Ltd)*

student contemporaries who wore size nine boots were heavily questioned by police looking for the Yorkshire Ripper even though we would have been twelve years old when the killings started! The Ripper himself was interviewed and strongly suspected on a dozen separate occasions before he was finally caught. The detectives had the wrong approach. They had one set of (card index) data for men with size nine boots, a separate set of data for lorry drivers, another set for kerb crawlers and so on. They compiled more and more data without effectively cross-referencing it for useful patterns.

Even apparent patterns need to be tempered with intuition. If there's a market for hot tea and a market for iced tea it doesn't necessarily follow that there's an opportunity gap or an exciting new category called lukewarm tea.

In the first television series of *Cracker* there was an episode where the police had drawn up a psychological profile of a shopkeeper's apparently motiveless killer as young, disgruntled and unemployed. Fitz (the hero) points out that the killing took place at 6.30 a.m. and questions why anyone would get out of bed that early if they were unemployed. He suspects the killer was a tired, frustrated shift worker on the way home, points out the bus stop a hundred yards away and suggests they interview everyone who uses those bus routes in the early morning. This turns out to be the right approach and very nearly catches the baddie.

Intuition is all well and good but detectives, like musicians, cooks and artists, are most effective when they improvise from the base of a solid underlying competence in the craft skills of their respective trade. So what are the basic tools of the advertising strategists' approach to quantitative data?

The big questions

When developing advertising strategy, the Big Questions are very useful as checklists that you keep referring to, for example the classic planning cycle;

Where are we now?
Why are we here?
Where could we be?
How could we get there?
Are we getting there?

If you can answer these questions then you've got a good picture of where your brand is at. They are very useful checks but they don't really get you started on that pile of retail audit data. (Where are we now? = 74 per cent Co-op distribution in Anglia = So what?)

At a less macro level it helps to bear in mind the questions that you will ultimately need to answer in order to write an advertising strategy and thence a creative brief. An advertising strategy can be defined as a formal statement of:

Who exactly are we talking to?
What do we want them to do?
What exactly can we tell them to influence them?

To get to this point you need to have a thorough understanding of the market under the following headings:

1 Market economics and competitor analysis
2 Consumers' relationship with the product/service category
3 Consumers' relationship with the individual brands
4 Consumers' relationship with the advertising

This should enable you to write an advertising strategy, creative brief and evaluation plan.

Thought Starters

Here are some Thought Starters for each question area.

1 Market economics and competitor analysis

This area is vital. This is the investigation that management consultants charge big money for and that clients have criticized advertising agencies for not understanding. There's no point in developing strategies solely from a demand-side perspective. We also need to understand the supply-side realities:

- How big is the market?
- Is it growing or contracting? Why?
- Is this market related to others? How?
- How many competitors are there and what share does each have?
- What positions do they take up? Why?
- Are any doing particularly well or badly? Why?
- How important to each competitor is their presence in this market? Is it a core business or more peripheral?
- How profitable a market/brand is this?

Beyond the 'realpolitik' of the economics your understanding from now on should be as much as possible from the consumer perspective. Try to look at quantitative data qualitatively, asking 'What does this mean in human terms?'

Table 5.1

Brand	Share of the average consumer's last ten purchases
A	4
B	2
C	2
D	1
E	1

For example, an 'out-of-stock' figure probably represents 'a lost sale' but that's not the end of the story. Think about it in behaviour terms. It means the customer either didn't buy anything on that occasion or they bought a competitive product. Which do you think they did? Which competitor does your data suggest they'd have bought? Would they have liked it, started buying it on a more regular basis since their first choice let them down?

Perhaps they were already buying the competitor. Look at Table 5.1. Brand A has the highest share of a consumer's purchases in a category. They buy lots of it. It appears to be their favourite brand. It's probably the brand leader in the market by a comfortable margin, but are its customers 'loyal' to it? The majority of their purchases are not of brand A. Surely it is more useful, less complacent, to do as Professor Andrew Ehrenburg recommends and 'think of your customers as "mostly other people's customers who occasionally buy your product"'. Bearing this sort of perspective in mind, let's return to the Thought Starters.

2 Consumers' relationship with the product

- Who is the 'consumer'? – age, sex, class, region, lifestyle
- Who are the heavy users?
- How 'important' to the consumer is the product?
- What does the consumer feel about the category?
- From where do the opinions/beliefs/knowledge derive?
- What triggers people to enter this market?
- What is the decision-making process?

3 Consumers' relationship with the individual brands

- How is the market structured in terms of brands? Why is it this way?
- What distinguishes the competing brands from each other (function, form, price, packaging, etc.)?

- What do consumers 'know' about the various brands? Why?
- What makes consumers choose between brands? What are the patterns of brand choice? Trade-offs made?
- What sort of consumers relate to our brand? Why?
- How does the consumer relate to our brand? Why?
- In what sort of repertoires does our brand sit? Why?
- What strengths and weaknesses does our brand have?
- What opportunities/threats exist for our brand? In what areas?
- What is the current brand strategy? (If there is one.)
  - Price
  - Packaging
  - Promotion
  - Distribution
  - Product

4 Consumers' relationship with the advertising

- How do consumers regard the advertising in this category?
- What issues are prominent in advertising for the category or for our brand?
- What is the relative importance of advertising to this category?
- What is the advertising history of the category?
- Which brands tend to be advertised and which do not? Why?
- What is the pattern of spend? Why is it that way?
- Do any advertising conventions operate in the market? Why?
- What is our brand's history in terms of advertising (both in terms of amount of support and the content)? Why has it been that way?
- What position do we take up in the light of any conventions? Why?
- What strengths/weaknesses does our brand's advertising possess?

Now (and only now) that you know what questions the data detective must ask you are ready to approach your data. It makes sense to start with an audit of what your information bureau, agency team and client has already got.

This will probably arrive as a pile of reports stacked in the corner of your office which grows remorselessly every day so that it appears to take on a life of its own. (Sometimes, if you listen carefully, you could swear you can hear it laughing at you.)

Waste not a second. Divide and rule it. Cut it into smaller piles. There are three points in a brand's life where measurement is particularly useful.

When it's produced
When it's bought
When it's consumed

(For some services such as catering, the three stages happen simultaneously.) It can be useful to try to sort your data according to which of these measurement points its data are centred on (although with many research companies horizontally integrating (e.g. retail audit data and domestic panel data) this is becoming more difficult.)

When it's produced

Market study reports by companies such as Mintel and Euromonitor are very useful primers for an overview of the market, the main companies and basic consumer information. Company reports help you to see who's who and what other interests the main players have. Government data can be a treasure trove of information about the size of markets, long-term trends within them, legislative issues affecting them, predictions of further growth, etc. A client's 'ex-factory' data will tell you what has been produced. For service companies there will generally be measures of insurance policies issued, hotel 'bednights' sold, etc.

In several established markets the main players pool their sales data through an industry organization. For example, the Society of Motor Manufacturers and Traders allows members to see what they sold and what their competitors sold on a daily basis. The ex-factory data and the consumer data may not match up exactly. This could be because the ex-factory data capture is not exact but it could well be due to factors such as grey market imports where the same products are bought abroad in bulk and imported by individual traders rather than the official UK sales company. This sort of trade creates measurement problems in markets from high-fashion clothing to car tyres and, most recently, to take-home beer and wine.

When it's bought

Retail audits such as Nielsen or IRI either take retailers' electronic data or go into stores to observe what is displayed. They then crunch this information and present it in many useful ways. For example, at first sight Table 5.2 is just 140 numbers on a page. In fact it is packed with information that opens up a world of investigative possibilities. Have a good look at it before you read on. Think about what it shows and about what other thoughts it starts and lines of inquiry it might provoke.

MATs

To start with, Table 5.2 makes a useful point about MATs. Moving Annual Totals are frequently used to summarize the current state of a market.

Table 5.2 *Product class X – Sales share, GB, Nielsen Grocery Service (£ 000)*

	MAT 48946	Sep. 1989	Oct.	Nov.	Dec.	Jan. 1990	Feb.	Mar.	Apr.	May	June	July	Aug.	Sep.
Sales Y % CHG														+17
Market total	48946	3537	3833	3931	4412	3585	3689	4392	4294	4215	4224	4247	3992	4132
Brand A	19.9	22.0	20.8	19.3	18.9	19.0	19.4	20.7	20.1	19.7	20.8	21.2	20.8	17.5
Brand B	0.5	0.4	0.4	0.4	0.4	0.4	0.5	0.5	0.4	0.5	0.5	0.5	0.5	0.6
Brand C	4.6		4.4	4.3	4.3	4.7	5.2	4.9	5.1	4.8	4.6	3.9	4.4	4.5
Brand D	0.5	0.3	0.3	0.6	0.7	0.9	1.0	1.2	0.8	0.4	0.2	0.1	0.1	0.1
Brand E	17.7	18.1	18.2	17.3	17.4	17.2	18.0	17.3	17.4	16.9	16.1	10.6	18.2	22.2
Brand F	2.4	1.9	2.1	1.9	2.0	2.0	2.0	2.2	2.6	2.7	2.6	2.8	2.6	3.1
Brand G	1.6	1.1	1.0	1.0	1.3	1.3	1.5	1.6	1.6	1.7	2.3	2.2	2.2	1.0
Own-label	46.2	42.4	43.1	45.6	46.1	45.4	44.5	44.3	46.4	47.7	47.8	47.8	47.7	47.7
All others	6.8	13.8	9.7	9.0	8.9	9.1	7.9	7.3	5.0	5.6	5.1	4.9	3.5	3.3
	Sep. 1990 Latest 12 mths	Sep. 1989	Oct.	Nov.	Dec.	Jan. 1990	Feb.	Mar.	Apr.	May	June	July	Aug.	Sep.

They are aggregated data for the previous twelve months, so if one data point is August 1995 to July 1996, the next will be September 1995 to August 1996, etc. In Table 5.2 MATs to September 1990 (the left-hand column) shows Own-label taking the highest share of sterling sales and brand A having the highest share of the branded sector (19.9) ahead of brand E (17.7). However, looking across the month-by-month sales figures we see the market dynamics in more detail, revealing the steady rise of Own-label and of brand E. Brand E is the current market leader. Its rise mirrors brand A's decline. Have brand E's sales come from brand A? Very possibly but we'll need to look at some consumer panel data (see later) to confirm this.

They aren't necessarily in direct competition. It may be that brand A is the old cash cow of a brand leader which has not received enough marketing and advertising support to fend off the appeal of Own-label and has become not much more than a 'manufacturer's own label' while brand E may be the new premium brand which is either growing the market or taking share from somewhere else, 'All Others' perhaps.

Value versus volume

Certainly the market is growing by value, up 17 per cent year on year as the figure at top-right shows. Is this value growth coming from volume growth, more of this stuff being bought? We need to look at volume sales to find out. It may just be that a general price rise, perhaps the cost of raw materials has been passed on to the consumer so that although value has risen 17 per cent, volume may have declined by a greater amount. Perhaps the value rise is attributable to consumers trading up to more premium priced, higher-quality variants. Is that what's been happening? Was brand A slow to reformulate? The value summary tables (shown) together with volume summary tables (not shown) give us enough data to work out relative price positions in the market (Table 5.3). In other words, brand F is premium priced. Its value share is 124 per cent of its volume share.

Table 5.3

	Value share (%)	Volume share (%)	Value/volume index
Brand C	4.5	4.7	0.95
Brand F	3.1	2.5	1.24

Price

Did brand A's price rise significantly in August? Could this explain the acceleration in share loss that we see? Why did any price rise occur? Is it made abroad and suffering from adverse currency fluctuations? Has it been having teething troubles switching manufacture and distribution away from its old formulation to a new improved formulation which may well take the market by storm in the next few months? I think we should be told.

Distribution

Distribution data by brand will help us get a better handle on what's been happening to the brands. If brand A has had excellent distribution throughout the year and its price has not been out of line with the market then its problems would seem to be to do with consumer preference shifting away from it. If it's been out of stock then we'd like to know why this was. Did a factory burn down or go on strike? Is it at war with one or more important retailers over the size of the retailer's margin and is the retailer delisting it to show they mean business? Look at the picture within each individual multiple.

Rate of sale

ROS is the usual way to look at relative demand for a brand. Brand A may have been selling well simply because it dominated distribution in the market. It's on sale everywhere. Brand E may not have been selling as well overall because of weaker distribution but where it was sold it may have been outselling brand A. Did the trade notice this superior ROS and, prompted by brand E's owners, give it wider and better quality distribution (e.g. more 'facings' on the shelf and/or more eye-level positions)?

ROS is the number of sales divided by the number of outlets. We usually also need to take into account the size of outlet. One Tesco hypermarket may sell more of the product category than thirty corner shops. 'Weighted (by either value or volume) distribution' takes this into account. It divides the ROS by the quality of its distribution. Technically:

$$\frac{\text{Average sales} \times \text{shop distribution}}{\text{Weighted distribution}} = \text{Weighted rate of sale}$$

Retail audit data will tell us enough to set up some working hypotheses which can be confirmed or refuted by other data sources. Don't overlook the immediate data source called 'the sales director'. It's always useful to attend those unglamorous retail audit presentations and ask the sales director(s) what they think has been happening. Now that the retail audit companies have moved to an account management system you'll also find the researcher presenting the data usually knows the market dynamics inside out and has a plausible explanation for most movements.

When it's consumed

At this point in the chapter you may be thinking that audit data tells you nearly all you need to know and that the hardbitten salesforce inhabit the real world while marketing and advertising only flutter about at a superficial level. 'Here come the Flower Arrangers' is how one of my client's sales directors likes to tease us. (Oh, how we laugh at this Wildean wit!)

But hold on a minute. We have only just started to investigate the market. We've not yet looked at our pile of data measuring the single most important agent in any market, the consumer.

Although it may appear that increased sales can be conjured out of a bit of wheeler-dealing on the distribution front, at the end of the day we need people, consumers, to actually buy the stuff otherwise all that behind-the-scenes trading effort could be pointless like in the old hippy adage; 'suppose they held a war and nobody came?'

Let's pause to remember a couple of marvellously simple common-sense rules:

There are only three ways to increase profit:

1 Sell more
2 Raise prices
3 Cut costs

There are only two ways to increase sales:

1 Get new people to use your brand.
2 Get your current users to use more.

So if we are setting out to strengthen a brand in order to allow it to sell more (including extend into other areas) or to raise its prices then we need to start by understanding our brand. Brands are metaphysical entities. They live primarily in consumers' minds. We need to find out who's buying our brand and how they relate to it.

It's time to turn to your third pile of data, the one that measures the brand when it's used. Up there with retail audit data, the other data

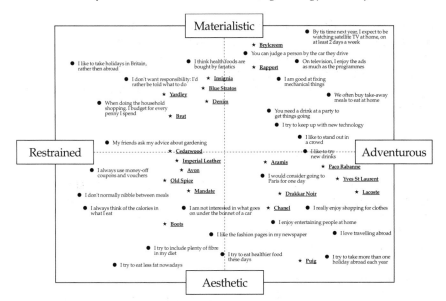

Figure 5.2   *Correspondence analysis*

source which is most widely used in the advertising industry is TGI. BMRB's Target Group Index is a huge self-completion survey. It takes at least three hours to fill it in and all you get is a £3 Marks & Spencer voucher but 25 000 people a year have enough goodwill towards market research to dutifully complete the questionnaire giving marketers (and sociologists) a goldmine of data. The survey asks people about their purchases and usage of products across a vast range of markets combined with their media consumption patterns, leisure interests and attitudes.

It is the Bible for media planning because it shows which media a brand's users are consuming. It allows for complex cross-tabulations. If you want to, you can find out how many Mars Ice Cream heavy users read *The Economist*, watch *Blind Date*, bought a lawnmower in the previous 12 months and agree that 'a real man can down several pints at a sitting'.

Segmentation studies are a classic use of TGI. Statistical techniques such as correspondence analysis allow you to identify a number of clusters of people within a given target market who have similar attitudes and behaviour (Figure 5.2). This psychographic analysis can be a very useful complement to TGI's standard demographic analysis.

An example

TGI's brand buying data should reflect the retail audit's sales data. However, every so often, you come across an apparent contradiction in the numbers. Let's not kid ourselves, despite what textbooks usually tell us, life isn't always straightforward and numbers sometimes don't seem to stack up. Things are often more interesting when they go wrong. Figures 5.3 and 5.4 are one such example. What do you do when the retail audit shows one brand share pattern and TGI shows a completely different pattern? Which one of them speaks with forked tongue?

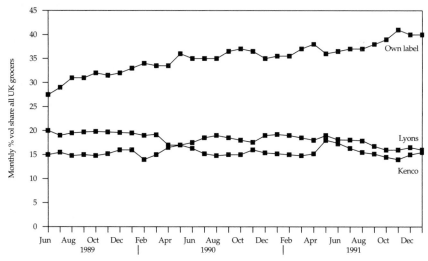

Figure 5.3   *Volume brand shares in the ground coffee market. (Source:* Nielsen)

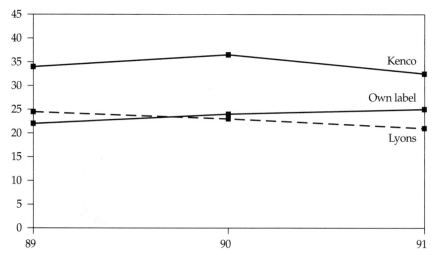

Figure 5.4   *Brand penetration as a percentage of all users of ground coffee. (Source:* TGI)

The first thing to do when you get this sort of breakdown is to go and make yourself a cup of coffee, breathe deeply and stay calm. The next thing to do is check the data's reliability. How big were the sample cells? Did the TGI data have any asterisks denoting statistically unreliable sample sizes? Next, start thinking about how the data are collected. Get hold of the original TGI questionnaire, use what you know about how people behave in this market and try to develop an explanation for the apparent contradiction. Here's my stab at it.

If in doubt TGI is probably less reliable for this particular market. We know from qualitative research and previous quantitative studies that ground coffee is a low-involvement market where purchase intervals for light users can be as low as three-monthly. Even when people do make a purchase the labelling can be confusing. They might buy 'one in a dark brown pack that's medium roasted and suitable for cafetieres. So light users possibly aren't that certain, without a visual prompt, which one they buy. Looking at the original TGI questionnaire shows that the ground coffee questions are asked directly after the instant coffee questions. People have just been prompted with the name Kenco. Very possibly they buy it in instant form because the instant coffee market is much more brand-name oriented. Maybe they see the familiar name of Kenco coming up and tick that box again (in error).

This would explain some of the data effect, but perhaps the explanation is simpler. The penetration data wouldn't necessarily reflect brand shares

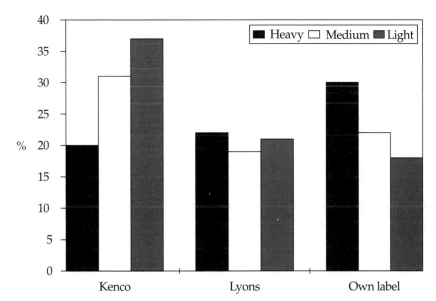

Figure 5.5 *Percentage of heavy, medium and light users who claim to use each brand. (Source: TGI)*

because penetration doesn't necessarily correlate with weight of purchase. It might be the case that much of Kenco's penetration is accounted for by light users. Indeed an analysis of TGI by frequency of use shows that this is the case (Figure 5.5). So although more people buy Kenco, they don't buy as much of it (TGI), therefore volume share is lower (Nielsen).

From this we can also start to develop a theory that people enter this confusing market via the reassurance of brand-name products, get to like ground coffee, buy and use it more often, get confident, notice that brand names are significantly more expensive than own-label and switch to own-label.

Feels plausible doesn't it? So off we go to test this hypothesis through other research and we've advanced from tearing our hair out to having a new hypothesis.

Volumetrics

TGI can be used to produce estimates of the volume of product consumption, hence the importance of different demographic groups to each market by using special analysis. TGI's own example covers the vodka market, and their analysis of regional variations in vodka consumption highlights the importance of Northern Ireland to volume sales in the vodka market.

The first stage in carrying out a volumetric analysis is to translate the claimed frequency of drinking vodka into an estimate of units drunk. Table 5.4 shows the frequency scale given to TGI respondents, and the volume equivalent used in this case. To convert frequency to volume, the 'default' translation scale for the vodka market has been used, which is pre-set into Choices (BMRB's PC-based special analysis system). Users are free to alter such translation scales if required.

Table 5.4

Vodka: frequency of drinking	Estimated measures per month consumed
10 or more measures per week	46.2
5–9 measures per week	29.4
3–4 measures per week	14.7
1–2 measures per week	6.3
3 or more measures per month	3.5
1–2 measures per month	1.5
Less than 1 in last month	
(at least 1 in last 6 months)	0.2

Table 5.5

Row	Cell	Total	All users: Vodka	Volume: Vodka
Total	#Resp	25853	5441	5334
	(000)	44158	9514	40341
	Vert%	100.00	100.00%	100.00%
	Index	100	100	100
Standard region: Northern Ireland				
	#Resp	1239	334	329
	(000)	1104	269	2630
	Vert%	**2.5**	**2.8**	**6.5**
	Index	100	113	261
Standard region: Yorkshire and Humberside				
	#Resp	2259	382	373
	(000)	3795	677	1450
	Vert%	8.5	7.1	3.6
	Index	100	83	42

Source: UKTGIM 93
Table base: adults 18+
WGT: POPBUKM
Copyright BMRB 1993

BMRB's example, in Table 5.5, shows that in the UK there are some 9.5 million vodka drinkers, who between them account for over 40 million measures of vodka per month.

Broken down into region, we see that there is some variation in the concentration of vodka users throughout the UK. For example, 2.8 per cent of vodka users live in Northern Ireland (roughly in proportion to the 2.5 per cent of the entire UK population living there). However, this 2.8 per cent of vodka drinkers downs 6.5 per cent of all the vodka measures drunk in the UK – an average of virtually ten measures each, per month. By contrast, the 7.1 per cent of vodka drinkers who live in Yorkshire and Humberside consume only 3.6 per cent of the total volume.

Beyond TGI

TGI's utility lies in its sheer size. But collecting and processing all that information from 25 000 people takes time. From the first interview in one year's survey to your getting the data to look at can be an interval of up to eighteen months. In stable mature markets this isn't the end of the world but in new or dynamic markets it's a problem. Further quantitative and qualitative research is a necessary supplement to TGI.

Panels

Most FMCG panel data are collected by issuing the panel member with a barcode reading 'pen'. Panels are therefore pretty accurate records of major supermarket shopping trips. They enable similar types of analyses to TGI but with greater confidence about accuracy of data collection. Consumer panel data can be extremely valuable as a way of under-standing patterns of brand switching within markets. Panels show the same individual or household's purchase choices over time. You can see if the generation 'cohort' of people who bought, for example, Budweiser five or ten years ago are still buying it or whether as their 'life stage' changed (onset of family life brings changed values) they've moved on to new brands and a new 'cohort' of Budweiser customers has taken their place. This identification of whether cohort or life stage has the greater effect on your market is often useful and is a form of analysis for which panels' longitudinal data are ideally suited. Panels aren't just for FMCG markets. There are motorists' diary panels, teenagers panels and even panels of financial intermediaries.

Usage and attitude surveys

U&As are a useful way of delving deeper into how people relate to a brand. They are *ad hoc* quantitative surveys commissioned by you especially to look in more detail at your brand. U&As can be used to discover how many of the brand's users use it in certain ways, what repertoires it sits in and essentially any of the questions from the earlier list which still remain unanswered. I suspect that U&As aren't conducted as frequently as they were ten or twenty years ago because a combination of qualitative research and a good tracking study is often capable of meeting the same information need.

Tracking studies

Tracking studies are often the principal ongoing source of quantitative data. The first studies were originally set up by Messrs Millward and Brown as a better way of tracking advertising's effectiveness. Before tracking studies, the typical method for measuring advertising effects was a 'pre and post' survey.

Pre and posts measure consumer's attitudes to and images of a set of brands before you advertise and then again a few months after your campaign. These timings are your timings and may not reflect competitors' advertising cycles. Just after your post measure the main competitor might bring out a very effective new campaign but if you've already spent the research budget on your two surveys you have no way of measuring the effectiveness of competitors' activity.

Tracking studies collect continuous data. A hundred or so people are interviewed every week and the data are studied on a rolling four-weekly basis to measure factors such as:

- Brand awareness
- Advertising awareness (both spontaneous and prompted)
- Brand image
- Brand predisposition (likelihood to buy)
- Recall of advertising
- Recall of claims made by the advertising
- Recognition of unbranded ads and the degree to which they are attributed to the correct advertiser.

Tracking studies have evolved away from their initial focus on advertising to a focus on the brand. This makes them increasingly useful in the development of new advertising strategies. In this respect one of the most useful questions is the predisposition or 'brand strength' measure. In many markets predisposition can be shown to be a good predictor of future sales and if you can isolate the main influence on predisposition you're halfway to a strategy already. The Alliance and Leicester case from the IPA's *Advertising Works 7* shows a relationship between sales, propensity and awareness:

> 'We find that although predisposition tends not to change very quickly, it is a reasonably accurate predictor of a society's share of the market. The correlation is not exact, but we would not expect it to be. Factors such as relative price (i.e. interest rates) and, importantly, branch location will modify the extent to which potential use is converted into actual use.

> We also find that propensity to use correlates well with awareness; in particular, with spontaneous awareness [Figures 5.6 and 5.7]. This continues the intuitive reasoning which says that people are happiest using household names.

> Note: in the figures the share of propensity to use has been calculated by taking the percentage of adults who would 'consider using' a given society and dividing it by the total of each of the top eight societies 'considering using' rating.'

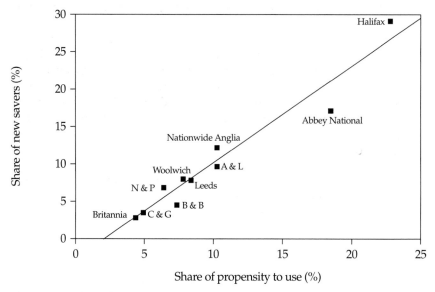

Figure 5.6   *Share of propensity to use for savings and share of new savers (1990).* (*Source*: FRS, April 1990 (propensity)/full year (new business))

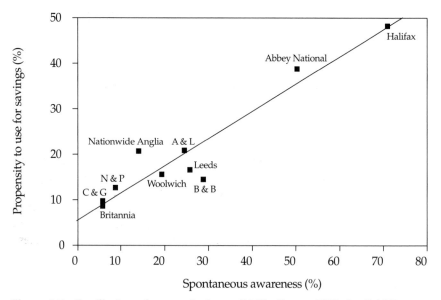

Figure 5.7   *Familiarity and propensity to use (1990). (Source*: FRS, April 1990 (propensity)/full year (awareness))

Measuring predisposition with other elements (generally price) held as a constant can be an excellent measure of brand strength and very probably future sales success.

During 1995 the newly arrived Orange mobile telecoms brand was still relatively weak in sales and distribution terms and was accordingly disparaged by its rivals. (My agency was invited to pitch by two of those rivals.) I presented the data in Table 5.6 to the Chief Executives of both Mercury One2one and Vodafone and on both occasions it had the desired effect of focusing the conversation on the need to start investing in their brand rather than relying on trading muscle to keep Orange at bay:

If you decided to buy a mobile phone and all of the brands in Table 5.6 had very similar prices and offers, which of the suppliers would you be most likely to choose?

Table 5.6

	%
Orange	27
Cellnet	22
Don't know	19
Vodafone	16
Mercury One2one	13
None of these	2

Base = national sample of adults who use a mobile phone nowadays and/or expect to buy one in the next five years.
Source: NOP 1000 Adults Omnibus, 4 June 1995.

This question wasn't conducted via a tracking study but via an omnibus survey. Omnibuses are surveys that are conducted regularly and on which anybody can buy questions. It's a cost-effective way of asking a few questions because you share the set-up and fieldwork costs with other 'passengers'. If your market isn't changing rapidly, buying into an omnibus every quarter can be a cheaper alternative to tracking studies.

Designing questions

When writing questions for inclusion on an omnibus, or for any other use, remember to think about;

- How you want to use the answers
- How you would react to that question if someone asked you
- How to keep the respondent interested and motivated to help.

The last issue is too often overlooked, particularly in relation to image grids. We generally ask too many questions, force people to go through list after list of things they don't know or care about. Imagine being grilled by twenty minutes of questions such as:

To what extent would you agree or disagree that Shell Unleaded is 'becoming popular among people like me nowadays'?

Do you: Agree strongly? Agree slightly? Neither agree nor disagree? Disagree slightly? Disagree strongly?

And to what extent would you agree or disagree that Esso Unleaded is 'becoming popular among people like me nowadays'?

Do you: Agree strongly? Agree slightly? Neither agree nor disagree? Disagree slightly? Disagree strongly?

And to what extent would you agree or disagree that BP Unleaded is 'becoming popular among people like me nowadays'?

Do you: Agree strongly? Agree slightly? Neither agree nor disagree? Disagree slightly? Disagree strongly?
etc.
etc.

No wonder Judie Lannon once defined the answers to such questions as 'that response which the interviewee senses would most quickly release them from the instrument of torture known as an image battery'.

The respondent often doesn't have very strong views about a brand. They are not as committed or 'loyal' as we like to imagine. In markets characterized by a great deal of inertia you may find it useful to ask provocatively worded questions to get any sort of response at all. A provocatively worded question such as 'When did you stop beating your wife?' can bias towards a particular answer but you can ask an equally biased question from the opposite perspective (rotating the order of asking). If people agreed with both questions then it would demonstrate their lack of strong opinions on the issue (see Table 5.7).

Take it easy with your questions, less can be more. Always use the vernacular and always pilot your questionnaire on your neighbouring colleagues to see how it sounds.

Table 5.7

'If people had any sense, they would close their bank accounts and use a building society instead.'

Agree strongly	12%
Agree slightly	12%
Neither agree nor disagree	16%
Disagree slightly	44%
Disagree strongly	26%

'Building societies are very limited. Most working people also need a bank account.'

Agree strongly	36%
Agree slightly	27%
Neither agree nor disagree	8%
Disagree slightly	15%
Disagree strongly	11%

Source: NOP Omnibus, 3 April 1994

Conclusion

It is amazingly easy to waste lots of time just swimming aimlessly in data. Don't just collect it for its own sake, When developing advertising strategy you are not the uniformed police constable who collects and files information, you are the detective who has to make a case out of it. Constantly develop and test hunches and hypotheses. Keep pursuing lines of enquiry. Keep asking yourself 'and this means that...'

One day you'll feel that your current hypothesis about:

Who exactly are we talking to?
What do we want them to do?
What exactly can we tell them to influence them?

is the 'right' one and go with it. Then you'll call it the strategy and 'sell' it to your immediate customers, your creative teams and clients.

To get to this end point, to get any sort of use out of quantitative data you need to have an approach, a set of questions which can act as a route map through the statistics. For example, I have grouped some questions under the following headings:

1 Market economics and competitor analysis
2 Consumers' relationship with the product/service category
3 Consumers' relationship with the individual brands
4 Consumers' relationship with the advertising

This chapter has been about using quantitative data in the context of formulating advertising strategy. Advertising is about using mass communications to engage with people and either reassure them that their behaviour/attitudes are right or cause them to want to change their behaviour/attitudes. Always try to look at your quantitative data qualitatively, asking 'What does this mean in human terms?' At some point you are going to want to get inside people's minds for a greater understanding than quantitative data can provide. If you haven't already read it you should turn next to the chapter about qualitative research.

Overview: Chapter 6

This chapter on qualitative research is also taken from the IPA's Stage 2 Campaign Planning course and was first presented in 1983. Roddy Glen is, in my view, one of that small elite of outstanding qualitative researchers with whom it is always a pleasure to share a project, and usually an enlightenment to hear a debrief from.

It would be fair to say that, in comparison to most other 'stages' of the qualitative market research process, analysis and interpretation are not given enough prominence in terms either of general discussion and debate or in the planning and scheduling of specific projects at the time they are commissioned.

Client's don't ask about A&I much, or discuss it with researchers, preferring instead to concentrate on those more visible parts of the process for which they can be held evidently accountable. For the researchers' part, the more projects they can do in any period, the more money they make, so the less time-consuming each one is, the better.

As the UK economy in the late 1990s reheats, and economies in some other parts of the globe go into overdrive, two significant effects seem likely:

- Time pressure on qualitative projects will increase further, as a result of growth in demand and of the way in which the research community responds to this, initially, at least (heavier workloads, quicker working, more juniors)
- Declining experience and understanding of the qualitative process among 'new generation' clients and agency planners, themselves relatively junior and under increasingly heavy workloads

There will be little to encourage introspection, and more incentive to press on with the business of growing the bottom line.

In this chapter Roddy therefore has two aims:

1 To outline the processes of analysis and interpretation as they would *ideally* be conducted, thus providing a benchmark of sorts, to which new buyers and sellers may refer
2 To demonstrate that 'interpretation' in particular is not merely the regurgitated 'voice of the consumer' on the demand side but a

process which extends from the initial request for research right through to intelligent discussion of the issues which emerge.

The intelligence of Roddy's writing style reflects the depth in which he has explored this subject. The relevance of his conclusions also seem to me to have applicability beyond the field of advertising research.

6 Analysis and interpretation in qualitative research: a researcher's perspective

Roddy Glen

Clients cannot be blamed for feeling that in buying qualitative market research (QMR) they are making a leap into faith. How do they really know what they are getting? (Indeed in some instances how do they know *who* they are getting? An important consideration in an industry where brands tend to exist, for the most part, at the level of the individual.) How can they tell if it is 'good' or 'bad'? Most importantly, how can they *ensure* that it is 'good'?

It seems all too often to be pretty haphazard, with outcomes which may be equally idiosyncratic. As a client, you may be present for the meetings prior to the fieldwork at which the objectives, methodology, sample, stimulus material and details of topics to be covered are discussed and agreed; at the interviews themselves (particularly if they are group discussions); and at the debrief presentation. But what you don't see is that part of the process in which the *meaning* of what was said in the interviews is judgementally determined through processes of analysis and interpretation. *That* tends to take place at times and in places which are the researcher's 'private territory'. In a way it parallels the creative process in advertising, where the client has an 'input' role at the start of the process, a 'receiving output' role later in the process, and very little contact with it in between.

It's not surprising, then, that the analysis and interpretation parts of the overall QMR process are among the least talked about. Clients, being more focused on the debrief, generally ask few, if any, questions about them. Researchers for the most part volunteer nothing either, which is a little more curious as it is mostly their skill at delivering insights upon which their reputations are maintained, as opposed to their ability actually to conduct the interviews. It's as if 'A&I' is too delicate an area of the process to withstand more than the most superficial discussion.

It remains mysterious; a sort of 'black box' into which go the data from expensive interviews and out of which comes a view of the market, the brand, the advertising, the packaging, etc. which appears at times to bear little relation to 'what respondents said'. Little wonder if there are some clients who are suspicious of it.

So how does it work? How should it work? What 'rules' are there about how it should be done?

This chapter seeks to illuminate this rather dark area of QMR, and is divided into three main sections:

1 Orientation and inputs
2 Functional issues – the mechanics of the process
3 Interpretation of consumer responses

Orientation and inputs

Most of the better qualitative researchers enjoy not only the collecting of data (and the attention they get when conducting group discussions and when presenting the findings) but also the activities of *hypothesizing, conceptualizing* and *interpreting*. The spirit of enquiry excites them, as does the *achievement of meaning*.

They deal in *ideas*, not 'data', and they are constantly attempting to split those ideas to see what they contain. In contrast to quantitative research, they chase significance, not incidence. Of particular importance is the realization that *interpretation is integral to the progression of a qualitative research study, and not a distinct stage*. This is worth examining in greater detail.

In the past, there was a tendency to think of a qualitative study as proceeding in a sequential but discrete manner. It would start with taking the brief and then go to the stage of data collection, followed by analysis, which was then followed by interpretation, leading to the eventual debrief. At each of these stages the researcher would be required to adopt a different mental 'mode', be it passive, absorptive, active, expansive, intuitive, etc. I am sure it's possible to *attempt* qualitative research in this way, but I am equally sure that it won't be much good. Insights will almost certainly be missed which could have been gained in the early stages of the study and which could have been of vital importance in shaping the thinking in subsequent stages.

Nowadays most practitioners believe the analysis and interpretation of qualitative data cannot be divorced from the earlier stages of a study. Sensitive interpretation begins at the briefing and design stages and the study progresses in the form of the continuous development, evolution, refinement (and often rejection) of *hypotheses*. Stephen Wells (1991) calls these 'rolling hypotheses', which seems a fair description. The good qualitative researcher, then, switches into interpretative mode as soon as the project is mentioned, and becomes fully mentally engaged with it as early as possible.

There are several stages where 'rolling hypotheses' and *active* thought are particularly important:

- The brief
- Project design elements
- What respondents 'say'
- What it all might mean
- What it means in terms of the 'Client's Thing' (the 'supply-side' structures, such as the advertising, the packaging, the product concept, the market, etc., whatever is the focus of the enquiry)

It is difficult to overestimate the importance of the first two. What happens at this stage, when the enquiry is being defined and designed, and what the researcher understands of 'the mission' is crucial. There are several different kinds of potential input, from various of the parties involved, and they each require interrogation and interpretation for the project to work optimally. Not all these inputs will fall into the researcher's lap, however, and it is important that he or she actively seeks access to all of them.

The brief

It may well be necessary to ascertain the political 'spin' on a brief and to attempt to 'decode' it. As Wendy Gordon and Roy Langmaid (1988) point out, there may be an overt brief and a 'covert brief', especially where more than one party has a direct interest in the outcome of the research. (Client marketers and agency; client NPD department and marketers are two of the most common axes here.) There are also a great many questions which may usefully be asked by the researcher at the start of a project. The answers to them, and indeed the need to ask them in the first place, all form an integral part of the process of interpretation which runs throughout the enquiry:

1 What decisions will the client/agency be using the output to assist with? (A good way, this, of sometimes getting a more succinct articulation of the brief!)
2 What other information does the client or advertising agency have which forms the context for the enquiry and therefore its findings (brand positioning, brand-share trend data, advertising tracking performance, etc.)? Odd though it seems to have to mention it, the Advertising Strategy and/or the Creative Brief are just such pieces of information where creative development research is concerned. It is surprising how many 'CD' projects are done with inadequate reference to these vital benchmark documents.

3 What models does the client have concerning the issue area? How do they think these might work, and what doubts do they have about their hypotheses?

This last area is one which can sometimes be contentious. Clients sometimes fear that the researcher's judgement and equanimity will be compromised if too much of the background is shared with him or her at the outset. I prefer to take the view that we're sufficiently grown-up and professional nowadays for this danger to be very remote. The disingenuously empty brief usually conceals a can of worms which the research is unlikely to remedy anyway, as well as being insulting to the researcher.

Of particular importance in creative development work is the need to understand not only *what* the proto-advertising is trying to communicate (per strategy and brief, as mentioned above) but *how* it seeks to go about this, in terms of the creative structures it employs. This is a question which unfortunately too few agencies are ready to answer at the briefing, and which has been known to send board account directors into an impromptu interpretative frenzy of their own.

Project design elements

These include:

- The sample
- Any stimulus material
- The topic guide
- The role for, and choice of any projective techniques.

The extent to which the researcher gets to determine these varies tremendously, depending on:

- The type of project (NPD, creative development, etc.)
- The brand history
- Its research history particularly (need for continuity, etc.)
- The relationship between the researcher and the buyer
- The internal culture of the commissioning client or agency.

Interpretation at this stage often takes an anticipatory as opposed to a rationalizatory form, in that much of the thinking that goes into designing a piece of qualitative research is concerned with deciding:

1 The best quotas (what kind of respondents will help us test our hypotheses best?)
2 Interview order (how can we arrange it to get the most out of each issue area while not having those covered earlier spoil it too much for those covered later?)

3 Stimulus material (what form should it take to be most easily and unambiguously understood by respondents?)
4 Projective techniques (which would be useful, appropriate for the type of respondent and not too time consuming?)

Whether we like it or not, all of this involves hypotheses about how people relate to the market sector, the brands, the packaging, the advertising, as well, of course, as about what they may not understand, what they may learn in the course of the interview, and how they may behave during it.

In summary, interpretation, in most instances a close relative of common sense, should be regarded as a continuous process, running throughout the entire qualitative study. The more questions you ask yourself at the outset, the more hypotheses you evolve, the more you attempt to anticipate responses, the more you interrogate the product or repeatedly view the advertising before going 'into the field', the richer will be your relationship with what happens in the interviews.

I sometimes think it's better to regard the whole process as one wherein we are being asked to *think* and to clarify some issues, and *as part of this* the client is paying for our stimulation in the form of access to relevant groups in the community via structured conversation.

Functional issues – the mechanics of the process

Although the activity of interpretation should run throughout any project, it is nevertheless the case that at some points in the process there are large data inputs, and these require to be 'digested' in some coherent way. The most notable of these is the point after completion of fieldwork.

At this stage the researcher has accumulated a pile of tape recordings, a few notes made after each group, notes from any observers of the groups, possibly a transcript or two if time has permitted, and a collection of hazy memories of the interviewing experience interspersed with recollections of fatigue, motorway service areas at night, and white bread sandwiches lovingly prepared by northern night porters.

What do we actually *do* with all this? Here, two principal types of problem arise. Alan Hedges (1983) identifies them as:

1 Functional – how does one cope with this mass of data? How does one break it down and digest it? It can be a daunting prospect.
2 Interpretative – how does one decide what it means? What to take literally, and what to believe? How to decide what it all adds up to? And how then to relate it back to the structures the client can work with?

There are three main areas of interpretation of consumer responses, which involve increasing levels of conceptual thought, with the functional activity called 'analysis' coming immediately after the first stage, which is itself an integrated input to it. The overall order of the stages of the process is as follows:

- Interpretation (Level 1) – What do respondents each feel and mean?
- Analysis – Sifting, differentiating, separating, sorting, ordering the data
- Interpretation (Level 2) – What patterns emerge, and what do *they* mean?
- Interpretation (Level 3) – What does it mean re the 'Client's Thing'?

While noting that the first level of interpretation occurs before and during the activity of analysis – indeed it takes place in the researcher's head as each interview progresses, a point I will return to – it is best to consider the two types of problem separately. This section deals with those which come under the heading 'Analysis'.

There is no magic formula for coping with data, no unique prescription for success. Everyone has to develop their own personal style of working. It is worth here considering the options available at this stage in the process. Some are much more satisfactory than others, and you should be aware of the trade-offs which pertain when deciding which method of data organization to use (see Figure 6.1).

Tapes

After the interviews, a complete aural record of them exists in the form of the tape recordings made. You can use these in any of four basic ways:

1 To listen to and make notes from, of an interpretative sort. The researcher notes the content in paraphrase form, and records observations in a margin. These observations are of a hypothetical nature, and may also be remarks about patterns arising or commonality with events on other tapes.
2 To listen to and make complete verbatim transcripts. The researcher may at the same time make notes in the margin as described above.
3 To send out for full verbatim transcription. The idea here is that the researcher receives back a full written transcript of the group discussion/depth interview from which they can subsequently work. Transcripts are useful as a source of illustrative quotes (for the report).
4 To listen to while following what is said on a full verbatim transcript. This is perhaps the best and most thorough method of content analysis, and allows the researcher to re-experience the interview and make

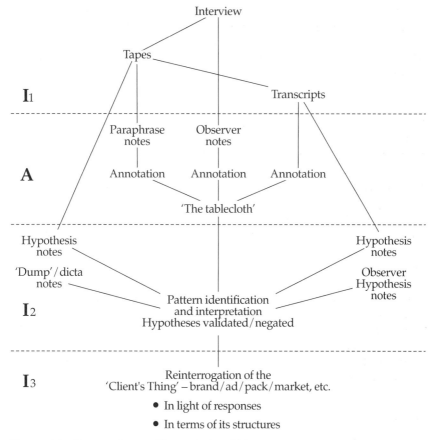

Figure 6.1 *Process stages – 'the mysterious bit'*

remarks on the transcript and on an 'hypotheses notepad'. Better sense can be made of the transcript this way – repeated remarks can be traced to individuals and a better feeling for consensus or disagreement can be obtained.

It is important in my view that researchers listen to some of the tapes, to invigorate the nerve-endings; to rekindle the 'buzz' of the interviews. It is essential to remind oneself of the ways in which respondents expressed themselves and of the *tone* of different parts of the discussion (flat, enthusiastic, chatty, hostile, etc.), the silences, the terminology, etc. If *forced* to make a limited selection, it is probably good to choose tapes of interviews in which views were expressed which were in some way puzzling, and those where the proceedings crackled along, rich in comments which were particularly stimulating. The dangers of this should be clear, however. We are more likely to base our interpretation on more vividly recalled data, and hence bias is highly likely to creep into the process as a result of selectively reviewing them. It is *not* best practice.

One great benefit of listening back to the recordings is that in addition to hearing what was said (and not said) again, the researcher can restimulate the thoughts *they* had during the interview, but had no time to examine. This, for me, is vital. I find I often have thoughts 'in the heat of battle' which, if not major insights or end points themselves, are frequently good beginnings of productive trains of thought. By the end of an evening's fieldwork, I've forgotten half of them.

Much of this is *not* accessible through simply reading transcripts – specially those parts *where people do not say what they mean or do not mean what they say*. In the UK today, the media has changed both what people know about and the way they speak. Ordinary people know something of surrealism. Understatement has long been an English verbal character-istic. Irony has more recently become a common expressive mode. 'Everyone's Dali now' and 'It's quite good' are both dependent on inflection for precise interpretation. Try them in front of the bathroom mirror, with different 'voice musics' and you will realize how much transcripts cannot offer.

Transcripts

I personally use these only infrequently, finding them less restimulating than tape reviewing. This is because I'm an audial person, more than a visual one. Full verbatim transcripts are favoured by many researchers as the 'source' from which they conduct the analysis and interpretation. This is always assuming that there is time enough between fieldwork and debrief for transcripts to be made, and for the researcher then to conduct a comprehensive analysis of them.

When reading full verbatim transcripts, the researcher should devise some way of beginning a distillation process in respect of the content. A system whereby marks, comments, abbreviations, etc. are written in the margins of the transcripts is a good one. This 'coding' of the transcripts can then save a great deal of time at the next stage.

When reading transcripts, as when reviewing the tapes, the researcher should refer constantly to *the objectives* of the research and, second, to the *topic guide*. The objectives are the agreed framework within which the client expects the findings, conclusions and recommendations to be couched. You should never stray far from them. While always referring to these 'guides' the researcher can write on the transcript thus:

- Summarize a majority view/behaviour/attitude
- Underline comments or quotes which illustrate this and code them in the margin for ease of retrieval

- Pick out a minority viewpoint
- Ignore obviously eccentric comments
- Annotate responses by type, using your own 'system' of codes and abbreviations, e.g: for positive or negative responses, comprehension problems, good illustrative quotes, etc.

You can also annotate in a more interpretative way by summarizing sections in the margin, e.g. hero unaspirational; presenter patronizing/insincere; proposition incredible, etc. These would be interpretative comments based on the responses to a series of questions or projectives.

It is useful again to have a parallel 'hypothesis notepad' when reading and annotating transcripts. This may be used as a respository for such interpretative comments and for jotting down, in no particular order, hypotheses, 'profound' thoughts and tentative conclusions. It is good discipline to use this pad only for 'global' thoughts and observations, not allowing specific quotes or responses to be mentioned. These notes will later provide a very useful series of ideas and frameworks through which the 'findings' may be appraised, and perhaps even explained and presented.

Thus at the end of this (time-consuming) process all the transcripts may be read quickly by looking at the annotations, and the interpretative framework is beginning to build.

Once this stage has been reached, you are ready to gain a more coherent overall view of responses, patterns, attitudes, etc. One good way preferred by many researchers is then to transfer the notes made on the transcripts (or from listening to tapes) on to a very large sheet of paper.

Table 6.1   *The 'tablecloth'*

Topic areas	Cells	25–34 BC1 South	35–50 BC1 North	25–34 C2D North	35–50 C2D South
Sector appeal Brands aware (spont). Brands used/in repertoire Differences between brands Brand A – personality Brand B – personality etc....					

I call this the 'tablecloth'. This sheet will be ruled into rows and columns, each column representing an interview or group. Each 'row' represents an area of the discussion, either literally (in terms of *responses*) or in hypothesis form. It may be highly mechanistic – simply a charting of responses which may then be examined for patterns – or it may be more interpretative (Table 6.1). The completed grid can then be marked, perhaps using different-coloured pencils to highlight response patterns, attitudes, behavioural traits and comments which appear to support or negate various of the rolling hypotheses.

From here, conclusions may begin to form, although only on a superficial level. It is the combination of this discipline and the application of hypotheses and conceptual frameworks of various sorts from which conclusions of a more penetrating and usable sort will emerge.

Notes taken by skilled and briefed observer

The opportunity sometimes exists for two researchers to attend the interview. It can be very useful if (and only if) both of them are fully briefed as to the objectives of the study and the proposed method of investigation of the various issue areas. One may take notes during the group as the other conducts it. These notes would ideally be as nearly as possible a full transcript – but may in fact be a mixture of verbatims and, if there is time, observations, hypotheses, conjectural thoughts, etc. This method of working is more suited to experienced researchers who will, by virtue of their experience, be more able to generate hypotheses quickly and judge the mood and tone of the interview as it proceeds. Importantly, it is *not* a substitute for the subsequent listening to tapes (or at least some of them), nor for the subsequent analysis of full verbatim transcripts. It does, however, come into its own when there is little time allowed between the completion of fieldwork and the debrief presentation. In such cases – which ought to be regarded as *in extremis* – the notes thus made would be 'distilled' down in the manner already described so that patterns, behaviours, attitudes, etc. can be clearly identified.

One of the characteristics of QMR, which some might say is a weakness, is the fact that it is usually the potentially idiosyncratic product of one mind. Most companies do not have a sufficiently robust margin that they can double-head all the fieldwork. Double-heading a project with a colleague is, however, something I think everyone in the business should experience, so stimulating is it when you come to interpretative tasks. It is an excellent way of hothousing issues and generating secondary and tertiary thoughts and ideas, much as respondents do in groups.

'Dump' notes and/or dicta-tapes

A good habit to cultivate is the *immediate* recording, either on tape or in written form, of the researcher's impressions, thoughts, feelings and hypotheses *after each interview*. These should be made after (not during) the interview, and should be brief. They should endeavour to capture something of the mood or spirit of the group so that when it comes to reading the full verbatim transcript the feeling or 'buzz' of the event is rekindled to some extent. I use a tape to 'dump' the thoughts I had while conducting the interview, so that I needn't worry about forgetting them. These notes should not be 'findings' as such, but should constitute the collection of hypotheses which will 'roll' throughout the study. You should also be sufficiently flexible to record suggestions for methodological revisions to the study as well. The benefit of making such immediate post-fieldwork notes is that they start the hypotheses 'rolling', and focus your thinking in a beneficial way.

One further very important point is worth making about the process of analysis and interpretation. As Wendy Gordon (1983) says in her paper on this subject:

> *Whilst the fieldwork is in progress or after the groups or interviews are completed you will find that a subconscious process of interpretation takes place. Thoughts will creep into your mind whilst you're driving. Whilst cooking a meal a sudden flash of insight on a particular aspect of the study will hit you like a bolt from the blue even though you were unaware that you were really thinking about it. These subconscious interpretative thoughts are like gold dust – value them and treasure them.*

This is absolutely right. Like a process of fermentation these thoughts occur spontaneously and unbidden, *and you could not have had them had you not experienced the interview or group*. Trust them. They often take the form of very important hypotheses.

In summary, the process of content analysis is one for which there are no short-cuts. It takes time and concentration. It cannot be rushed or skimped. Only when it is done thoroughly can you be confident that you have not been superficial or impressionistic. Your understanding may not be quite the same as someone else's but it *is* based on sound procedure.

You have reached the point where, as Wendy Hayward (Robson and Foster, 1989) describes it, you have held on to the data and now you must let it go. We each have our own metaphor for this part of the process, as it's difficult to describe otherwise. It is one of the areas which inexperienced qualitatives find the most alarming because it's almost counter-intuitive. Their difficulty is that they daren't stop looking at the trees for fear they will forget some part of the wood. The way to see the wood, however, is to get above it. Time to fly...

Interpretation of consumer responses

When we reach the post-fieldwork stage, where a mass of raw qualitative 'data' has accumulated, we should have some ideas already about what certain parts of it might mean. Much interpretation, however, still remains to be done, in order to create meaning out of the apparent chaos of the 'data'.

Analysing and interpreting qualitative 'data', however, is not just a matter of semantic content analysis, but of looking for *meaning* – the music as well as the words. There are three levels on which the interpretation of interview data operates in QMR:

1 Interpreting what people say to get to what they mean
2 Interpreting what the whole thing might mean
3 Interpreting what this means in terms of the 'Client's Thing'

Interpreting what people say to get to what they mean

This level of interpretation, of course, occurs both during the interviews and at the start of the whole process of post-interview analysis and interpretation, when listening to tapes or reading transcripts. In the interviews we are, as moderators, constantly having to respond to what is going on. We listen, assess, seek elaboration, probe, prompt and generally make on-the-spot judgements about *what* is being said and *how*. We don't have questionnaires, but are instead much more flexible, being both proactive and reactive. This is similar to the interpretative activity that we all carry on whenever we converse with anyone. The difference here is that our conversation has a purpose which goes beyond simply understanding what is said.

Qualitative researchers inhabit, by virtue of their primary task, a world which lies between *people* and *things*. We attempt to understand and illuminate people's *relationships* with things, usually with the purpose of assisting the proprietors or creators of those things in strengthening this relationship in motivational terms. *Meaning* is ascribed by people to things. It does not reside inherently in products, brands, advertisements, or any *thing*. So meaning is a construction, and is the only reality that matters, in market research at least.

There are difficulties involved in establishing the meanings people place on things, however, and merely analysing what people *say* is unlikely to overcome them. These problems arise because in the research situation we are dealing with:

- People (!)
- Respondents
- Users/non-users of certain types of products or services

In these multiple capacities, people are likely to be unreliable conveyors of meaning, and the good researcher will develop (with experience) a greater understanding of people in these 'roles' and the pressures they experience which contribute to this unreliability. People:

- Are often poor at expressing themselves
- May be inconsistent and self-contradictory
- Often have not thought about what they believe or why they do things
- May not want to admit to others (or even to themselves) how they feel or behave, and hence may distort or even lie
- May be subject to group or other social pressures
- Are in an artificial situation (i.e. they are *respondents*, being interviewed).

In groups they behave in ways which further act to conceal the true meaning of their relationship with the subject of the enquiry. Frequently they:

- 'Follow a leader'
- Feel obliged to be critical
- Are defensive, lest they appear stupid (a big fear!)
- Compete for attention
- Seek to agree
- Fight for informal leadership

In short, they don't/can't always say what they mean, and don't always mean what they say.

A good researcher will develop a sensitivity to these group dynamic factors which attend and affect the group process, as well as gaining a basic knowledge of 'body language', allowing them to interpret what various postures usually mean – particularly those to do with acceptance/rejection and agreement/disbelief. With experience, too, of working across many different markets, and (yes! it's allowed) drawing on their own experience as a consumer as a start point for hypotheses, researchers can develop a sensitivity to the conventions, totems and taboos of various product fields. In this way there is a greater chance of reaching a better understanding of people in their roles as consumers, users, non-users etc.

Mini-case

In the late 1980s the Meat and Livestock Comission ran a television campaign in support of British pork. It featured lighthearted vignettes of families being served different pork-based dishes (visual recipe suggestions). The family members were shown looking eager and enthusiastic at the arrival of the dishes, and their attraction was rendered humourously visual by showing them leaning over sideways towards it. The proposition offered to the viewer was a dual one which sought to encourage greater *reliance* on pork as an attractive dinner meat, and which underpinned this with the idea that pork is (perhaps surprisingly) *lean*, and therefore healthy. The endline was 'Lean on (British) Pork'. Research was examining some potential new scripts for the campaign.

Respondents in groups said they liked the ad, that it was 'quite good', and generally had no difficulty in replaying the communication. When asked what it was saying, it was striking how many people replayed the communication almost verbatim from the strategy document. It would also have been easy to miss the equally striking number who prefaced their response with the words 'I suppose...'

The proposition was not in fact adopted by most respondents. This was in large part because, as expressed via the commercials, it was something most people found counter-intuitive. At the time of research, the prevailing opinion of pork was that it was a fatty meat.* Additionally their perceptions of the visual 'joke' and, more particularly, of the reason for it (a visual-semantic bridge – often dodgy in my experience) seemed to mean that it remained as a *perceived intention* rather than as anything more enrolling. Being nice people, however, they made a concession for it.

The word 'suppose', used in the way they used it, has a very special function. It means something like 'I can see what they're trying to say, and can imagine that there may be some people, more easily amused than I am, who would enjoy the way they've gone about it. It doesn't quite make it for me, however, and so I don't really feel obliged to take it that seriously. Points for trying, though.'

Advertising to which the audience condescends may ultimately be only a little better than that which patronizes the viewer.

---

* It is fair to say that the campaign was never expected to change people's minds overnight. It was in fact the start of what was recognized by the Meat and Livestock Commission as necessarily a long-term education process, which has, with perseverance through the subsequent years, been measurably successful.

The problems of interpreting what respondents *mean* from what they *say,* and what they *think* from what they *say and do,* are aggravated by the fact that qualitative interviews rarely deal with the more cut-and-dried areas of attitude and behaviour, and have to cope with intangible or even subconscious attitudes and motivations.

Our job, then, is to build up a picture of each individual, and of how they affect and are affected by the interview situation. We then try to understand how they each view the things they are asked to consider (market, brand, advertising, packaging, propositions, etc.) and to gauge the levels of enthusiasm, commitment, and sincerity with which these views are held. What do they seem involved with? What do they block? What 'language do they use? How honest are they being? How consistent are they being? When are they being ironic or disingenuous, and when to take them literally?

Most researchers have had the experience of playing a piece of proto-advertising only to be told by respondents that the message was that the brand could be enjoyed or used by everybody. In a few cases (e.g. Coca-Cola's classic campaign) this may be *part* of the intended communication. In most cases, however, it is a response offered, sometimes disin-genuously, because it is not instantly apparent what the real message is. Here, the researcher has to be alert to the possibility of respondents hoping that this answer will prevent any further questions about something they find too difficult or obscure.

It's fair to say that in making those assessments, common sense is the main guide, and that we are essentially using the same tools as we use in everyday conversation, only using them more intensively and more objectively. The 'antennae' which we develop in childhood to interpret others' moods and dispositions are simply deployed here in a different way which does not have ourselves as the end-beneficiary. The process can be made to sound more arcane and mystical than is in fact the case, and it's true that a balance has to be maintained between being fanciful and being over literal or naive. It is likewise important, as Alan Hedges (1983) points out, to realize that the process has no definite end-point, in terms of the attainment of *'the answer'*:

> It's important to dispel the fallacy that there's a hard, cold, clean pristine Platonic Truth underneath it all if we only had the analytic tools to scrape away the surface junk. Underneath that muddled, chaotic, inconsistent surface there may well lie a muddled, chaotic, inconsistent reality. People are ambivalent, untidy bundles of latencies, not clear-cut and deterministic machines.

Interpreting what the whole thing might mean

Once you've decided what you think people mean, what conclusions do you draw from it? What patterns emerge from across the different types of people in the sample which might confirm or negate the various hypotheses you have been examining? How do the response patterns stack up with the conventional wisdoms surrounding the issue areas? This is a higher-level interpretative problem, which involves making judgements about the application and the decision-making context of the study.

An example illustrates the two levels of problem. Suppose you show people some advertising and they claim to dislike it. You may have a problem on the first level – that of deciding if they said what they meant and meant what they said. Can you believe their comments represent their real feelings? Were they reacting to the *style* of the stimulus material rather than the content of the ad? Did the group setting invite people to assume more critical postures than they felt? Were they led by one strong hostile voice?

But there's also a problem on the higher level. Assuming you conclude that they genuinely disliked the ad, does it actually *matter* that they don't like it? Is that an appropriate 'test' for an ad in the particular sector involved? If it was doing all the right things in terms of communication and seemed likely to be impactful and memorable, isn't that the overriding consideration? In recent research into new advertising for Christian Aid this was precisely the case, with few people liking the ads, and a great many being provoked in other ways entirely. The intention was to create disturbance and discomfort, which would lead to outrage and, hopefully, action.

At this second level the objectives both of the study and of the advertising become important. What do the former ask you to do? Are you just supposed to be *describing* people's responses? Or are you supposed to be *explaining* why they say what they say, and what implications it has? Are you expected to 'evaluate' and 'provide guidance'? The more you try to judge and explain, the more you get involved in the higher-level interpretative problems. But the less you try to judge and explain, the more your client is left grappling with the interpretation of evidence he or she can't possibly understand as well as you do. Consistent responses such as 'It'd be better if they kept it as a cartoon', 'People will be offended' and 'It's aimed at (another target group)' are not uncommon, and invariably require judgements as to their ultimate relevance.

It is not simply enough to describe people's responses in most cases. To do so is to remain in the realm of reportage as opposed to that of interpreted findings, and on the level of *specifics* as opposed to achieving a more useful *general* portrayal of the nature of their relationship with the issues or material under investigation.

The researcher's task at this stage is not simply to present the client with a join-the-dots 'picture' of how people claimed to feel about the brand or the advertising, but to deal in *boundaries, lines of generality,* in a more conceptual way.

Interpreting what this means in terms of the 'client's thing'

In taking the project forward from our interpretation of the aggregated views of the consumers interviewed, we need to establish how these various interpretations or conclusions relate usefully to the client view or model or to their 'Thing' – be it a new product, packaging, advertising or the market itself. The key frequently lies in the following activity:

Reinterrogating the 'Client's Thing'
– in structural and conceptual terms
– in light of the responses

The important word here is *conceptual*. For it is concepts, abstract notions, general ideas which embrace or illuminate many specifics, which enable us to make more sense out of the world and consequently to make decisions, the purpose of which we are clear about.

As researchers we come into contact over time with many product fields and types of advertising. As professionals it is our duty to be curious about these, and to be students of them. We will begin to evolve mental maps, models, typologies which may assist in the interpretation of qualitative 'data'. Some are little more than straightforward 'checklists' of areas for examination, others are more evolutionary in nature. For example, in an attempt to understand 'the market' within which a brand operates we would examine:

> Users
> Usage patterns and occasions
> Purchasing
> The role and importance of brands
> Salient evaluative criteria for differentiating between brands
> Brand positionings on these dimensions
> Brand images, personalities, essences
> . . . and so on

Within each of these areas there may be further known subdivisions which are expressible in concept form, albeit in 'jargon', e.g.

Purchasing:
| Premeditated | Impulse |
| Distress | Stock-keeping, etc. |

Within each area of marketing activity there may be numerous hypotheses we wish to test, e.g.

- That consumers see the market as divided into the same categories as does the manufacturer's marketing department (a good one this, with spirits and fortified wines, countlines and moulded bars)

- That the salient criterion for differentiating between brands is taste
- That brand loyalty is high
- That the market is an added-value one, showing price positivity
- That purchasing is always premeditated
- That the advertising must always show a typical usage occasions, or type of user, etc.

The litany may indeed be a long one.

There is a similarly long (although nowhere does it seem to have been written down) list of types of advertising platforms or structures, each of which is likely to give rise to key issues with which consumers will be concerned, e.g.

Type	*Issue*
Expert testimonial ⎤	
User testimonial ⎦	Credibility
Celebrity endorsement	Identification with user, credibility
Knowing-brand-in-conspiracy	Targeting, identification
Humour	Branding, targeting, identification
Cartoons	Targeting

We can learn to identify these types of advertising, and watch to see if the 'predicted' issues arise, and put responses in better perspective accordingly.

Researchers should have, as intelligent people, a stock of concepts by which distinctions may be made, and models constructed which move towards explaining why respondents responded in the way they did. A few examples are:

- *Product values-centred advertising* (e.g. archetypal old-style washing powder advertising, whisky and bitter advertising which major on heritage), as distinct from *user-values centred advertising* (e.g. most 'knowing-brand-in-conspiracy with ad-literate audience' model advertising, advertising which targets by means of style)
- *Adopted Proposition* versus *Perceived Intention* (cf. 'Lean on Pork' mini-case above)
- *Identity* (issues around *who* I am/*who* I want to be) versus *Disposition* (issues around *how* I feel/*how* I want to feel). A lot of advertising effort is spent trying to convey the nature of a shown brand-user's experience. It is often the case that the audience never gets as far as considering this, because they get hung up on the protagonist's identity.
- *Relevance* and *Credibility* – the two most common *boundaries* operating in respect of propositions and brand positionings.

- *Denotive* (overtly expressed, or 'spelled out') versus *Connotive* (implied or indicated by commonly understood associations) communication – these are usually both present in advertising and packaging. How do they work with respect to each other? Are they relevant and credible?

In advertising we should attempt to separate and gauge the contributions of:

1 The *communicative content* (the strategy, albeit in synoptic form)
2 The *vehicle* (the core creative idea used to convey the intended message)
3 *Executional detail* (the specifics of the articulation that is given to the vehicle)

Using the sorts of conceptual distinctions and frameworks mentioned, such reinterrogation can be most revealing. Aspects of the brand or advertising which were hitherto not obvious may suddenly become apparent. They may not be intentional, and may never be recognized by the owners or creators of those things, but it may be that consumers and audiences pick up on them at levels they find difficult to articulate.

This is the most exciting part of qualitative research – the sudden understanding of why people appear to react in the way they do in respect of a particular product or advertisement, and then the development of a model of the 'towards a general theory' sort. Once this reinterrogation is completed it is usually not difficult to see why responses were the way they were. A model that explains this can be built, which can be used to guide the development of the brand or advertising. I'll end with a case history which illustrates some of this.

Mini-case: Halifax 'house'

When asked in qualitative interviews what advertising people can recall for banks or building societies, this commercial always gets an early mention, and almost always has a very positive reception. I don't know what weight of airtime it has received, but I do know it is now quite old. It seems to have become a 'classic', at least within the sector, if not among all UK TV ads of recent years.

The sort of things, in no particular order, that people say about it *include* (not a comprehensive list) the following:

- Easy to recall who it's for, because of the 'X'
- It makes you fell they're nice people at the Halifax

- They are the biggest, so your money will be safe there and they won't muck you about
- They care about people, perhaps a bit more than some of the others
- The advert doesn't talk down to you, or make out that you're stupid
- It's very watchable, with all the different people gradually making up the house
- It gives a very nice warm feeling, seeing it, with all the people working together to make a home
- The music says it all – it's about 'home' and has words that fit very well.

These sort of comments include some which are about perceptions of the brand (consumer perspective) and some which are about the ad itself (viewer perspective). The comments demonstrate that the ad is successful in respect of the main indices of *relevance* (i.e. 'my kind of stuff', both as an ad – *rewarding*, and as a brand – *beneficial*), *credibility* and *distinctiveness*.

They do not, however, explain by themselves *why* the commercial seems so effective, and scores so well on quantitative tracking measures. The responses are *consequences* of the way the ad has been written, and in order to understand *that* we need to look at it in terms of its *structure* and the internal relationships between its various elements.

Examining the components by themselves may take us a bit further in terms of divining the success of 'House', but, like cataloguing the responses and comments it will not take us all the way there. The film is made up of lots of ordinary-looking people who are cleverly organized and filmed jumping up on each others' shoulders and finally forming themselves into a house. We know it's not absolutely for real, but find the apparent process fascinating, as well as the result. The music runs throughout, and is eminently suited as an accompaniment, in terms of both its content and its tone. The people then jump down and rearrange themselves into a giant 'X', which reminds us of the Halifax (Figures 6.2 and 6.3).

The voiceover says, in the middle of the film and towards the end, something about having helped over a million people in the past five years to find the right mortgage scheme, and how the advertiser has lent more money to more people for more mortgages than anyone else. 'So if you want to get into a new home, you'll know who to talk to.' We do not perhaps listen closely to it, but take out an overall reassuring feeling that the Halifax is *big/experienced* and *nice/caring*. This message combination is interesting not least because it includes elements of both *attribute* and *attitude*.

The structural headings I use – *brand, proposition, vehicle* and *execution* – are not new. They are all concepts familiar to those who

Figure 6.2

Figure 6.3

work with ads or in advertising itself. I then try to identify what each is, or is made of. What is different is that in that process I attempt to examine the extent to which they are consonant, or contained within each other. My contention is that the closer-knit they are in terms of association and meaning (i.e. their capacity to represent significant aspects of each other) the more likely is the ad to communicate well.

The model, it should be said, does not seem to fit *every* type of commercial – testimony to the very diversity of creativity – but it seems to illuminate this one well.

The presence or absence of relationship between these structural components (although not the degrees to which these occur) can be shown quite dramatically using a type of Venn Diagram, which simply has four circles. I arrange them as in Figure 6.4. Fairly obviously, where

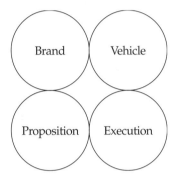

Figure 6.4   *A Venn Diagram*

a meaningful interrelationship in terms of what viewers perceive seems to exist, I show the circles overlapping, and where none seems to exist there is no overlap. It follows from this that the most robustly structured scripts will manifest as four overlapping circles, which create a 'flower' shape in the middle. In fact, this is a cruelly stringent 'test' of the ostensible 'efficiency' of a commercial, and very few actually achieve this degree of tightness. The Halifax 'House' ad, however, seems to be one which does (Figure 6.5).

The Execution elements are powerfully interrelated with the others, as well as bringing tonal values of their own which are constructive to the whole:

- The people are ordinary, like you and me. We can relate to them.
- The direction chooses to focus in on them in close-up, and this creates a feeling of the celebration of the individual. We are facilitated in one of our favourite pastimes – people-watching. It is greatly charming, and indicative of a corporate attitude which acknowledges people as individuals.
- The music, as well as being melodic and quite well known (especially if you are over 35!), is lyrically apt for the communicative intention. It is tonally cosy and reassuring. And it ends with the line 'Now everything is easy 'cos of you', just in time for the sign-off to imply ownership of the second-person pronoun.

Figure 6.5 *The overlapping circles of the Halifax 'House' ad*

- The people (still a living example of cooperation) form themselves into the 'X' – the (long-ago) well-chosen brand logo.

The overall piece emerges with a reassuring tonality, along with a nobility of spirit and an elegant simplicity of form. All the four component areas contain something meaningful of each other, giving rise to a superbly consistent communication of both the proposition and of positioning through felt brand values.

Conclusion

What I hope I have shown in this chapter is that analysing and interpreting qualitative data is both more complex and potentially more fun than many might think. It is also more essential than some seem to believe. As opposed to simply occurring after the fieldwork, the interpretative process begins with the first contact from the client or agency and continues throughout, taking in project and sample design, content briefing, the interviewing itself, as well as the subsequent sifting and sorting of the data.

Hypotheses which you intuit at the outset, and which you then develop, refine or reject, are a core part of the process. The more questions you ask yourself, and the more hypotheses you try out, the richer will be your relationship with what happens in the interviews and, ultimately, the more robust will be your conclusions.

There is no satisfactory substitute for immersing yourself thoroughly in the data – tapes, transcripts, notes and thoughts of your own and of any skilled and briefed observers. Different researchers find different methods best for them. It's a personal thing.

Often there is not enough time to undertake all the procedures I have discussed here, but in 'short-cutting' we should always be aware that that is what we've done and by how much we've done it.

That said, it is equally important to develop an ability to rise above the data once they are sifted, sorted and differentiated. The ability to make intuitive leaps with confidence once the data *patterns* have been assimilated is a crucial part of the interpretative process, and one which takes time and experience to grow into. In interpreting qualitative data in this way, you should be courageous. You should trust yourself, and believe in your own experience.

The responses in the tapes and transcripts are only *part* of the overall process. They do *not* provide the conceptual frameworks, but they do give clues about the dimensions which are important in such frameworks, and they do give indications as to where problems appear to lie.

Interrogating the 'Client's Thing' in terms of its structures both before fieldwork (hypothesis generation) and in light of responses is vital, for two reasons:

1 As qualitative researchers our job is not simply to try to understand people alone. We seek to illuminate the *relationships* between people and brands, advertisements, packs, markets, etc. So why be satisfied with only one side of the story?
2 By achieving and communicating the required understanding in terms of *supply-side* structures we are enhancing the usefulness of the research to the client. It then explains what is happening *in terms of* the client's end of things. It provides explanations, diagnoses and guidelines in terms of the structure of the 'Client's Thing' – and that is what he or she is able to change, not the people. It's in a *user-friendly* language, and may not involve the mention of specific responses at all.

Lastly, what I hope I have *not* said is that if you don't do all of this you're not doing it well. That isn't necessarily so. It behoves us all, however, to be aware of by how far we fall short of the rigorous professional ideal when yet again we are faced with the need to deliver in three days findings which in academia might be felt to need three months.

References

Gordon, W. (1983), Paper given at The Analysis of Qualitative Data, AQRP One-Day Event.

Gordon, W. and Langmaid, R. (1988), *Qualitative Market Research. A Practitioner's and Buyer's Guide*, Gower, Aldershot.

Hedges, A. (1983), Paper given at The Analysis of Qualitative Data, AQRP One-Day Event.

Robson, S. and Foster, A. (eds) (1989), *Qualitative Research in Action*, Edward Arnold, London.

Wells, S. (1991), Wet towels and whetted appetites or a wet blanket? The role of analysis in qualitative research. *Journal of the Market Research Society*, **33**, (1), January.

Overview: Chapter 7

The advertising development process within the agency resembles a communications 'relay race'. The creative brief represents a pivotal phase in the chain, marking the point where the strategic understanding gleaned by the account team is passed on. It is the point at which the understanding of the client's problem becomes distilled into a form that makes it clear what the advertising solution is required to achieve and provides inspiration for the creative team. It therefore represents the single most important contribution the account team can make to influencing the power and creativity of the advertising.

Creative people have to generate original ideas on the back of thinking done by other people. They must turn the thinking in the brief into a piece of communication that solves the problem. A successful campaign idea is the result of inspiration, intuition, and experimentation built on the foundation of logical analysis and the footholds for inspiration the brief provides.

The value of the brief is defined entirely by how useful it is to the creative team. To maximize value the brief needs two key properties: directionality, and inspiration. The directional elements are those which elucidate the nature of the problem the advertising is trying to solve and what it needs to achieve. The inspirational elements are those which provide a foothold, a place to start the process of creative generation.

This chapter examines some real creative briefs and discusses the issues encountered in writing briefs in real life. It also highlights the role of the briefing and the context of working relationships between account team and creative team which maximize the chances of a successful outcome. This chapter, originally presented on the IPA Stage 2 course (Campaign Planning) in 1990, is an excellent and well-argued point of view (from the perspective of one of the UK's most highly regarded planners) of the fulcrum of the advertising process.

7 Creative briefing

Gary Duckworth

Briefing in the advertising process

Client companies employ and pay advertising agencies because they enable them to solve brand problems and exploit brand opportunities. Advertising is a functional instrument, designed to achieve specific objectives, as earlier chapters on strategy have outlined. The reason the brief is so important is because much money is going to be spent on the campaign that emerges from it. So the agency has both the opportunity to create something that works and the responsibility to ensure that it does.

You can consider the advertising development process as a kind of relay race (Figure 7.1). The essential job of the first part of the chain – let's call it strategic development – is to take an understanding of the client's business, their consumers, their marketplace, their brand, etc. and from all this come up with a clearly defined role for advertising to play in building their client's success.

Creative briefing is pivotal because it represents the stage in the advertising development process where the strategic understanding developed by the account team reaches the people whose job it is to really crack the creative problem. But this strategic understanding has to be transmuted into a form the creative people can use, so that it becomes a useful tool and inspiration for the creative team. The essence of creative briefing is that the initial understanding must now be distilled, and then passed on in a way that provides a foundation and the beginnings of inspiration for a solution.

Figure 7.1 *The relay race*

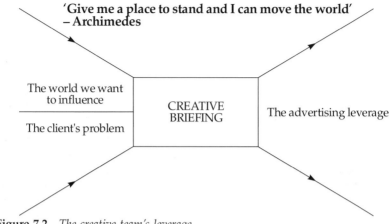

Figure 7.2   *The creative team's leverage*

Archimedes and the lever

Archimedes said: 'Give me a place to stand and I can move the world'. He was explaining the concept of leverage, whereby a small force exerted at the right point is magnified through distance to move an immense object. The brief is the place the account team gives the creative team to stand in their quest to move the world – i.e. to shape the decisions and perceptions of the target group out there in the real world (Figure 7.2).

People outside advertising often make the erroneous assumption that all advertising works. The truth is that some works and some doesn't. Some creates an enduring brand asset but some offers a few fleeting seconds of entertainment and is then forgotten forever. In this respect, creative briefing is the pivot of a process that may or may not end up producing a satisfactory result. It marks the point at which the understanding of the problem becomes distilled into a form that makes it clear what the solution is required to achieve and provides some inspiration for the creative mind to work with. It is the point of where the account team exert the maximum leverage on the eventual advertising outcome because the briefing represents a *passing on* of understanding and of ownership of the problem from one part of the agency to the other. Someone else is taking over the bus.

From here on, it is going to be the responsibility of the creative team to devise a campaign which, when it finally emerges, will do the job it is supposed to do. Many other people, further along the process, will play a role in shaping the campaign – planners and researchers, media and production people. But it is the creative team who will *originate* the solution.

So the briefing represents the single most important contribution the account team can make to influence the power and creativity of the advertising. Two important consequences follow:

1 *The rudder and the supertanker* The rudder on a tanker is only a relatively small part of the ship, but a few degrees change of trim in the bearing of the rudder to port or starboard can make an immense difference to where the supertanker ends up over the course of a voyage. Similarly with a brief, a steer to the team that is off-course can make an immense difference to the eventual creative outcome.
2 *The oil and the engine* I have observed that the brief represents a passing on. The brief is a tool for the benefit of the creative people: an instrument to make the job of the agency's most valued and talented people as easy as it can possibly be for them to exercise those talents. The lubrication in a car makes it possible for the engine to work to its best ability – its value is defined entirely by how well it enables the engine to do its job. The value of the briefing is defined entirely by the value it provides to the creative team in originating an advertising solution.

I hope this point seems obvious. The fact is, sometimes there is an unhealthy tendency for account teams, and especially planners, to 'fetishize' the brief. The brief becomes treated as some precious, almost mystical object, filled with intellectual cleverness or obscurely written guidance. It becomes treated as something important in its own right, an end in itself.

There is the enduring myth of 'The Great Brief', which is apocryphally believed to lie behind great campaigns. I've investigated this issue, and traced backwards to the original brief from some justly famous work.

The brief that originated the Levi's campaign was:

What must the advertising say?

501s from Levi's are the right look and the only label.

And why should the consumer believe it?

Because they represent the way jeans should be worn today; and because they are the original jean, indelibly associated with the birth of teenage culture in the 1950s, and its finest expressions since.

Tone of voice

Heroic
Highly charged
American (but 'period')

The brief that originated the 'Heineken Refreshes the Parts' campaign was 'refreshment'.

What is interesting about both of these briefs is that they are simple and to the point. But I don't think either could be accused of expressing some profound philosophical insight. And though you can see in both cases how the campaign emerged from the brief, you can't see the campaign idea in it. The brief is a start – a vital start, but only a start.

Wittgenstein observed that the study of philosophy was like a ladder: you climbed it to reach a certain point of enlightenment, but once you had attained that point you could throw the ladder away. All briefs end up in the bin.

Principles of a good brief

I'm going to start distinguishing here between the *brief* – i.e. the written communication which goes to the creative team, and the *briefing* – i.e. the context of dialogue and discussion that goes on around it when the briefing meeting takes place (Figure 7.3).

Figure 7.3   *The difference between the brief and the briefing*

So what is a good brief

People often say that advertising is a blunt instrument. Imagine a brief for a blunt instrument – it wouldn't run to many pages. It would say something like: 'About two feet long, wider at one end than the other, made of wood.' Whereas a brief for knitting a jumper is a complex of tiny elements, that reveal the end result slowly as we follow it, a creative brief needs to give the big picture quickly and directly.

Direction

Inspiration

Figure 7.4 *The two key properties of effective communication*

So it has to be clear and simple if we are to stand a chance of producing effective communication. There are two key properties it needs: to be *directional* and *inspirational* (Figure 7.4):

- A creative brief gives guidance to a team who are going to produce a piece of communication that *does* something, something that will intervene in the external world. The directional elements of the brief are those which define the task – what the advertising needs to achieve, the problem it is trying to solve. Plus the kind of people it is talking to, how they think, feel and behave. In a nutshell, the directional elements of the brief are those which give the creative team a clear understanding of the problem.
- The inspirational elements are those which give the creative team a springboard, a jumping-off point for originating the campaign idea. They include the 'tone of voice' elements, the kind of 'feel' which the advertising needs to have – soft and cuddly, or cold and sharp, etc.

Every agency has its own creative brief form, as part of its working processes, and each designs the brief in different ways, giving the sections different names because each agency likes to think it is unique and special, but the essential components nonetheless bear a strong family resemblance (Figures 7.5 and 7.6).

Bartle Bogle Hegarty

Creative Brief

CLIENT _____

BRAND _____

THE PRODUCT IS:

THE BRAND IS:

1. THE ROLE OF ADVERTISING:-

A. WHAT DO WE WANT PEOPLE TO DO AS A RESULT OF SEEING THIS ADVERTISING?

B. HOW DO WE BELIEVE THE ADVERTISING WILL WORK TO ACHIEVE THIS?

2. WHO ARE WE TALKING TO?

3. WHAT IS THE SINGLE MOST IMPORTANT THING THIS ADVERTISING SHOULD CONVEY?

4. WHY SHOULD PEOPLE BELIEVE THIS?

5. WHAT PRACTICAL CONSIDERATIONS ARE THERE?

DATE	
JOB NO.	
1ST REVIEW	
FINAL SIGN OFF	
CREATIVE DIRECTOR	
TEAM LEADER	
BUDGET ESTIMATE	£
MEDIA	

Figure 7.5   *A creative brief form*

DUCKWORTH, FINN, GRUBB, WATERS

BRIEF

What is this brand called?

Who do we want to buy it?

Why should people buy this brand?

Requirement:

Signature   **Date**   **Traffic**   **Date**

Duckworth, Finn, Grubb, Waters Ltd. 41 Great Pulteney Street, London W1R 3DE. 0171·734 5888 Fax 0171·734 3716
Registered in England No. 2377231. Registered Office 41 Great Pulteney St. W1R 3DE.

Figure 7.6   *Another creative brief form*

The sections of the brief fall roughly into these two areas (Figure 7.7):

**DIRECTION
GIVING**

**INSPIRATION
GIVING**

Figure 7.7   *Interaction of the two key properties of effective communication*

- *Why are we advertising*? Role of advertising. What is the advertising doing? What do we want people to think?
- *Who are we talking to*? Target group. Type and outlook of person, not just demographics. Their behaviour with respect to our objective.
- *What are we saying*? Proposition/main thought plus support
- *How are we saying it*? Tone of voice, brand identity
- *Executional guidelines* Things to avoid. Things you must do
- *Requirement* Media consideration/requirements. Timing

Giving clear directions

If the advertising the creative team produce is to shape the perceptual aspect of our world, we must begin by giving them a picture of how it is currently shaped and the shift in perception the advertising needs to achieve. Let's pull the focus back here and examine the concept of giving clear directions – how directions can be helpful or unhelpful. Suppose you're lost on your way to visit some friends who have recently moved. You stop the car and ask directions from somebody passing by. Here are two different replies you might receive:

- *Reply 1* 'Moreton Road. You definitely mean Moreton Road not Marsham Road? Okay. You're not far away. Continue straight along here about 400 metres and take the left after the Red Lion pub.

Continue straight on over a narrow bridge and just continue. Eventually you get to another main road with traffic lights – turn right, and it's first on your left.'
- *Reply 2* 'Moreton Road? Moreton Road. Now let me think. Funny you know, I've lived round here all my life – yeees, I know. It's the one near where they built the new school my daughter goes to. If I'm not mistaken. You'll need ... Now wait a minute so go right after the school. Wait a minute. That's Marsham Road. Moreton, Moreton, No, I tell a lie, go along until you ... take the second right ... or is it the third? Anyway it's on the right somewhere then ... Or maybe there's a quicker way altogether. If I'm right...'

Reply 1 is clear, crisp, and highly functional. It establishes the goal, briefly sets the context and then provides clear directions so the person hearing it knows unambiguously the right thing to do. Reply 2 is well intentioned but that is about all that can be said in its favour: it rambles, it adds detail completely unrelated to the task in hand. It goes off on a completely misleading tack: it considers alternatives, but fails to opt in favour of any one in particular. The person receiving it is no better off than where they started, in fact they may be worse off because they are more confused. Bad creative briefs can have the same effect.

Here's a real-life example of directions, where people have paid attention to clarity, because these are for a situation that could be critical: these directions used to be on cards in London Underground trains:

What to do if you see a suspicious unattended package

1 Don't panic
2 Pull the red emergency handle at the next station.
3 Get your fellow passengers off the train. Alert a member of staff.

Here is what the card does *not* say:

What to do if you see a suspicious unattended package

It is quite possible that a tumult of conflicting emotions will course through your mind: concern for your own safety, your loved ones, regret that you'll never finish those dining-room shelves. However, research and years of experience have shown that the optimum response is – don't panic, rend your garments or vent your resentment at God's vindictive capriciousness.

Can you explain it to your mum?

So the writer of the brief has to do all the homework, understand the problem in depth, then simplify and distil, so the directions become clear.

If you put too much in, people will get lost. One simple test I apply when I'm engaged in this exercise is to ask myself if I can put the problem in three short sentences. Can I express it in a way (and using language) that my mum would understand?

Here's an example of just the direction element of a brief I wrote for a campaign for the Sunday newspaper *The People*.

Why are we advertising?
People don't think of buying *The People* because it's very low profile. If they do think of it they assume it's a less sleazy version of the *News of the World*, or have no clear picture.

We need to put the paper back on the Sunday newspaper map and give it an attractive identity which reflects the paper as it is today.

The issue of language

The passage above is deliberately written in ordinary language. It's very important, as the distillation of our strategic thinking reaches the team whose job it is to 'translate' it into a piece of communication, that the language we use changes and doesn't use 'marketing speak'.

For example I could have written the same kind of directions for *The People* brief, but in this kind of language:

Why are we advertising?
The product has a severe saliency deficiency so it does not get into the target's consideration set. The leading brand sets the category values and our brand is perceived as a 'me-too' because of these dominant associations. Alternatively, a proportion of the target segment have a dissociated perceptual set with respect to the brand.

The campaign objective is to increase saliency and to communicate a brand identify which is motivating and more appropriate to the product's experiential manifestation.

Some people find this kind of language tempting because they feel it sounds 'clever', in just the same way many academics write using obscure jargon because they feel it helps their career advancement if they have an intellectual image among their peers. To a greater or lesser extent all professional disciplines develop their own language, and there is a value to this because they need words for concepts that are not part of our everyday discourse.

If you work in the marketing or advertising business you may be able to remember the shock you had when you first saw an example of 'marketing speak', e.g.: 'The everyday cheese that meets your needs for mildness with flavour.' After a few months you forgot how weird this language is because you learned to use it habitually as a working tool. While this may be fine for certain professional purposes, the danger is that if we get wrapped up in the cleverness of our own words, we run the risk of a breakdown in the communication process because the creative teams do not generally use this kind of language. Nor indeed does anyone else.

A similar kind of issue often arises with the description of the target group. Because we have so many tools for analysing people's behaviour in markets, all of which use 'code', there is a tendency to be sloppy and to continue to describe the target group in this code in the creative brief, without translating it back into something more recognizable:

Target group
The target group are 30–45 BC1 adults, 80:20 men:women. Living in Acorn areas J-K, and with a median income of £30 000 pa. Attitudinally they are achievers and secure conservatives.

The difficulty with this is you don't feel you know the people you are trying to reach. Here's an ordinary-language example from a brief for a London Fire Brigade campaign:

Why are we advertising?
To get people who assume they'll escape in a fire to realize that they really do need a smoke alarm. To jolt them into considering smoke alarms.

Target group
All ages, tend to be on lower incomes. Elderly people, young singles, young marrieds with children. Don't think about fire. Think it will start slowly and they'll hear it/smell it. Assume they'll wake up/get out.

The more we use language rooted in the real, ordinary world, the better equipped the creative team will be to communicate with it in our campaign.

The structure of the brief

Just because the brief is written in ordinary language does not mean it is mundane or prosaic. On the contrary, it is a highly structured set of instructions and ideas.

The centerpiece of every brief is the 'proposition' or main thought which describes the essence of what we want to communicate. The key to good proposition writing is to keep the proposition brief, singleminded and simple. As a rule of thumb, once you've written it, you need to look at it and ask yourself: 'Could I write an ad from that?' – just a simple, straightforward idea of what your proposition might just look like when turned into an advert. So you can work out if what you've ended up with is a useful working tool for a creative person. If *you* can't write an ad from it, it's unlikely anyone else can.

The role of the proposition is to encapsulate the *main* thing you want to communicate, not to contain everything you want to say:

- Do say: The Honda Banzai is the family coupe with great performance.
- Don't say: The Honda Banzai coupe combines performance, reliability, economy and cat-like roadholding with sporty good looks and room for a family of five.

It is important to take the responsibility for the brief being single-minded. If your strategy development has left you in an ambiguous position, and you are not sure what the core communication needs to be, it is not acceptable to use the proposition as some kind of selection box for the creative team to make their own choice. If you can't agree with your client whether the proposition is 'thickness' or 'a range of flavours' you need to do more strategic homework and distillation to get to a resolution. If you put 'A range of thick flavours' all you are in effect doing is avoiding the decision and dumping the responsibility for the strategy on the creative team.

I'm a great believer in giving people a concrete thought rather than an abstract one, because an abstract one can so easily end up just being vague. This is a particular issue with brands built on emotional imagery – for example, fashion, perfumes, cosmetics, or confectionery. You don't necessarily have to have a 'fact' to be concrete.

A perfume example
Do say: The essence of the East
Don't say: Floating and beautiful

A confectionery example
Do say: Private moment
Don't say: A unique taste experience, full of indulgence

A snack example
Do say: Big crunch in a neat, light gold square
Don't say: A totally different kind of crisp

I've had a lot of discussions with creative teams about 'Can you express the proposition as a headline, should it be 'creative'? and so on. I've had mixed views back. In fact I now work with one creative director who finds this helpful, and one who doesn't.

Here's the same brief, for Granada TV Rental, so you and your creative team can make your own minds up. The proposition is written in two different ways, but the support doesn't change:

'Creative' version of proposition
Why buy a millstone when you can rent a milestone?

Support
If you rent from Granada you can stay always up to date. Nicam, widescreen and satellite

Plain vanilla version of proposition
Renting from Granada is more sensible than owning.

Support
If you rent from Granada you can stay always up to date. Nicam, widescreen and satellite

The support

If the proposition represents the kind of understanding or conclusion we want the target group to come to, then it needs to be backed by evidence – the support for the proposition. This should be one of the most inspirational elements of the brief, because it gives the creative team ideas or product points that can be dramatized creatively. It's an area where doing your homework into the brand and its performance or history can unearth some really interesting fact or 'nugget' and give the creative team a really powerful jumping-off point.

Proposition
If you don't have a smoke alarm you won't stand a chance.

Support
Foam furniture goes off like a rocket (Figure 7.8).
Fills the house with poisonous cyanide and carbon monoxide gases and dense black smoke which chokes you in seconds.

Tone
Urgent and frightening

Tone

The 'tone paragraph' is there is to give guidance on the 'feel' of the advertising – the tonal ambience of the communication. Should it be

Figure 7.8   *The hidden dangers of foam furniture fires dramatized by an ordinary chair which comes alive and breathes fire*

'short and sharp' or 'soft and seductive'? I'm using clichés here deliberately to illustrate the point, but in reality the tone paragraph aims to be specific to the circumstances and needs of the brand.

I always try to give myself a rule that you can only use two words for tone. Even one will do fine as long as it's well chosen. So what you don't write is:

Tone
Warm, reassuring, yet jaunty and audacious.

Because it is nonsense.

The awful example

I've made up bad examples so far to illustrate my points, but here's a fine example of true-life waffle which led to a TV campaign that spent a significant sum of money and vanished without trace. The brand has been disguised to protect the guilty.

Proposition
Brand X ground coffee. Its distinctive character stands out from the rest.

Brand character
X is the sort of character everyone admires – he's warm, friendly, sociable and approachable, yet retains a distinctive style so that he stands out from the crowd.

Tone
A distinctive and different treatment from any other ground coffee advertising that gives contemporary relevance to the brand in the real lives of our primary audience.

This brief gives us some classic guidelines on how not to do it. The proposition is hackneyed. There is no support given as to why we should believe it. It sounds like it could apply to a lot of products, rather than specifically a coffee brand (there appears to be nothing relevant to coffee in it). Language is used portentously but unhelpfully ('distinctive and different'). It employs the kind of phrase making ('contemporary relevance') that nobody apart from people writing creative briefs ever uses. We all make mistakes.

Mandatories

Sometimes you need this section in the brief – essentially it's there to set out what the advertising must include. A mandatory might be a genre convention where the received wisdom suggests that some creative element is essential to success – for example, a beautiful hair shot in a shampoo commercial. Or it might be the regulatory financial rubric you have to show in a commercial offering mortgages.

Alternatively, you may have learned something that has to be avoided. For example, in the Fire Brigade brief we had a mandatory not to show children in the ad because research strongly suggested that those in households without children – e.g. the elderly – were likely to interpret the message as 'not aimed at me'. Their response was 'That's right – people with children at home should definitely get a smoke alarm'. Yet statistical analysis showed that the elderly were in fact one of the highest risk groups, whereas smoke alarm ownership was most advanced among homes with children.

The requirement

This is where you specify what format the campaign needs to take. And it is important to be clear. There's no use in your creative team producing a brilliant script for a 60-second TV commercial if the media budget will only support 30 seconds. Giving the creative team a clear idea of the number of executions you need in press or posters helps them to focus their minds on the task.

More complex brands, still simple briefs

Different advertising problems emerge over time as new types of brand owners come to the marketplace. Twenty years ago we had largely FMCG brand problems to solve – yoghurt, frozen peas, crisps, detergents, etc. Now we have retailers, TV channels, telecoms companies, banks, airlines, and cars as well. These often present more tricky problems to analyse because understanding what the advertising needs to do (i.e. understanding the directional element of the brief) is tougher. It remains just as important to stick with the distillation process, but sometimes the structure of the brief needs to change slightly.

To launch Daewoo cars in the UK we had an overall positioning we wanted the advertising to achieve: 'The most customer-focused car company.' There were a very large number of differences between what Daewoo offered and what other car manufacturers provided. None of these differences was in its own right big enough to build the entire brand on, but taken together they added up to something very distinctive. This kind of brand has been well described by John dalla Costa (in *Admap*, January 1996) as a 'Velcro' brand because it has a lot of little 'hooks' which add up to an overall 'perspective.'

To simplify the communication task for the creative brief, we divided all this list of difference into four primary categories (we called them core values). For the launch campaign each core value had its own support (see Figures 7.9–7.12).

Guidance versus rigidity

The best way to describe the brief is as a kind of structural pattern. While it is a set of instructions, it is not like a knitting pattern code that gives an exact and complete guide to the final garment.

The brief offers guidance, but falls short (or should fall short) of prescription. This is because it needs to allow the creative team the latitude to exercise their insights and creative imagination. A brief which is too rigid, and requires the creative work to be a literal translation of what it says is likely to lead to advertising which fails because it is dull and uninspiring.

It is the power of the creative idea which bring the proposition to life and dramatizes it to us so that we have the chance to interest the target group in what we have to say. The creative team originate the solution, not the brief writers. After all, if writing the brief solved the problem, we wouldn't need creative teams. But someone has to actually do it. And it is in this that the risk and challenge of the advertising process lies.

DUCKWORTH, FINN, GRUBB, WATERS

BRIEF

What is this brand called?	Daewoo

Who do we want to buy it?
Broadly: All motorists
Specifically: Prospective buyers of saloons and hatchbacks costing £8-12k

They want a nice new car with the minimum of hassle. We need them to understand and be impressed by Daewoo's refreshingly different approach to selling cars.

Why should people buy this brand?

Daewoo is a different kind of car company because we're hassle-free.

Why should they believe us?

1. We have unique Daewoo showrooms, no dealerships
   - designed to help you relax and enjoy visit; café area, interactive displays, creche for kids, welcome to get in cars and poke around
   - staff who help if you want them to and won't if you don't
   - long test drives arranged at your convenience

2. We agree a re-sale price when you buy the car so you can always sell it back to us without any risk
   - purchase prices are fixed, no haggling, so no-one gets a better deal than you

3. We give 4 years free servicing, 4 years free AA membership, a 4 year mechanical warranty and an 8 year anti-corrosion guarantee with every new car (we can afford it because we have no middlemen)

4. When your car needs to be serviced we come to collect it and leave you with a new top spec courtesy car, free

5. On top of this we want to recognise the trust shown in us by our first UK customers, so everyone buying a Daewoo in our first three months will have their car replaced by an identical model, new, in August (so it's 'N' reg).

Requirement:
TV for each area mentioned above
Press to add detail where needed
Outdoor likely to be wanted to add street presence

Signature	**Date**	**Traffic**	**Date**

Duckworth, Finn, Grubb, Waters Ltd. 41 Great Pulteney Street, London W1R 3DE. 0171-734 5888 Fax 0171-734 3716
Registered in England No. 2377231. Registered Office 41 Great Pulteney St. W1R 3DE.

Figure 7.9   *A Daewoo brief*

Figure 7.10 *This commercial talked about the comprehensive package available on Daewoo cars because dealers don't 'take a cut'*

Figure 7.11

Figure 7.12

The briefing

Creative people: what are the target group like?

Given the brief is designed to communicate with the creative team, they are in fact the target group for the brief. Creative people have different orientations to their work. They are conscious of what their peer group will think. They know their work will be on show in public. Imagine how you would feel about your own work if you knew it was going to be widely publicized, there for everyone to see. It is a very different feeling from the feelings of those earlier in the advertising development chain.

Another important difference is that far more of what they actually produce comes from the self. If you are an account planner you have the raw material of research to work from, you have your spreadsheets and models. If you are an account manager you have a process to manage, a team to coordinate, and a client to look after. If you are a creative person you start with a brief, you own life experiences, and a blank piece of paper.

Anyone who has ever been on a creative role-reversal course (I recommend it) will know how difficult it is to produce an original advertising idea in response to a brief. Briefs come from the logical, analytical area of life, but advertising communication is a process that goes beyond the rational, that uses symbols and emotional understanding, so a good advertising idea inherently uses non-logical processes.

A good idea emerges out of the brief, synthesizes it, and goes beyond it. Creative people have to generate original ideas on the back of thinking done by other people. They must turn the thinking in the brief into a piece of communication that solves the problem. A successful campaign idea is the end result of inspiration, intuition, and experimentation built on the foundation of logical analysis and the footholds for inspiration the brief provides.

Because their work comes from the self, from their intuitions, emotions and hunches, they have to be committed or these creative processes will not operate. If they do not find in the brief a convincing explanation of the problem, they will tend to produce dull work because they are operating mechanically. If they do not find it useful, it will fail to engage their imagination, and they will tend to ignore it.

The critical nature of the briefing

Because the creatives' emotional commitment and morale is so important, the briefing – i.e. the context in which the brief is delivered – is all-important (Figure 7.13). To create the right working environment for the briefing there are a number of circumstantial factors that significantly influence whether the briefing is likely to be productive.

First, it really makes a difference to have good relationships between the people who write the briefs – account planners and/or account managers and the creative department. If the agency culture is cluttered with unhelpful stereotypes – e.g. planners are 'boffins', creatives are 'prima donnas' – it is very difficult for both sides to have the mutual

Figure 7.13   *The importance of the briefing – the context in which the brief is delivered*

respect needed for a successful outcome, because everyone will be in their corner emotionally, defending their egos (not to mention living up to their stereotypes).

Second, do you, the brief writer, know your creative team as people? Do you talk to them outside of the work context about music, football, ads they admire and so on? How can you brief someone effectively if you don't know the people you are talking to? More to the point, the chances are that you can communicate with them better and they will trust you, the more you know them. Just like in real life.

Always remember, *you* haven't cracked it, *they* are the ones who originate the solution.

Making the briefing interesting

Let's start with a question here. Why should your advertising be interesting if your briefing isn't? Ever been inspired by hearing something really dull? It may only be for a trade ad, but every brief is important given that it has a job to do.

I once heard of an account director who was asked to brief the creative team on a DIY product which filled holes in walls. He walked into the briefing with a hammer, smashed a hole in the wall, and then mixed the product in front of them, using it very successfully to mend the hole in the wall. And then walked out. It's a good story. It doesn't really matter if it's true or not, because it illustrates some great insights. First, it was dramatic and entertaining. You wouldn't forget a briefing like that. Second, it gave the creative team a really good idea of what the benefit of the product was. Third, it was a brilliant way to create commitment to the product so the team could feel enthusiastic about solving the advertising problem.

So what can you do to bring it to life? Sadly, not all the things we advertise can be so convincingly demonstrated. Nonetheless, there are lots of ways you can bring things to life. Perhaps a video of people talking about what they like about the product, or how it helps them in their work. Perhaps photographs to show the kind of people the campaign is aimed at, or a few quotes from research of their views.

Maybe you can experience the product directly if it is something like a mobile phone, an airline or car. If it's a bar of chocolate you can always eat it. If it's a store you can wander round and buy something, talk to the staff. Maybe do the briefing in the store or driving along in the car. None of this will necessarily end up directly in the creative work, although it's possible that one of these experiences may spark something off. But the briefing will be more memorable and chances are that the creative team will absorb more.

The briefing gives you the chance to embellish and amplify what you have set down formally in the brief. Don't use it to sneak in extra things that suddenly occur to you, or clutter and ambiguity will rear their heads. A briefing is a performance of an existing script, not a chance to suddenly write a new one.

The team will probably have questions, and you may need to do some more work or thinking. It may be that something they observe helps you understand more than you've got to so far. I've frequently had the experience of talking through a brief with a team, only to find something somebody says gives me the insight to improve it.

And when the creative team have heard enough, don't hassle them about how they're getting on. All of us have had the experience in a briefing situation when you feel you have enough to go on, at least for now, and creative teams need the space to go away and let it all sink in. Maybe they'll want to talk more later. You have to let go of the responsibility for solving the problem and recognize that the baton has been passed on . . .

Reacting to the work

When you get the campaign idea presented back to you, remember the point about the personal element, so if you have points or criticisms, act sensitively. First, though, just make sure you create a clear visualization of what exactly is supposed to happen in the ad. Creative people, because they have worked hard on the idea and have got so close, sometimes neglect to explain it fully. Ask questions if you need to.

I think you have to start by reacting to it spontaneously – laugh, cry, whatever. Just imagine the ad in a break, or a newspaper. Remember, the people seeing your ad aren't going to be comparing it to the brief you've written. They're just going to be in their everyday lives when suddenly this ad comes up in front of them. What will they take out of it? Even if it's not 'propositionally perfect', it may well still accomplish the task you've defined. If it's not the kind of idea you expected, try to understand its potential.

Make sure you distinguish between the idea and the execution. There's nothing more frustrating for a creative team to take you through their campaign idea, only to find you querying some trivial executional element which is not fundamental to the script.

If you have problems with it, be articulate about your reservations so your views can be as constructive as possible, and if it really isn't right, now in the meeting may not be the best time to say so. Maybe you need to do some more thinking and come back with a more considered view about what needs to be done. If you've got problems with it, be articulate about your reservations so your views can be as constructive as possible.

Remember, you are all working together to get a result. When the advertising is right, everybody wins.

And finally

There are no great briefs, only great ads.

There are no great briefs, but there are a lot of bad ones.

A good brief is probably about as good as a brief gets.

Good luck.

Overview: Chapter 8

This chapter is essentially concerned with giving suggestions on how to write a creative brief, based on the way it's done at HHCL & Partners, the agency Steve Henry founded in 1987. It is taken from a speech given annually since 1990 on IPA Stage 4 (Better Account Direction), a course aimed at improving the craft skills of account directors with four or five years' experience in the business.

After a general introduction, Steve looks at the concept of 'being different – for the sake of being better'. He goes on to make five suggestions for writing a creative brief:

- Decide which rules in your marketplace can be broken
- Forget the 'USP', and look for the brand personality
- Define the 'target market' so that you like and respect them
- Write 'creative starters'
- Make your brief inspiring

Steve Henry's style is highly personal, often controversial but always entertaining. Which is probably why his advertising is as successful among the mass market as this chapter is when delivered to the much smaller audience of account directors – who receive its freshness with rapture.

8 Creative briefing: the creative perspective

Steve Henry

(If you want to make a difference, make it different)

Introduction

About seven years ago, Leslie Butterfield asked me to give a talk at an IPA course, aimed at '4-year-old' account directors, on the subject of writing creative briefs. This was an unusual request for at least two reasons. First, I'm a copywriter by training, not a planner or an account director. So I don't write creative briefs. However, like all writers, I like to think of myself as a strategist manqué, so I thought ... what the hell, I can handle it. (Basically, I believe that if you put enough manqués in front of enough word processors, one of them will eventually write a decent strategy.)

But the second reason was perhaps more interesting. At the time of the request, HHCL enjoyed a unique reputation in the advertising industry. Our work seemed wilfully complex to most people in the industry – 'different for the sake of being different' was probably the most common accusation levelled at us. The fact that clients gave us interesting and increasingly high-profile accounts to work on seemed to puzzle and annoy our critics. Perhaps it was the radical inside Leslie which urged him to invite me to speak; perhaps it was a competitive streak in him – and he merely hoped that I would make a prat of myself in front of some highly impressionable young people. More likely, I think it was just that Leslie recognized that something interesting was going on at HHCL.

Criticism

Because, while we didn't enjoy having criticism levelled at us, we liked the idea of being different. In fact, we felt that you had to be 'different' to survive, and thrive. So we adapted the phrase aimed at us and made it our credo to be 'different – for the sake of being better', and this applied to nearly all the processes of working at HHCL.

However, it's outside the orbit of this chapter to go into all our structures and processes. (Although, when I was giving the talk, people usually spent a lot of time asking about them.) And it is also outside the orbit to discuss fully our agency's beliefs about total marketing, about getting outside the 'advertising box' to produce what we call '3D marketing' solutions. Because the briefs on the course were very clear in being 'advertising-only' projects.

That's realistic ... because quite often briefs are limited like this. But clearly, you can have a lot more fun if you allow yourself to think about all the media available to you, and attempt to solve a marketing problem by exploring all the marketing avenues there are. And, in passing, I would like to say that I hope the terms 'above-' and 'below-the-line' will soon be banished, as agencies face up to the fact that there are a whole range of new opportunities which must be taken for our clients – including amazingly sophisticated direct marketing-, PR- and IT-based solutions.

But enough of the waffle. The purpose of my talk was to pass on five thoughts which we used at HHCL to help our project teams create interesting, inspiring, and distinctive creative briefs when applied to 'advertising-only' projects.

First suggestion

Find out what everybody else is doing in your marketplace. Then do something different.

When you approach a particular client's problems, take a long look at what the competition is doing. I ask our planners to form a mental picture of what the most typical communication looks like in that marketplace, and then write it down, so that we can all discuss it.

Limiting ourselves to TV advertising, we can all come up with 'typical' images in most markets – here are two current examples.

1 The car market. The received wisdom here seems to be that 'to shift metal, you've got to show metal', and as most cars increasingly come to resemble each other, so too do most car ads – the same low-angle shot of the tyre holding the road, the same three-quarter rear profile (which seems to flatter the common design of most modern cars), the same long and winding road, and probably an interior shot showing the steering wheel as if such an item were a unique luxury in modern cars. Product 'bunny', usually mentioning the ubiquitous 'ABS', is intoned by one of three or four favoured voiceovers. This is a crude overview – but whichever sector of the car market you're working in should

throw up several more specific 'rules', which the advertisers feel they must adhere to ... or die.

2 The jeans market. This has been dominated by Levi's for many years now, with a frothy mixture based (by and large) on three basic formulae – Americana, sex and music. Any jeans ad which includes two of these three basic ingredients (and most, sadly, embrace all three) can only be copying the great Levi's campaign. It's an interesting fact that it is Levi's themselves who have, while adhering to their successful formula, actually shown the most originality in the form of jeans' ads – by varying the music, or by playing variations on the basic strategy, or merely by using the most radical film directors. It seems to me that nearly everybody else just mimics them. (And imitation is the sincerest way of saying you haven't got an original thought in your head.)

The sort of questions you might like to ask yourself about your market are these:

● Does everybody do 'funny' ads?
● Does everybody do ads with music in them?
● Does everybody do ads that are deadly serious?
● Is there a typical consumer in the ads?
● Is there a typical way to describe or show the product?

Or (moving away from TV advertising)

● Why does everybody else use TV advertising, and is there another medium we can dominate and make uniquely ours?

For instance, we achieved record sales for our car client, Mazda, by using interactive posters and press. While everybody else threw money at the TV companies, to create the clichés described above, Mazda went a different way – and, in a very depressed market, achieved a 40 per cent year-on-year sales increase (Figure 8.1). You have to find out the 'rules' – in order to break them. You have to find out what everybody else is doing – and do it differently.

Why should you do this? On a glib level, you're doing it because you're writing a 'creative brief' – and you should be creative. On a much more serious level, you're doing it to grab the high ground for your client. To be competitive for your client. And to help your client to win.

Most briefs, in most agencies, simply describe the status quo. And that, by definition, is where everybody else is. At HHCL we describe the status quo as follows:

What is = what was.

Figure 8.1

Anita Roddick once said something similar. She described conventional research as being like a rear-view mirror. It told her where she'd been. It couldn't tell her where to go next.

So, find out how the marketplace is currently 'working'. Then grab the high ground for yourself, by breaking some rules. Not all the rules – at least not all the time. And picking the right rules to break is the key (and most adrenaline-pumping) challenge. But if you play to the rules that exist out there, you're playing on somebody else's pitch. You're automatically at a disadvantage.

Of course, breaking rules requires confidence. And confidence has been at something of a low ebb in the marketing industry recently. But you still have to do it.

If you need any more persuading, look at one very simple, but very frightening, statistic. It's recently been claimed that the average person in Britain is exposed to 1300 commercial messages a day – from their wake-up breakfast radio station, through the logos on every carrier bag and T-shirt they encounter, to the last commercial on late-night TV before they've finally had enough and close their eyes for the day. And the same research claims that the average Briton remembers only two of these messages. Why should they remember more? A commercial message is asking you to spend money or change a habit. People by and large don't like doing either of these things.

The human brain can adapt to most changing environments – and it's adapted to today's highly commercial environment by learning how to screen out our messages. In research groups, people might say they *like* certain ads – a typically funny lager ad, or a celebrity endorsement which tickles them – but really getting through to people takes a lot more than this. People no longer just ignore advertising – they've learned how to 'pigeon-hole' our messages so that the brain absorbs, then ignores, our expensively produced efforts. You have to get under people's defences. And the best way to do this is to do something unexpected.

Of course, it still has to be palatable – you have to check that people want to come with you to this new place. But it can't be overemphasized how important it is that your message is distinctive. (For those of you who want to know the provenance of that alarming statistic, I'm afraid I can't help. I can only remember that I read it somewhere! But advertising can never be a scientific endeavour; you just know that what I'm saying makes sense. Don't you?)

As an addendum, beware of people who are 'brave in hindsight', by which I mean the kind of people who say things like 'Hey, I love that Tango work – let's do a Tango for our brand.' This sounds brave – but it's the opposite, because it's copying a formula that's out there, and the most it can expect to do is a percentage of what the original work did.

It's like in Hollywood (where the writer William Goldman said that the golden rule is that 'Nobody Knows Anything'). To counteract the fear involved in launching any new film, most executives will fall into the seductive trap of commissioning a sequel. ('Hey, that worked. Let's do it again.') But the money people in Hollywood finally figured out that sequels usually only gross (at tops) about 60 per cent of the original film. Number 3 in the sequence grosses 60 per cent of that, and so on. Of course, that still makes sequels attractive – but are you happy to create an effect in the marketplace that is just 60 per cent of what your competitor has already achieved? If you do, please leave the room and allow me to cry quietly for a moment.

Incidentally, I now know what to say to clients who ask us to do 'another Tango'. First, I tell them that they deserve something unique. And second, I take them through the process which Tony Hillier (our original Britvic client) went through in buying (or rather co-creating, since his involvement was so crucial) the original work. He looked at a brand which was selling a million cans a day, and decided he could make a difference to this figure. (There's confidence for you.) Then he looked with us at the typical soft-drinks advertising of the time (which could be summed up in the visual image of boy meets girl on American street while sun shines and *fire hydrant goes off*) and decided to reject nearly all the rules therein. In other words, he decided to break the rules of the marketplace, and grab the high ground for his brand. Together, we created an advertising campaign that used street-credible, British humour for the first time in soft-drinks' advertising (Figure 8.2). We also tried to avoid showing fire hydrants, wherever possible. We were rewarded by an increased sales figure of one-and-a-third million cans. A day.

Figure 8.2

The second suggestion

Forget the logical proposition. And find the personality of the brand instead.

There used to be something in advertising called the Unique Selling Proposition, which necessitated going down a list of the brand's qualities until you found something unique and then concentrating on that. This led to such advertising claims as 'Treats – they melt in your mouth, not in your hand'. Unfortunately, a lot of people in the business still believe in this approach. And it's a mistake. Which is not to say that it was always a mistake, because, despite the almost transcendent meaninglessness of the Treats claim, the USP was a useful approach at one time.

But those times have changed, because competitive insulation is now more or less dead. That's what we said when we launched our agency in 1987, and one of our very first clients was able to confirm this for us, with an amazing story.

Aiwa, the Japanese electronics company, invented DAT – Digital Audio Tape – and were copied within six hours. If they'd briefed us to tell people about the 'USP' of DAT, it would have been *unique* for less than a morning.

Lead times in the fashion industry, to take another example, are down to less than half-an-hour.

These days, if you invent a better mouse-trap, the world probably won't beat a path to your door. The chances are that someone like Alan Sugar will copy it, put it on the market at half-price, and the path to your door will remain woefully overgrown, like the 'before' half of a hedge-trimmer advertisement. If your client has a competitive advantage, it will be copied.

But this is a tricky area. Every time I said these words to my class of 4-year-olds, some of them would look worried. It feels comfortable to put in a logical proposition. It's something concrete to hang your hat on, or rest your case on. (There's a mixed metaphor for you!) It helps to make the whole business feel more objective and quasi-scientific (which is very reassuring, in a world of unknowns and unknowables).

Also, clients take pride in their product 'breakthroughs'. 'Aha,' you can hear the brand manager exclaim, 'we've finally got chocolate that won't melt in your hand. Let's see those other agencies copy *that*.' But if consumers want non-hand-melty chocolate, your competitors *will* copy it. I'm sorry, but they will.

Lots of people have coined their own versions of the USP. One very memorable expression of it was the phrase 'interrogating the product until it confessed to its strengths.' At one time I felt that this was a brilliant concept, but I believe that it is no longer as relevant as it once was. What consumers are really motivated by now is the personality of the brand.

At this point of the speech, I always used to ask my audience how they chose their company cars. (Assuming they were allowed that luxury and that latitude.) I know how I chose my first one. I did my homework. I read the trade mags, and discovered that

Car X was faster 0–60.
Car Y was better on head-room.
Car Z was best on fuel economy.

But I soon got bored and confused with all this, and bought a Volkswagen Golf, the one with the red line round the radiator. Because that was the early 1980s, and that was a great yuppie car to have. The personality of the car was absolutely right for me (and other sad proto-pseudo-yuppies) at that time.

I believe that great car advertising has always realized this. Look at the brand personalities built by, at various times, Volkswagen, Volvo, and Audi or, even more relevantly, BMW. A fabulous campaign, which has been built on a whole host of logical propositions. But I would argue that what is really being sold in every BMW ad is the *personality of the brand* – in this case, a personality which cared passionately about every detail of its engineering.

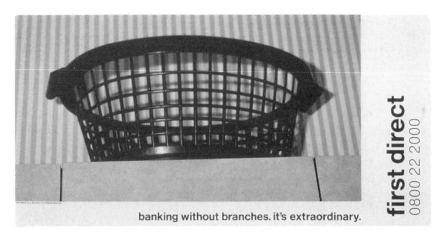

banking without branches. it's extraordinary.

first direct
0800 22 2000

Figure 8.3

For further proof, look at the distinct lack of logical propositions in some other brilliant campaigns. Look at Oxo, or Peperami, or Guinness, or our own agency's launch of First Direct.

First Direct was launched almost as you would launch a fashion label. The bank had no high street presence, and 'existed' only in terms of the perception created by its advertising. We created a personality that was quirky, provocative, individualistic – and appealed to our target market of 'early-adopters' in such a way that we attracted 100 000 accounts in our first year. This was the target set by First Direct's parent company, Midland Bank, and it seemed at the time an almost impossible target because we were dealing with a bank that had no high street branches, and we knew that only 300 000 people switched bank accounts each year. But we achieved that target – by creating a unique brand personality (Figure 8.3).

So that's what we look for in our creative briefs – a description of what we christened the Unique Selling Persona. (Actually, as a piece of neologism, this was a bit of a cock-up. By using the same initials as the Unique Selling Proposition, we made sure that our term wouldn't stand out as the strategic breakthrough it surely was. But never mind. These things happen ... At least it stopped the rest of the industry from catching on quite so quickly.)

So, if you follow this reasoning, you'll see that

The hops in the beer don't matter.
The stitching on the T-shirt doesn't matter.
The interest rates in the bank don't matter.

Of course, your client has to get those things right – that's the hygiene factor. And you can sprinkle a bit of logical argument over your

Figure 8.4

concoction – but don't believe that a logical proposition is going to sell your product by itself. Put all the stuff about interest rates etc. in if you want to. But make it subservient to the personality of the brand. That's what you're really selling.

This seems to me so crucial that I think it constitutes a definition of what we are all doing in this industry. I believe we are in the business of creating distinctive, appropriate, impactful *tones of voice* for our clients – and each one has to be different for each brand we work on. That tone of voice can then be used across all the client's marketing communications – from the trade brochure through to their web-site. Another client we've worked with demonstrates this point further.

When we won the Martini account, we realized that they already had a very distinctive tone of voice – but that it was no longer deemed appropriate for modern drinkers. Searching for a logical proposition was never part of the game. But by concentrating on their brand personality, we were able to understand the root of the problem. What we had to do was reframe their existing (and inescapable) tone of voice in a way that motivated a new generation.

We took their heritage – the drink of the 'beautiful people' – and put a modern twist on it. By saying that you had to be beautiful to drink Martini – and, moreover, by suggesting that most people would require cosmetic surgery to achieve the desired level of pulchritude – we effectively owned and mocked our property at the same time (Figure 8.4).

The marketing generated enormous amounts of PR – but what did it do for sales? At the time of the appointment, our client said that we would be performing a miracle if we slowed down the sales decrease which had been happening for the previous fifteen years. In fact, since the advertising began, sales have increased 10 per cent. We all rubbed our eyes in disbelief when the figures first came in.

But, as I say, this *is* a tricky area. Increasingly, more and more agencies have understood the importance of a brand personality over a logical proposition, (which means that I've got into fewer and fewer arguments with the 4-year-olds listening to me telling them this). As a result of this, I've started to think that maybe it's time to push the pendulum back again. Maybe we should revert to logical propositions – to be different.

Who knows? Everything I'm saying here will only be right for a small period of time, before the world turns again.

The third suggestion

Except possibly suggestion number three, which will always be true. *Define the 'target market' so that you like and respect them.*

David Ogilvy once said 'the consumer is not a moron. The consumer is your wife.' I'm going to ignore the inherent sexism in that remark, because I believe it was just a product of the time he was working in. The point is that this is a fabulous piece of advice – and one of the most crucial things for everybody in marketing to think about.

For a long time, the advertising industry has defined its 'target market' using ghastly, patronizing jargon, like

'The consumer is a C2 housewife, living at home, with two kids.'

or

'The consumer is a young professional, age 25–30, living in a flat in London Docklands.'

The point about both these descriptions is that you don't *like* the people involved. Even the small pen portraits sometimes offered up are no better – they're usually attempts to pigeon-hole and somehow belittle the people you're interested in communicating with. You cannot advertise to people you don't like and respect.

This seems such an obvious point, I'm amazed more people haven't clocked onto it. Think about your personal experience. If you're at a party, and you find yourself talking to someone you're not interested in, how effective are you at communicating with them?

Incidentally, I think this is one of the reasons why it is now so difficult to advertise to a large section of the population – a group of people you might call 'Middle England'. These people, usually middle-class, often women, are responsible for buying millions of pounds' worth of products every day. The advertising industry has patronized them for so long that they're not interested in having a conversation with us any more. Try to talk to them in research groups about moving the advertising on, and they're like bored partners who can't be bothered to talk over the cornflakes any more. Too many years of men in white coats talking down to them about meaningless 'secret' ingredients has rendered them so fed up with advertising, they don't think we're ever going to change. But we can change. And the key is to treat every sector of the marketplace with respect.

Incidentally, it's worth looking at the terminology we tend to use about the people we want to talk to. The phrase 'target market' is inherently hostile, aggressive. The term 'consumer' is more than a little derogatory – it's only one step up from the very insulting 'punter'.

At HHCL we try to use the word 'customer' as often as we can – as a term of respect. (But I must admit that old habits die hard, and I often find myself still using terms like 'target market' and 'consumer' because they're so well-recognized. But that's just because I'm lazy – and there's really no excuse for it …) The point is that this area constitutes probably the biggest mistake the advertising industry makes. By patronizing the people we want to talk to, we've created, in a large number of market sectors, a fundamental breakdown in communication.

Let's take another difficult market sector – business people. In traditional research (done one-on-one because they're all far too important to join any group!) they'll tell you that they like to be treated with respect and with a business-like tone of voice. Hence the deadly boringness of most business-to-business advertising.

But if you do sensitive research among business people, you find that – surprise, surprise – they have the same sense of humour as the rest of us. And this was the breakthrough that allowed us to relaunch Mercury Communications to a business audience, using empathetic humour, a trend I expect to see copied by everybody else in the market, now that we've established that business people do smile occasionally.

At HHCL we like to do media-based research with our audience. Because if you find out which TV programmes and films they like, and which newspapers and magazines they read, two things happen. First, you know the media to employ when you want to talk to them. Second, they become more human and more interesting. Personally, I also like to know which books they read, what music they prefer, and if there are any other cultural things they get into – because then I can rip those off for the creative execution. So find out what makes them laugh. What makes them cry. What they think about current affairs. The point I am making is to treat your customers – both clients and 'end-consumers' – with respect.

When I first got into the industry, one analogy was always being used about our profession. It was said that we were like lawyers, being paid to put the best case forward for our clients. But that's so defensive. It has the effect of making the client look like some poor, bent, second-hand car salesman, clasping his sweaty hands in the dock.

I prefer a different analogy for our business. It's like when you're giving a dinner party, and you want to introduce people to each other who've never met before. You find something which you know they both share an interest in – whether it be the music of Van Morrison, the short stories of Raymond Carver, or even (God help us) the difficulty of finding a good school for the kids. And once you find that topic, you can leave them to get on with it, knowing that there's a good chance that they'll get on. Crucially, it doesn't matter if the other guests join in or not.

To jettison this rather clumsy analogy and revert to the business of marketing, precision targeting is the name of the game. Your media should deliver your desired audience, so that you can have a (relatively intimate) conversation with the people you want to talk to. It doesn't matter what anybody outside of that audience thinks about your advertising. (Unless – and this is an interesting caveat – part of your marketing strategy is to be 'overheard' by other people. This can be very valid, but it doesn't detract from the point I want to make, which is that it is vital to like the people you're communicating with.)

This again is a tricky area for some people, because the advertising industry is full of people who don't really want to be in the advertising industry. They're ashamed of it. (Who was it who said 'My mother doesn't know I work in advertising; she thinks I play piano in a brothel'? It could be any one of hundreds of people in our industry ...) People like this produce ads which their mates laugh at. They try to appeal to people other than their desired audience. That's a dangerous approach, because it's seriously unprofessional – but it's also something else. It's the first sign of being boring. So, try to avoid it for a few years anyway.

The key thing is to find out as much as you can about your customers, and then describe them in a way that motivates the creative people. If you then find that the creative team are slagging them off, try to get rid of them. They're never really going to enjoy working in this business, anyway.

The fourth suggestion

Put in creative starters i.e. write your own creative ideas to your own creative brief. It only needs to be a sentence or two for each idea to describe how your strategy might look in its final medium. Limit yourself to about seven creative starters at the most. Some people at HHCL get a bit carried away at this point and write up thirty creative starters. But that's just showing off. Doing this is a good test of how interesting and actionable your strategy is. It's also a good test of how collaborative your creative team is, because a lot of them will reject anybody else's ideas – and I think that's stupid.

It can't be overemphasized, throughout this process, how important it is to be collaborative with your client and with the rest of your agency team. Try not to be too possessive about your role in the process – and encourage other people not to be too possessive about their roles either.

To give you one example from HHCL. It was actually an art director who came up with the final wording of the strategic breakthrough on the AA, rechristening them 'the fourth Emergency Service'. In this instance, the planner was able to enjoy the traditional creative director's role – saying 'that sounds great, let's do it' and then enjoying a lot of reflected kudos. In this case the reflected kudos consisted of a client enjoying record levels of recruitment because they were brave enough to go with such a bold repositioning. Membership levels rose from 7 million to 8.5 million people in just two years.

This is a great strategic idea – and it could have come from anyone in the team. Similarly, with creative ideas. If you're creative enough to write a brief, you're creative enough to write creative ideas, and that plethora of the word 'creative' in this sentence says something itself. Everybody in this industry is 'creative'; we really need a new word to describe the people who are charged with coming up with proposed conceptions and then executing them. Any suggestions, gratefully received.

But meanwhile, onto suggestion number five. The final suggestion.

The fifth suggestion

Make it inspiring. Make your brief inspiring. Believe in the power of the brief, which is to address fundamentally important business issues in a creative, innovative way. What I *don't* mean is this – don't shove in loads of jokes, or write it in some 'funny' dialect. Don't try to disguise a boring piece of thinking by dressing it up in funky clothes. (Incidentally, I would also beware of too many diagrams. Sometimes they're incredibly valuable and insightful, but more often they're just a way of jazzing up the obvious. Planners as a breed seem to have an undue fondness for some of the geometrical shapes available on the Powerpoint program. I don't know how many other writers in this book have had recourse to this method of communication, so I hope this doesn't come across as a cheap dig. I've seen Leslie's draft of his chapter, and I consider his 'diamond' model an honourable exception to everything I've just said!)

Don't make your enthusiasm shallow. I recently saw a brief from another agency which included, as its proposition, the line 'PHWOOOARR, they don't half taste good'. It looks enthusiastic, but actually it's just very poor camouflage for the most boring proposition there ever was.

Derive your energy from the challenge of making your thinking fresh. If (following suggestion number one) you can show the creative team how to break the rules – and which rules you can break – they'll love you for it. That's what good creatives want to do, not out of some unreconstructed infantile desire to break things in general (at least, hopefully not) but because they instinctively know that that is how you get through to people.

Be ambitious. Be confident. Believe that you can really change the marketplace. Hopefully, your clients will also share your enthusiasm. The best ones will – and they're the ones you should be working with, if you're bright enough to buy the very important, nay seminal, piece of work you've got in your hands right now!

Let me summarize some of the things I've said in this chapter.

1 Find out what everybody else is doing in your marketplace – and decide how you are going to do it differently.
2 Don't look for logical propositions – look for and describe a brand personality.
3 Describe the 'target market' in non-patronizing ways, so that you like and respect them.
4 Put in creative starters – to demonstrate how actionable your brief is.
5 Make the brief inspiring – by making your thinking fresh and unexpected.

That's probably the most important point of all. If I wanted to sum up everything I wanted to say in one sentence, it would be contained in point five. Another way of expressing point five is to say this:

Write the brief with the intention of changing the world.

Overview: Chapter 9

The role of Account Director is a very difficult one to define. Essentially it requires a person to be a jack of all trades and to be pretty nearly a master – or mistress – of all of them.

To be a generalist, harnessing the talents of others with more specialist, and therefore more easily defined, roles within the team, is not easy. This is particularly the case because the job requires the raw material of intelligence and application to be coupled with diplomacy and a certain willingness to allow the egos of others to be satisfied before one's own.

In this chapter, Bruce Haines (one of the best account directors I've ever worked with) looks at the human qualities needed to accomplish this duality, often overlooked by some in Account Management who fail to realize that the key to their own success is heavily dependent on the relationship they have with other departments – in particular, those in the Creative Department.

The Creative people's requirements of those in Account Management, Bruce argues, is quite simple. They want Account Handlers to manage the client relationship in such a way that the chances of their best work appearing is enhanced. The best creative people realize that having a sympathetic relationship with the Account Handler within the agency is also a good way to help work go through. Few of the best and most confident creative people respond well to bullying or patronizing attitudes. On the other hand, they do not much like the obsequious Account Handler who hangs around the Creative Department agreeing with all that the creative teams say.

A relationship based on mutual respect and regard for each other's discipline is needed and achieving this is the key task facing Account Handlers. They must feel themselves responsible for ensuring that this exists and take pride in the results that spring from it – happy and productive working environment, excellent strategic thinking, outstanding creative work and a long lasting and profitable Client relationship.

This chapter, presented at a conference in 1995, is drawn in part from Bruce Haines's talk on the IPA Stage 3 course ('How to get the most out of your clients') in the same year, and also from Bruce's numerous contributions to the IPA Stage 4 'Better Account Direction' course.

9 Managing creatives

Bruce Haines

Rewriting the title

Some time ago I was invited to speak to a group of people on the subject, 'Managing Creatives'. The conference organizer said some flattering things to enthuse me – 'I understand that you have worked with some pretty difficult creative people and managed to get some good work out of them, would you like to tell our audience how you do it?'

I accepted the invitation and began to panic about what I would say immediately after I put the phone down. I would consider myself an instinctive rather than a trained manager and, as such, I am distinctly disinclined to analyse how I do things. In the light of what I had just agreed to do this raised a bit of a problem because it quickly became apparent that I had no idea how I did what the title of the speech suggested, nor, for that matter, had I any idea how other people did it either.

In such circumstances it is always useful to question the appropriateness of the title. To do this, I thought of the Creative people I have worked with and quickly came to the conclusion that if indeed I had managed any of them – and I wasn't too sure about even doing that – then I must have been a pretty inconsistent manager because I had enjoyed, or not enjoyed, very different relationships with all of them. So that gave me a problem with the first part of the title.

The second problem was a niggle that I have always had. I hate it when those people who work outside of the Creative Department call those who work inside it, 'Creatives'. I know that they are 'creative', but that's a different thing. 'The Creatives' (as in 'Oh God, I've got to tell the Creatives that the Client has blown out their work') suggests a different kind of relationship from that where they are known as the Creative Team for example or, collectively, as the Creative Department or even Creative People. I may be oversensitive to this but 'creatives' seems to me to be a patronizing term. This could, of course, also stem from the attitude of the people I have known who use that terminology who always seem to want to put 'creatives' in their place. Whatever the reason, I have grown to dislike it as a nomenclature and so have a double problem with my given subject.

Because this is my chapter, I have decided to change the title. This now becomes:

Working with creative people

I could have added 'A personal guide to self-survival' but then I would be guilty of pandering to the myth that there is something peculiarly difficult about working with creative people. This is simply not the case – at least in the collective sense.

Over the last twenty years I have worked in various capacities, as Account Manager, Account Director, Client Services Director, Managing Director, CEO, Partner and mostly friend with five Creative Directors of renown and the many creative people who worked for them. If I were to write a list of their names the first thing that would become evident is that the only thing that links them as people is the fact that they are all creative. Just like any group of people, they all have their strengths and weaknesses, although in this particular list, strengths vastly outweigh weaknesses and I count myself fortunate to have worked with all of them. But the fact remains that they are people first, creative second and I probably worked differently with all of them.

So are there any commonalties that could form the basis of a lesson in how to work with creative people? Rather than examine my list for clues, let me first redirect the focus and look in more depth at the other side of the relationship – me, and people like me who work principally in Account Management.

Earlier, I said that I considered myself to be an instinctive kind of manager and very bad at self-analysis. However, in the interest of providing as informative a chapter as possible, I have looked in the mirror and offer what can only be described as a highly subjective view of the subject.

Let me first return to the word 'instinct'. It is certainly not my intention to suggest that we cannot improve our understanding and management of this relationship with training and advice, but it has to be said that the raw material of the Account Manager's character does play a large role in whether that advice will be fruitful or not. I claim no false modesty here but there *are* non-creative people who *can* work successfully with creative people and there are non-creative people who cannot. In the end, it is rare that the successful management of this particular relationship can be learned from scratch.

So what do I feel are the basic qualities for successful Account Management?

Attitude

It is pretty much essential to have the right in-built attitude to work in Account Management. As an aside I make the obvious comment that this attitude has to be matched by a basic ability to do the day-to-day job. I use the word 'job' advisedly. There was a period when some of the Account Directors and Managers who worked for me talked incessantly about their careers. They were much more interested in how quickly they could join the board (regarding it as a career stage) than in doing the job well enough to get there by the assent and approval of their colleagues. 'Do the job and you'll have a career, concentrate on your career and you'll have no job' I would tell them merrily. But I did understand the frustration that many of those Account Handlers felt. Account Management is a discipline that always seems to get better over time at an exponential rate. With age and experience the job gets more and more glamorous until that magical stage when 'Management' beckons and Account Handlers in Agencies, good and bad, get promoted away from the Client and away from the job of producing Advertising. That, I can tell you, is many times more frustrating than watching those ahead of you getting the glory.

But back to the beginning. Because so much of the Account Manager's day is made up of rather tedious process, being efficient and making sure the wheels don't fall off, it surely must be the case that these usually intelligent young people do the job for reasons other than the joy of making sure the job number is opened and that the contact report is delivered within twenty-four hours or that the MEAL analysis is completed. It doesn't take a rocket scientist to work out that the creative work and the relationship that account people have with the people who produce it provides the added extra. Indeed it is the relationship between creative people and those who work with them that forms the heart of the reason why client companies, for the most part, are unsuccessful at creating their own advertising.

Most clients in most marketing departments cannot provide the environment where creative people can create. Why should this be? To a large degree, I think it's about ego. Those of us who work in advertising know full well that we only have a business if we please our clients. And, of course, clients are also privy to this information.

We may wax lyrical in credential presentations about being business partners and 'service without servility' and some of the luckiest of us may conduct our client relationships in the spirit that those words suggest. But in our hearts we know that the client has the whip hand because in the end, it's his or her money.

So, in much of the day-to-day management of our client relationships we subjugate our egos to that of the client. This does not mean that we are, or should act like, weak people without courage or opinion. In fact, only those who have a great sense of self-worth and strongly believe in their own abilities can really do the job. It simply means that we work in a service industry. It may be *our* creative work, but it's his or her brand and, because they are paying for it, *their* advertising and sooner or later most clients like this to be acknowledged. And, given the nature of the job, this acknowledgement in whatever form it is expected will most likely be made by someone in Account Management.

The Account Handler is, in essence, an ego coordinator. We have to balance the demands of those people we know want to be able to demonstrate the demands of their ego publicly – the client, very often the Planner and almost certainly, those in the Creative Department.

The intelligent Account Handler gets his or her pleasure in other ways. We get our pleasure from the knowledge that the total job of running the account has been done successfully. This can often be a rather private pleasure and the degree to which Account Handlers can be satisfied with this secret and all too often *self*-acknowledgement is often an indicator of that person's skill in the Account Management discipline. More specifically, I believe that the degree to which an Account Handler can control his or her ego is in direct relationship to the success that that Account Handler will have in working with a creative team. We have to be able to judge the moment, to raise issues when the time is right. Right, that is, for the other person in the relationship. To conduct our working day by being proactively reactive. To lead by asking others to go first. To become the generalist specialist. It is our job to manage a sea of apparent contradictions and that, I can tell you, is not easy. It is *particularly* difficult if you are the kind of manager who *has* to have instant and continuous recognition for doing your job well. Difficult, because so much of what we do is invisible.

I have now worked at Leagas Delaney twice, once from 1986 to 1992 and again from September of 1994. Some time during my sabbatical I had dinner with Tim Delaney to be told. 'When you were there I had no idea what you did but all I know is that it's not being done now and I miss it'. That may be the best compliment I've ever received. This quiet way of working, making your own private satisfaction, is something that not all Account People can do well.

Respect

There are *some* Account Handlers who think that the business would be much better off without creative people at all. They *sort* of realize that they need them but can never quite admit it. When written as baldly as that it may appear absurd but people like this do work in our industry. These people by their actions and thoughts show no respect to our creative colleagues, those who are the designers and manufacturers of the only product that we make. And respect is an essential component in this very potent mix.

These are the kind of people who talk about the Creative Johnnies, the Long Hairs, the Creatives. They call them by these names in a patronizing way and often do so to establish their own superiority in an agency's pecking order. They behave in this way because they cannot bear not to be the ones getting the public reward and recognition that comes with being successful in our industry. They sit in the Grosvenor House and quietly resent the Creative Team – usually young, often socially inept, very often highly paid, going up to collect the gong. I have never understood this.

A few years ago I watched as our Creative Services Director assembled the Agency's submissions for the Campaign Press Awards. I was ecstatic at seeing this mountain of quality work all lined up to be packed. 'Look at it all, Sarah,' I said 'Isn't it fantastic?' 'Yes' she said 'And I see pain in every one'. And she was right. We had all of us, in every department, suffered the pain that comes with producing work of high quality – but no one had experienced the degree of pain that the creative teams had felt giving birth to it.

Every time a creative team gets asked to answer a brief they know that they face the possibility of something going wrong. They hardly ever start the process with the expectation of things going exactly as they wish – and that is the case whatever the team, however good the agency.

This can partly be explained by the process of creating modern advertising. The client can kill it. Six housewives in a group discussion in Bootle can kill it. The lack of budget can kill it. The Director can kill it. The road to air date is strewn with rocks that could possibly prang the idea.

But even greater than this is the fear that they may not be able to think of anything at all. That if they do, it might be a bummer. That all their peers will snigger and point. That this may be the time they might produce a disaster and it will be – by the very definition of advertising – a very public disaster with their name on it.

This is not something that affects anyone else working in an agency. No-one sniggers over a boring strategy or timing plan. These things are essentially private things. The creative person suffers in public and this, in my book, excuses a lot of the pain that creative people sometimes seek to inflict on their colleagues.

The degree of pain that *they* feel has to be understood if you have any chance of working successfully with high-calibre creative people. Once understood, it gives the manager the capacity to tolerate and indeed forgive the worst excesses of the creative temperament.

Not everyone can do this. And those who fail, often fail because they never understand the most basic point. The key issue about managing creative people is not about managing creative people at all. It is about

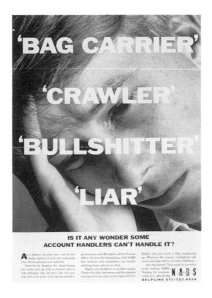

Figure 9.1

managing everything and everyone else around them. I believe that the key to managing a successful creative business is to manage the whole rather than the parts. If you concentrate on managing the Creative department in isolation you will be doomed to failure.

As a manager the first step to ensuring that creative people are happy and productive is to ensure that you hire the right people for all the other departments of an agency. People who have the right attitude. People who appreciate that what creative people do is inherently worth while and important and that creative people themselves are worthy of the same level of respect that those people expect for themselves.

I do not underestimate the difficulty that many non-creative people find in accepting this. After all that I've said thus far, it may come as a surprise to many of you but I do in fact acknowledge that creative people can be difficult to work with, as the ad in Figure 9.1 for NABS graphically demonstrates.

All I do as a manager of all the people in our agency is to provide an environment within which a group of talented and opinionated people are able to do what clients cannot do – produce outstanding advertising. What that often means is acting as referee. As a manager I believe that I have to see both points of view. And as a social democrat I have no problem doing this. What it often means is, on the one hand, explaining – and often excusing – the attitude of the creative person to Account Managers, Planners, media people, the lady who makes the coffee, and, on the other, telling the creative person not to be such a pig when dealing with people who are their colleagues and who all do a job that *they* couldn't begin to do.

Now, as I say, this is not always easy. Creative people are not always easy to respect and in some very rare cases, even to like. Some Account Handlers deal with this little difficulty by attempting to go native. Respect is wonderful – toe-curling obsequiousness is quite another thing. These Account Handlers seek to curry favour with creative people by trying to appear to be as much like them as possible. They will empathize with them on all issues, join in the ritual slagging off of the client, the agency management and all manner of things that they think creative people get exercised about. This usually backfires when the chips are down.

A long time ago Chris Wilkins sat guru-like in the Y&R bar, surrounded by adoring Account men and women. He asked if they would prefer to be Account Handlers or creative people. Seeking to please, nearly everybody said 'Creative, of course'. 'Well,' he said, 'You're all a fat lot of good to me. I've got a department *full* of creative teams. What *I* want are Account Handlers who want to be the best Account Handlers in London.' Far from wanting Account Handlers to be like them, the best creative people *know* that they need help and know that the better the Account Handlers and Planners, the better the help they'll get.

Steve Henry of HHCL told me of a Road to Damascus experience. When he and his partner, Axel Chaldicott, worked at GGT they would consciously write advertising that they knew the Account Management department would find impossible to sell. 'Let's see if he can get that one through' they would grunt as a hapless Account Manager went off with the art bag. Then it gradually began to dawn on them that very little of their work was being made *and* that the account people worked for the same company. *And* that the *good* account people, the ones with influence, didn't want to work with them. They sued for peace.

So here's a basic but vital lesson to remember. Creative people, despite the pain of producing it, want their work to appear, and the clever ones know they have more chance of that happening if they work with the best Account Handlers and Planners. What they want is for people in other departments to be good at their own job and not try to emulate the role of the creative person.

So what are those skills that are admired by creative people and indeed other disciplines? Some time ago I was at an IPA meeting where we were discussing a course for Better Account Direction. We were asked at that meeting to write down a list of qualities that good Account Directors should possess. Most of the Planners round the table produced lists which consisted largely of professional skills – strategic insight, under-standing of markets, numeracy, etc. Those Account Handlers present mostly concentrated on people qualities – leadership, diplomacy, team building, etc. It was an interesting exercise and reflected, I believe, the added value that good Account Direction can bring to a project. Yes, of course, Account Directors must have all of the skills demanded by the Planners – but in essence, those are the ones that are inherently rational and very responsive to training. The softer, more human qualities identified by the Account Handlers are more difficult to learn.

Imagine running an important pitch. In the end it comes down to the Account Director to keep all the specialists on the right track – utilizing all those rational skills. But that will count for nothing if all the specialists are on different right tracks. That's where those people skills come in, enabling the Account Director to play the 'ego coordinator' role we discussed earlier. But does that make it seem as if the Account Director rules the roost to the exclusion of others? Only if he or she is a fool.

Consultation is a prime requirement of successful Account Direction, and that means listening – listening all the time to judge the situation, to measure the mood and to involve all disciplines in the process. Once everyone feels involved, colleagues in Planning, Media and crucially in the Creative Department will, in return, want to know what the Account Director thinks.

It is a common misconception that creative people do not value the views of Account Handlers. They *want* us to have opinions. A colleague of mine, an Account Director, worked with Dave Trott at GGT. He tells the story of an Account man – not him, you understand – being asked by Dave what he thought about an issue. 'I don't know' he nervously replied. 'Well, neither do I' said Dave, 'So that's that then, goodnight'.

It is a common misconception that creative people want complete freedom to do whatever they want on a project. Freedom sounds exciting but for most creative people it can also be a big and frightening thing. In reality they want freedom – and direction. Our job is to provide the solid strategic base, the supporting platform on which they are free to roam about and perform. But, as with any stage, it is essential that they know how far they can move before they fall off the edge. It is our job to tell them this. Freedom, but within established parameters. The parameter is often something that will be settled by Account Management and the client.

The relationship between creative people and client is also something that requires careful monitoring. If you listen to creative people talking of clients within the confines of the Creative department it is sometimes not so pretty. Get the same creative person in a room with a client, however, and the tiger becomes a pussy cat.

One of the greatest problems an Account Manager can have is dealing with the client who thinks that *his* problem will be solved by putting the creative team in the room with him. I can remember one meeting where I was at one end of the table defending a piece of work that a client was attempting to destroy and David Abbott was at the other end quietly sketching something on a pad. As the conversation got more heated he held up the pad and asked solicitously of the client: 'Is this the sort of thing you want?' At which point the meeting ended with the client saying to me 'There you are, you see. *David* understands what I mean'. Unfortunately after the client left the room David, as I remember, was not quite as keen on the new idea as he was on the old one.

I am not against creative people meeting clients. Such meetings are usually beneficial but it is essential to understand that, when face to face, most Creative people aim to please clients and will often concede a point where an Account Handler will keep going.

One of the roles of Account Management is to manage the gap between the client and the Creative department, to reduce the width of it if at all possible but to be aware that it inevitably exists. I remember telling one group of Account people that their role was not to be waiters – taking orders from the client, running to the kitchen and expecting the Creative Director to act as chef and cook a prescribed dish. Creative people are capable of excellent strategic thinking and they should be included in the strategic process.

Trust

If included at the beginning of the process, the degree of trust between Account handlers and Planners, on the one hand, and creative people, on the other, will be greatly increased, and cooperation, speed and the chance of a successful solution all improved.

Responsibility

What this all boils down to is a shared responsibility in the production of an advertising solution, a grown-up partnership of recognized and respected expertise in different disciplines.

Honesty

But if it's grown up it has to be honest. This is the most difficult one of all. What do you do when you don't agree? That odd occasion when you don't think that the Creative Team is right? How do you cope with the occasion when you are asked to sell work that you can see is either wrong or maybe, and here you really do have to swallow hard, maybe just isn't good enough? What you have to do is risk the row and go for it.

The best creative people encourage constructive criticism. But this has to be earned. And it requires the creative judgement and taste of the Account Handler or Planner to meet the approval of the creative person.

No easy matter, and this usually needs to be demonstrated over time. Foolish indeed is the new Account Manager who marches in to the Creative Team and, just by dint of his title, arrogantly seeks to impress them with an incisive and wounding critique of their work. John Maynard Keynes once said that people are often at their most dogmatic when they are most unsure. I think he must have been thinking of creative people when he said that.

In going for it, just remember that despite the look of fierce determination on his face, the creative person may be as unsure as you are about the work. What they often need is an out, asking the Client for more time, providing a logical reason why the idea may not be acceptable or relevant. Here the Account Handler can really give support to the Creative Team – as long as the Account Handler has done his or her job and has the trust of the client.

All the words I have highlighted above are about relationship management. All or any could be used in any relationship – between people of any discipline. They do not depend on one party being creative – which may be a lesson in itself.

I've talked about respect, trust, responsibility and honesty. Let me add one more.

Pride

A creative friend of mine once started an agency with an Account man. It came to grief as a business probably for many reasons, but its demise as a relationship seemed inevitable to me when my creative friend spoke to me about his partner. 'You see' he said 'he just isn't proud of us or of anything we do'. Showing an emotional commitment to the work and being proud of your creative colleagues is, I think, the least we can do to thank them for the pain of doing something that we, quite simply, cannot.

So, what are the secrets of good account directorship and agency relationship management? Perhaps it's my social democratic leanings coming to the fore again but I believe that it is a question of balancing the basic requirement for organizational, bureaucratic skills with a dose of advanced diplomacy and common sense. One without the other and that much-sought after career advancement is unlikely to happen.

As Account Managers we all learnt the basic skills which got us to the stage of consideration for promotion. Those that proceed further are inevitably those who have demonstrated a capacity to do a different kind of job as an Account Director. To put it bluntly, those who do not learn that the job from that point on is about the care and motivation of other people will eventually lose out. Those who realize that if they help other people achieve what they want – the Creative Team and the client especially – will be rewarded with a job considered well done *and* a great career.

Overview: Chapter 10

This is essentially a 'how to' guide for young planners and account handlers. It is designed as a checklist to prevent disaster in the construction of a pitch rather than as a guarantee of victory.

Jim Kelly's chapter advances the premise that a pitch is a medium in its own right and that the sole object of the exercise is to win the business. It recognizes that pitches are an artificial process and all efforts should funnel towards the pitch date, not the air date.

Embracing this principle may result in behaviour in pitches which is not consistent with the ideal development and prosecution of an advertising campaign. Jim argues that this is acceptable under the circumstances, particularly if it leads to an appointment.

The ten-point checklist he proposes can look like a catalogue of the obvious and the axiomatic. But if you consider the full implications of all of these components and adhere to most of them, you will undoubtedly create a better pitch. The ingredient list for the professional pitch comprises:

No. 1   The Pitch Leader
No. 2   The Pitch Pow Wow
No. 3   The Timing Plan
No. 4   The Logic Chain
No. 5   The Idea
No. 6   Package Your Thinking
No. 7   Define the Role for Advertising
No. 8   Ask the Ultimate Question
No. 9   Make a Recommendation
No. 10   The Rehearsal

These guidelines are necessarily 'presentation-centric' but they do not ignore some of the vital stages of foreplay in the conduct of a pitch. Neither do they restrict lateral or innovative pitch styles but should allow them to be delivered on time and with the appropriate conviction and coherence.

What this chapter won't tell you, Jim concludes, is where to find one of the most crucial ingredients of the winning pitch; *the great idea*. Thankfully, some things can never be generated from a rule book!

This chapter was first presented on the IPA Stage 2 Campaign Planning course in 1992.

10 A Survival Guide to the Pitch

Jim Kelly

Introduction

The following is a faithful re-creation of a presentation which I have given at the IPA Stage 2 Campaign Planning course every year for the past five years. Its purpose was always twofold: (1) to give some immediate guidance to the fifty or so delegates who were about to embark on a stressful three-day mock pitch for a hypothetical account in syndicates of six and (2) to help give them an idea of just what steps were essential in the construction of a professional new business presentation when they returned to the real world, if you could call it that, of their own agencies.

My presentation took the form of a recipe, a simple enough metaphor and was always preceded with the caveat that it did not guarantee a winning pitch – that particular formula has still to be written. Modestly, though, I still believe that if these ten points are adhered to, they will inject some focus and sanity into what has been described as 85 per cent confusion and 15 per cent commission (you can tell how old that quote is).

In essence, it is a 'how to' guide but it does consider the philosophical as well as the practical aspects of pitching for new business. Its title was and remains:

'A Survival Guide to the Pitch'

I make no apologies for the somewhat melodramatic title of this piece but competitive pitching is still the most gladiatorial part of the advertising process. If you are lucky in your career you will be involved in many such contests and they will in turn be responsible for some of the highest highs, the lowest lows and definitely the worst pizzas you will ever experience in agency life. The outcome of the first dozen pitches in the life of a new agency will usually dictate its survival prospects and new chief executives pray for an early win as proof that the medicine is working.

Our ability to triumph in these tests of skill and stamina is still seen as the index of agency virility. Why else do we study the 'Campaign Business Performance' league so assiduously and why has the reporting of new business wins relied on the language of coups, scoops, nets and scores for the past twenty years.

Some commentators argue that the very drama of these pitches is what gives them their *raison d'être*, since they frequently require the senior management of a client company to attend the meetings and ratify the decision, thereby investing it with greater corporate commitment than if it happened in a less auspicious way. The announcement of a competitive advertising review by £50 million plus spenders like BT and British Airways can still attract national press attention, interest Ladbrokes and hypnotize our little industry for weeks.

In recent times there have been some mutterings in the press about replacing the grand pitch with relationship matching and other alternative courtship rituals but there seems little sign of these particular brains and beauty contests dying out just yet. In fact the EU law on competitive tendering for public contracts above a certain value, for example, indicates to me that pitching has a long and unhealthy future.

Surprisingly, then, given its central importance in the field of advertising endeavour the pitch is the subject of very little scholarly dissertation. Rarely if ever is this messy precursor to the planning of an advertising campaign referred to in the pages of *Admap*, for instance. Jeremy Bullmore, the great sage of our industry, covers every aspect of the business in his book *Behind the Scenes In Advertising*; but his analysis of pitching behaviour is scant except for this gem:

New business presentations combine tension, expense and absurdity in roughly equal proportions.

A greater insight, however, is provided by John Perriss, supreme commander of Zenith World-wide, who was fond of the dictum that:

There are six major media: television, press, outdoor, radio, cinema and . . . pitches.

The logical extension of this thought is that your prospective clients must be the sole target audience for this last medium and when you grasp the full implications of that you have the basic premise on which effective 'pitch doctoring' is based.

The strategic and creative thinking that goes into a pitch is highly artificial, telescoping as it does the ideal advertising development cycle into weeks or even days. No-one knows how much of the creative work shown at a pitch ever sees the light of day as advertising, but my guess is less than 10 per cent. So we might reason that it is a deeply wasteful process also.

However, this is not the case if we consider pitches as an end in themselves and not part of some greater advertising plan. In fact once we detach it from sensible campaign development we can appreciate that the overriding purpose of the pitch is to win the business. In the words of Vince Lombardi, veteran NFL coach: 'Winning isn't everything, it's the only thing.' I have been accused of cynicism as a result of this stance but after twenty years in the game I am forced to conclude that a great pitch that doesn't win the business is a contradiction in terms. It is utopian to believe that virtue will bring its own reward and that all you need to concentrate on is answering the brief, selling more of the client's product and improving the brand image.

While these issues may be convergent with the pitch, the subtext of how you deliver the primary messages may be more decisive in influencing the outcome of the contest than you think. So as you fix your sights on the D&AD pencil and the IPA Ad Effectiveness Award, don't overlook the little detail of getting appointed first.

This, then, is the realist school of pitching and with that precept firmly embraced you should now look to the preparation of your case (or cake, if we're sticking to our metaphor) and channel most of your intellect towards the pitch date, not the air date. As you do so you can take some solace in the knowledge that no-one in advertising, however experienced, has the monopoly on wisdom when it comes to pitches. This was brought home to me as long ago as 1979 when the biggest pitch in town was for British Rail and the grudge match of the day was between Saatchi & Saatchi and ABM. Late in the pitch cycle, John Bacon, the writer, presented his creative director Jeremy Sinclair with a possible strapline which was dismissed on the grounds that 'The age of the train is here again – will never win a pitch'. Alas, a few weeks later ABM carried off the prize with a line that was just a tiny variation of this. But at least Jeremy rejected it for the right reason, i.e. he thought it wouldn't win!

Anyway, enough philosophizing, you're on the shortlist, the pitch is in four weeks' time and the clock is ticking, so now what? The following list is, as they say, necessary but not sufficient for victory.

No. 1 The pitch leader

Every pitch should have a clearly identifiable leader (note the singular) and they have a daunting list of responsibilities which may be delegated only partially. These include:

Allocation of resources
Managing the time
Arbitrating disputes

Editing the presentation
Achieving consensus
Motivating the team
Taking the credit/blame

I do not propose to dwell on the methods by which leaders can carry out these tasks but it is important that somebody does and preferably somebody who is accountable for the outcome of the pitch! My experience of pitching in big agency environments is that the proliferation of management titles often means there is no shortage of candidates for pitch leader. Paradoxically this situation can result in a complete absence of leadership or accountability, but I digress. Assuming such a hero emerges he or she will probably call an initial meeting which I have called . . .

No. 2 The pitch 'pow wow'

This is best convened immediately after the client has briefed the agency and should involve the entire presentation team and any other interested parties. Please note that creative and media people are essential to the proceedings.

Its form and etiquette should be that of a brainstorming. This means everyone leaves their stripes and functional roles at the door. Within reason no idea should be scorned and no line of logic rejected at this stage. The word 'and' is a more appropriate conjunction than 'but' in these gatherings.

The object of the 'pow wow' is to develop the competing hypotheses about the solution to the brief and agree ways in which they might be validated and brought to life. It usually also throws up random ideas for presentation theatre as well. On the principle that first ideas are often the best ones in advertising it can even provide a breakthrough on day one. Lastly, someone, usually an account manager, has the task of writing up the minutes and circulating them to the pitch team.

No. 3 The timing plan

This might sound like a fairly routine piece of housekeeping but you would be surprised how many pitches have foundered on the rocks of poor timekeeping. The timing plan should have semi-sacred status and be agreed overtly with all members of the team. Like all good timing plans, it is worked backwards from the presentation date in order to allocate time fairly between tasks. It is enforced ultimately by the pitch leader. Ignore it at your peril or you'll be doing your first rehearsal in front of the clients, or ringing up and begging for a time extension, both of which I have done this year already.

No. 4 The logic chain

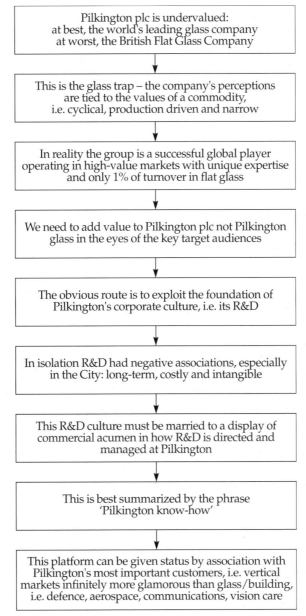

Figure 10.1   *The Pilkington logic chain (February 1989)*

If these first three ingredients boil down to applied common sense this next one is more proprietary. I have been accused of excessively linear thinking in my fetish for these devices but I am unrepentant. In essence, a logic chain is one page containing fewer than ten consequential and short sentences which sum up the argument for the pitch. It is a document which never appears in the presentation because it is the chassis for the *whole* presentation. If you can condense your argument into this form as early as possible in the assembly of the pitch it will have a variety of benefits: it can be a template for the rehearsal, or a vital reference at 2.00 a.m. when no-one can see the wood for the trees and eventually with a bit of elaboration it can easily become the management summary for the leave behind pitch document.

I have shown an actual logic chain for the Pilkington corporate pitch which GGT won against AMV and CDP in 1989 in (Figure 10.1) purely to illustrate this simplified form of argument, although you might feel it wasn't an overly complex one in the first place! This 'pitch on a page' was referred to throughout the run-up to the presentation and kept us out of the quicksand that corporate advertising strategy can very easily turn into (see Figure 10.2).

Figure 10.2

No. 5 The idea

The following ingredient has less to do with excellence in pitches and more with excellence in advertising. It is axiomatic in my view that where agencies add the most value to a client's business is in the provision of a central communication idea that sits above the individual media execution and becomes the centre of gravity of all the brand's marketing communications. Indeed my own agency was conceived and devoted to *the idea* as our primary product to such an extent that we charge for ideas separately to all other agency services.

Now it is not the remit of this chapter to explore the nature and definition of an advertising idea, but suffice to say there should be one, at the heart of every pitch. This is the nugget that wasn't in the client brief. This is the De Bono-like leap that frees the client's advertising strategy with one bound. This is the intellectual property against which all the brand's communications can be judged.

At some point in the last AA pitch Howell Henry Chaldcott Lury will have told the Automobile Association to stop being that 'verry verry nice man' and to start behaving like the fourth Emergency Service. It must have been a chilling moment, but it is an idea of such force that it requires very little executional elaboration. Imagine what it must have been like in the room when BBH told Häagen-Dazs that they were going to inextricably link their ice-cream to sensuality, yes, say it loud, SEX! It all looks desperately simple in hindsight, but then the best ideas often are. Once you have a piece of step-change thinking like these two examples at your disposal the construction of the pitch is pretty self-evident. But even if your idea is not of such quantum proportions it should still obviously be the centre of the argument.

The best pitch presentations are built from the idea outwards. Since this is ultimately what you are going to be selling, the logic of any pitch should rationalize both forwards and backwards from this idea. If you ever study a pitch document after a presentation it is rare that it actually offered more than three elements in total that would qualify as seriously original thoughts or insights into a marketplace. It is an all too frequent offence also that these nuggets are camouflaged under elaborate restatements of the client's original brief. When Aneurin Bevan accused Harold Wilson of being 'all facts and no bloody ideas' he could just as well have been critiquing a poor agency pitch document.

No. 6 Package your thinking

While on the subject of facts it is an easy temptation in pitches to show volumes of untreated market statistics and the accompanying workings in the margin as a way to justify the agency's assertions and evidence effort. I believe this is gradually being eliminated by the trend to shorter pitches, i.e. an hour or less, but in case it is not, you should be aware that the facts by themselves are silent. It is only the deductions that you make from them or the insights that you have which make them useful in a presentation.

If you accept the initial premise that clients are the target audience for pitching purposes then the analysis that you have conducted must be brought to life by resorting to:

Models
Signposts
Analogies
Memorable typologies
Themes/soundbites

All these should be designed to strengthen the argument and make it portable in the minds of the target audience – your client. It would be wrong to be prescriptive about the form these should take since everyone has their own style but the principle of how and why they work is inescapable. Please note charts with lots of arrows leading to boxes with words in them do not of themselves necessarily constitute effective packaging.

A very basic example of simplified pitch graphics is shown in Figure 10.3 and is a relic from an old Farley pitch. Ten years ago the sugar-rich Farley rusk that we all grew up on was *the* fastest-declining Nielsen-audited grocery sector. This unenviable feat was attributed to a variety of changes in the way that mothers approached feeding their infants. This 'nibbled-away rusk' was devised as an at-a-glance way of bringing the list of reasons to life.

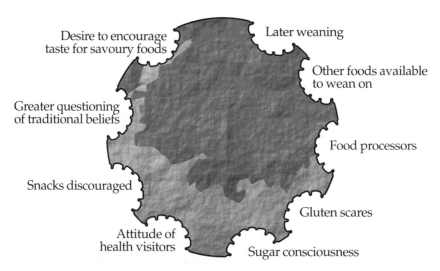

Figure 10.3   *The gradual decline of the rusk market*

Another off-the-peg chart which I would commend to you is the brand pyramid. This is a handy portmanteau device which allows you to sort all the various dimensions of a brand into their relative importance and roles. Figure 10.4 is one I made up earlier for Winalot Mixer. As you can see, it is a slightly more interesting pro forma, but it is a good mental discipline to fill in even if you never use it in the presentation.

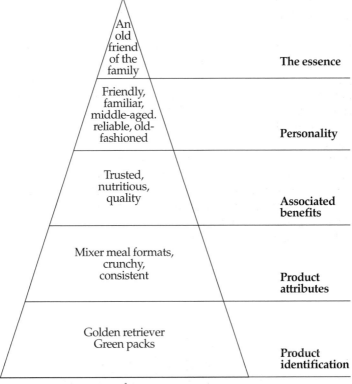

Figure 10.4 *The Winalot brand pyramid*

One particular pitch I was involved in which was more noteworthy for its pitch theatre than its long-term marketing thinking (the product failed in the test market) was for a new cookie from Lyon's biscuits called Ostlers. In the course of the presentation in order to convince the client that his cookie, at least at first sight, appeared unexceptional, we glued the new creation to a board containing at least a dozen competitive cookies and invited the brand manager to pick out his baby. He found one but failed to see the other two we had also secreted in there – phew. This pitch deployed the ubiquitous vox pop video as a means of dramatizing the real product truth which was that when you bit into one you couldn't tell whether it was a biscuit or a cake. This was the (short-lived) appeal

Figure 10.5

of the product and became the advertising idea for the pitch, i.e. to create the debate:

'Is it a biscuit or a cake?'

Another memorable piece of packaged thinking used in a pitch later went on to appear in a successful IPA Advertising Effectiveness Paper.

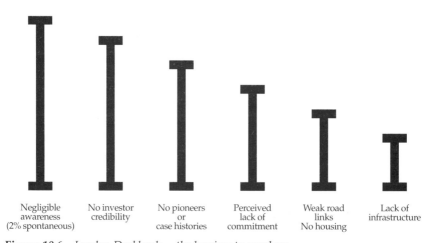

| Negligible awareness (2% spontaneous) | No investor credibility | No pioneers or case histories | Perceived lack of commitment | Weak road links No housing | Lack of infrastructure |

Figure 10.6   *London Docklands – the barriers to purchase*

This was for the London Docklands Development Corporation and was born out of desperation in the early hours the night before the pitch. After listening to a somnambulant debrief about the communications problems inhibiting the regeneration of London's Docklands Mike Greenlees (the pitch leader) was moved to utter these words to the presenter: 'You've got a big ball of wool here – but I don't see a cardigan'.

Mike went away and produced one chart called *the barriers to purchase* (see Figure 10.6) from which the presentation team orchestrated the whole strategy and I enclose it here in the form in which it appears in *Advertising Works 3*. Incidentally, GGT, as you will have deduced, won the pitch, one of the first in its life (Figure 10.7).

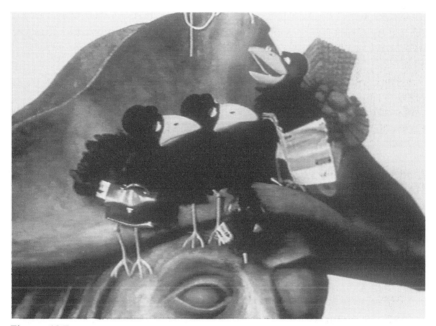

Figure 10.7

No. 7 Define the role for advertising

While it is difficult to generalize about the content of a desirable advertising presentation, it is also difficult to imagine that you could omit this ingredient and still have a credible presentation. This title also covers:

The advertising objectives
What outputs will advertising affect?
How will the advertising work?
Measuring the advertising

Until you have established the premise or model of advertising effect you are working to – it is difficult to assess any creative or media strategies in the resultant vacuum. It is also a prerequisite of any discussion over whether the budget matches the task that the task is clearly delineated and this may involve spending as much time stating what advertising cannot do as well as what it can. This 'choice' is rarely exercised in the client's brief and it is expected that the agency will have a viewpoint on this.

No. 8 Ask the ultimate question

This ingredient should probably precede some of the earlier ones but on the grounds that it is never too late to ask this question or indeed never too early I have included it here. The ultimate question is, of course:

'What will it take to win the business?'

The foregoing rules have been necessarily presentation-centric but obviously pitches are often won before the pitch day ever dawns. If you go back to the realist school of pitching there are other things agencies have to do to get appointed apart from answer the client brief. There are frequently hygiene factors like size and commitment to be considered. Are we too big for this account? Are we too small? Do we have any kind of resourcing or experience advantage to exploit? Of course, there is the important question of 'the relationship' and who is going to do the bonding and with whom on the client side.

Identifying one member of the client team who is going be more sympathetic to your agency cause to give unofficial feedback in the sometimes extended courtship period can be invaluable. These opportunities are largely case-specific and difficult to pontificate about except to say that such intangibles are usually lurking off-brief and need to be confronted openly.

Winning pitches are often mistakenly viewed as being disproportionately about how good you are at the black arts of what I have called 'strokes, coups and other manoeuvres'. Some more protestant and self-consciously ethical agencies frown on the kind of vulgar displays I am about to describe. My own view is that they have their place as long as they are relevant and meet one or more of these criteria:

Memorable or original
A discriminator
Stimulates audience involvement
Demonstrates commitment
So compelling they lead to an appointment on the spot

Alumni of the Charlotte Street Academy need read no further since 'the nothing is impossible' culture was always at its most inventive at pitch time. We've all heard the stories of how Saatchi & Saatchi put a Toyota in their reception area prior to round one of the pitch and how they put a second one in prior to round two (and yes, of course they won the business). Also it must be said that Saatchi & Saatchi were at their deadliest when they had been eliminated from a pitch. This usually prompted a complete overhaul of their effort overnight as in the case of one privatization pitch or indeed intercepting a sport shoe client with a fresh artbag while on his way to appoint another agency.

Mike Greenlees once knocked a hole in his agency boardroom wall to demonstrate the filling properties of a particular product from Polycell during a pitch. It might not have swung the pitch but it must have helped.

However, my favourite example of the stroke comes not from London or New York but from Austin, Texas.

This is the story of GSD&M in that city who had held the South West Airlines account for twenty years, having virtually grown up with the airline's president and founder Herb Kelleher. The appointment of a new marketing director inevitably caused some questioning of this cosy relationship and resulted in a repitch being called. The Richards Group from the airline's native Dallas was invited in to contest what became a grudge match of statewide significance over who held Texas's national airline. Richards raised the temperature by putting up a poster in front of the airline's offices with the pitch date on it and the claim that they had waited nineteen years for that day. But GSD&M were smart in that they asked themselves the ultimate question and came up with the answer. If you've held an account for two decades you are unlikely to turn up a blinding piece of insight that will revolutionize the business just in time for a repitch. Very wisely GSD&M went in to bat on their record and at the same time went on an emotional offensive.

First, they went back through the files and assembled every still photo of every agency barbecue, birthday party and softball game they had ever been on with Herb and the team. These they interspersed with footage of their former triumphs on the account. This was then edited to a particularly mawkish John Denver track in a video confection guaranteed to bring tears to the eyes of any God-fearing Texan. This was to be the scene setter to their presentation. But just in case that didn't do the trick they planned a big finish also. They composed a new anthem for the airline's advertising entitled 'Together We Stand'. It could have gone platinum in Nashville. In order to render it to maximum effect they bussed the entire 200 staff of GSD&M to Dallas and assembled them in the atrium at the airline's office to sing it.

At the end of their pitch they took Herb out on the balcony and as the agency burst into song Herb was almost moved to tears. Someone had the courtesy to phone the Richards Group who were due on that afternoon and at least warn them that they had, in effect, already lost.

No. 9 Make a recommendation

This ingredient once again is a statement of the obvious. A pitch is not a menu, it is a point of view and presenting a suite of options is risky when the client has six to choose from already. It may be an acceptable technique to show routes that you have eliminated particularly if they may have been espoused by a competitor. It is a cardinal error to let a client go away from a pitch and not know what it was you stood for or told them to do.

No. 10 The rehearsal

My advice here is make sure you have one and do it for real with all the passion you intend to muster on the day. Use non-presenters or even people uninvolved in the process as critics and devil's advocates. Time it. Don't be afraid to deconstruct it if it isn't working.

In the course of rehearsal one vexed question inevitably arises or, worse still, doesn't arise when it should. The dilemma is: do you let everyone who has worked on the pitch present in some way however small? There is no easy answer to this but I am sceptical about the level of coherence and dramatic impact achieved by these democratic 'jack-in-the-box' pitches. In the end I can only offer the quote by Steve Martin:

> *Some people have a way with words and ... some people not have way*

as a good rule of thumb for the pitch leader faced with this dilemma.

Lastly I will leave you with a collection of things not to say in pitches for no other good reason than countless people have said them already before you and they have passed into advertising cliché:

> *'We were really excited by the challenge of working on your brand'* – the opening gambit.

> *'Now I'd like to hand you over to the team who have been living and breathing your business for the past four weeks'* – the handover.

> *'We've done a huge amount of desk research'* – the market background.

'We thought we'd ask a few consumers what they thought, but, of course, this isn't proper research' – the vox pop.

'Here's the book of the film' – the document.

Postscript

By its very nature pitching encompasses all types of advertising and I concede that this recipe will not extend to every case but *some* of it will be applicable in *all* cases. Remember also that it was designed for agency staff of three years' experience or less. To the seasoned and innovative campaigners reading this it may seem facile that you can distil our voodoo art down to a ten-point plan.

In retrospect where it is deficient is in acknowledging the role of genius, pure talent, energy, conviction and individual powers of persuasion that can affect the outcome of any pitch however shambolic. In fact it may mislead those young people who have yet to sit in an actual live pitch into thinking that the process is a rather dry, logical and arid affair. (It is a particular hobbyhorse of mine that some of the larger training agencies are delaying the age at which their junior planners and account handlers are actually exposed to the real performance of the pitch as opposed to merely working on one behind the scenes.) So I will add one more ingredient as a gesture to this human factor in the form of a quote from an obscure American adman who said (or perhaps plagiarized) this about pitching: 'One man with a passion – is a majority!'

Overview: Chapter 11

The media presentation on the IPA's Stage 2 course (Campaign Planning) has historically been given by a number of luminaries of the UK media world, including Ken New of Abbott Mead Vickers BBDO and Jonathan Durden of PHD. I selected this contribution from Iain Jacob of BBH/Motive because it represented the best blend of strategy and implementation and, at the same time, gave an excellent overview of the dynamics of this exciting and rapidly changing arena.

In this chapter Iain examines the importance of media thinking to brand strategy, outlines the key guidelines for successfully developing a media plan and analyses the issue of media buying, as distinct from media planning. In covering these areas he also gives us a fascinating insight into the media world, and hints at some of the developments over the horizon that may reshape our thinking in the next decade.

This chapter was first presented on IPA Stage 2 in 1992, and remains, in my view, an outstanding contribution to the subject.

11 Making the most of media

Iain Jacob

Introduction

Don't you think it is strange that in an industry dedicated to consumer communication in the media that actual media decisions are left to a 'media specialist' or a media department? Shouldn't we all be media specialists?

But for those of us not in a media operation it is seemingly ever harder to stay in touch with media developments and how 'media specialists' actually work. Gone are the days when the account director could say 'this has to be on television' with any degree of confidence that this would be the best solution. Maybe the client should be using one of the now-available national radio stations, marketing via the Internet or making their own television programme and syndicating this to the relevant television channels.

For the next few pages I would ask you to put to one side any preconceptions you might have about this area called media. Forget, for a moment, its apparent complexity, the strange language of impacts, effective frequency and price versus pure station average in which it deals. Forget the idea that it is something best left to someone else.

One of the greatest ironies of the explosive change that we are witnessing in our media environment is that it is forcing us to reapply the first principles of sound marketing thinking in the way that we approach media for our clients' brands. For some years the media discipline has been bound up with conventional wisdoms that are now increasingly failing to deliver genuinely effective communication. Can we rely on the rules of television usage that applied to a four-channel environment to provide good solutions in a forty-channel satellite home? The current definition of readership – 'read or looked at for at least two minutes' – may have been acceptable for a one-section newspaper but are we confident that it tells us much about how people are reading the eighth section of *The Sunday Times*?

You are reading this chapter at a good time; a time when the conventional wisdom and traditional language of media is having to be challenged, a time when one of the greatest assets that can be applied when creating great media plans is that of common sense. This chapter goes back to first principles to ask, what should we be expecting from our media thinking? What guidelines can we apply to get there? And how is the industry evolving to meet the challenges of our rapidly changing media landscape? We will cover the following areas:

1 The importance of media thinking to brand strategy
2 Guidelines for successful media plan development
3 The issue of media buying
4 Why media has become dominated by media-dedicated companies.

The importance of media thinking to brand strategy

When Marlboro Friday happened there was much written about the death of the brand. Ironically the event went on to endorse the power of the brand. Philip Morris's position is stronger than ever in that market.

Despite extraordinary pressures such as own-label products, the new 'savvy' consumers, the costs of globalization, etc. well-managed brands continue to reward their owners disproportionately well. The Coca-Cola Company stock performance over the last few years is a vivid case history. In March 1996 they were named by *Fortune* as 'America's most admired company', largely for this performance. Not bad for a company whose founding brand would appear to be at the forefront of these pressures.

Companies are increasingly defined by the strength of their brands rather than simply the value of their manufacturing assets. Reebok is capitalized at $2.5 billion and has a turnover of $3.5 billion a year – the company doesn't own any of its own manufacturing facilities.

A brand is a relationship, a relationship that the consumer is willing to pay for over and above a commodity price. Brands remain one of the most cost-effective ways for a company to build consumer relationships. What Philip Morris had wrong prior to Marlboro Friday was the price/value relationship, the brand itself had retained the most enormous and valuable consumer franchise. The retailer brands have succeeded as they have built closer consumer relationships than many of the traditional products that they list and become enormously powerful brands in their own right.

So how does this affect the way you should think about media? The truth is that in the majority of cases the consumer is going to have a greater exposure to you and your competitors' brands in the media (in its broadest sense; television, retail, press stories, the Internet, billboards) than he or she does eating, drinking and driving it. It is across the media that much of this relationship is built.

Given that good brand companies are obsessed with the perfection of the product performance of their brand it makes sense for them to be obsessed with its delivery in the 'media' and how this is adding value to the brand. A good analogy is that of retail distribution. How many companies would describe their retail distribution strategy as trying to be everywhere despite the environment and what it says about the brand? Not many, but the founding strategic principle of plenty of media plans remains that of 'maximizing coverage at optimum frequency'.

Good media thinking is about building real, valuable relationships between the brand and its consumers, with the least possible use of resource. This may appear to be an absurdly obvious definition but ask yourself how your experience of media thinking matches it. In the UK an average individual is exposed to over 1000 commercial messages a week. Add this to the avalanche of other information you receive (how many e-mails did you get yesterday?) and then think about how many brand messages you remember. In this environment describing the potency of a media plan simply in terms of coverage and frequency in no way describes how it is effectively building this relationship. How often have you seen a media plan that had 85 per cent coverage at 5 OTS written on it and observed that everybody feels comfortable because the numbers are so big?

But believing these figures relate directly to real communication is akin to believing that your fellow-citizens remember those 1000 messages. The key questions to ask are: why should our target consumer notice the communication in this particular media plan? How does the media usage specifically help to build the relationship between brand and consumer? How does this plan give the brand an unfair advantage? How does it differentiate the brand? All questions that a marketeer is very used to asking in other parts of his or her business.

So why is this so relevant today compared with five years ago? Within our rapidly evolving media landscape there is the growing opportunity to build stronger brand relationships and genuinely help to differentiate between brands, and in many cases doing this with significantly less resource.

It is not unusual for media spend to account for over half of a brand's total advertising and promotion budget. It is inevitably the biggest single marketing expense for the majority of consumer brands. If you can significantly alter the price of building the consumer relationship in the media you can obviously have a pretty significant effect on the viability of profitably running a brand.

So what is changing?

For the consumer, media is quite simply moving from undersupply to oversupply. And many a consumer market has taken this walk. Media in the UK has been slower than many consumer markets to become more consumer driven, largely due to legislation restricting both development and ownership of the media. But given new technology and the development of legislation (still very restrictive), the level of oversupply is becoming quite remarkable.

In oversupplied markets consumers make choices. What is it that suits them? If you are into mountain biking there is now no need to buy a general-interest bicycle magazine and accept that there will only be ten pages on mountain biking somewhere towards the back of the title. You can now choose from three different mountain bike magazines (excluding the foreign imports), each one taking a slightly different angle on the sport. Is this phenomenon restricted to a few niche media? Hardly, look at the growth of men's magazines over the last ten years with the number of titles available up by 150 per cent from 1985 to 1995. Look at the numbers of consumers willing to pay for sports coverage on satellite television, look at the success of Classic FM, a relatively new commercial radio genre in the UK that happens to provide the highest reach of all the commercial national channels. Interestingly, in this environment we are likely to see the emergence of more genuine media brands (e.g. MTV or Virgin Radio). These brands will help consumers make media choices in this cluttered environment.

Research continues to highlight that consumers are, in the main, very comfortable with making these choices (especially the younger and the most economically active ones). They are, in short, increasingly choosing media that fits the contours of their lives, and once they have found these media they appear to relate to them that much more strongly. The media may no longer have the demi-god status of the old BBC – but they are often much closer to the consumer. Look at the growth of real interactivity – radio phone-ins, telephone chat lines, TV audience participation shows, the Internet, to name a few. Brands now have significantly more choice of media channels in which to build their consumer relationships.

How can this benefit brand companies?

In the past, with limited media outlets for a brand, the media process was largely a mechanical one often led by the necessities of media buying in a monopolistic media environment. The major opportunity for a brand to gain a competitive communication advantage was to outspend the competition relative to brand share or to come up with better ads, or of course both! Grabbing a 15 per cent share of voice (SOV) for a brand with a 10 per cent market share was a good sign of effective brand investment because the fact was that all brands were likely to be fighting within exactly the same media channels and time bands. In the limited television channel, limited newspaper section environment the standard syndicated media research was also a more reliable indicator of commercial exposure to the consumer than it is today.

With more discriminating media consumers we now have an environment where a brand can identify part of the media landscape that is particularly actively consumed by its target consumer and then go out and own this part of the media for itself therefore creating much greater cut-through to its consumer. What's more, if this strand of media reflects the positioning of the brand the media placement itself will enhance the brand's relevance to its consumer.

As with any opportunity there are a number of downsides. The media architecture built around a brand will increasingly determine how effectively the brand can communicate whatever the potency of its creative message. In a fragmenting media environment there is the temptation to dissipate marketing funds, chasing the traditional paradigm of maximizing coverage. Those brands that fail to secure a relevant territory within the media will find it increasingly difficult to secure a share of their consumers' attention as background commercial noise increases.

Brand companies that embrace the new media environment and challenge market conventions have the opportunity to:

1 Build a stronger relationship with the brand's consumer through genuinely brand-centric media thinking and deployment
2 Differentiate a brand from its competitors in the way that it uses the media
3 To do both these things for less money

The launch of Häagen-Dazs in the UK was an example of a brand both identifying a new route to its core consumer and exploiting an area within the media that supported the brand's core positioning. Prior to the launch of review sections in the national newspapers this option was simply not available to the brand and it would have been forced into fighting its much larger competitors on their own battlefield, that of television.

When Häagen-Dazs launched in the UK in 1991 they changed the rules of media choice for an FMCG launch. Conventional wisdom suggested that TV was the brand battleground – launch regionally, use TV to help gain retail distribution, role out to a national presence as the brand grows. But Häagen-Dazs was creating its own segment in the ice cream market – that of a super-premium adult treat (but not for a formal dinner party, one to be shared with a loved one!). Research highlighted that the core consumers who would become ambassadors for the brand not only had a great interest in arts, reviews, film, but they were also indulging this passion by reading the then newly launched review sections of the quality press. They read these sections during leisurely weekend time – they were an adult treat in their own right. By owning this area in the media for Häagen-Dazs, disproportionate brand cut-through was created (the brand launched nationally on less than half a million pounds of advertising) and undoubtedly surprised its major competitor Unilever. All premium competitors added together were outsold.

Figure 11.1

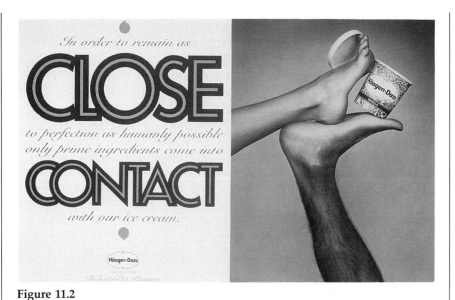

Figure 11.2

Today's media environment forces us fundamentally to challenge our basic operating conventions if we are to create the most effective brand communication platforms. Conventional rules concerning issues such as the investment levels required to launch or sustain a brand in a particular medium will increasingly be found wanting.

In 1993 Diesel jeans, a premium, street-fashion brand and a then regional player in Europe, accelerated its position enormously by refocusing media away from the cluttered environment of style press into television. In fact they focused almost exclusively on MTV, and despite a relatively low European budget, this focus provided a dominant presence within a directly relevant brand environment. This approach created greater brand standout for Diesel among regular MTV viewers across Europe, an important and opinion leading consumer group in this market, than for any other jean brand. This fundamentally helped Diesel reach their current position of a significant pan-European player. Prior to 1987 and the launch of MTV, Diesel would have been likely to remain in relative obscurity as a niche street brand for a much longer period.

Focus is not simply a requirement for small or niche brands, it is a necessity in today's media environment. Sustaining an ongoing relationship with a brand's core consumers is one of the greatest challenges for today's marketeers. It is not unusual for 20 per cent of a brand's consumers to account for 80 per cent of its profits. Today's media environment provides many more opportunities to ensure that a brand is more consistently and affordably turning up in front of its consumer heartland in the most relevant way. This does, however, demand a more realistic approach to the setting of the basic media performance parameters. For example, is it realistic for a brand to be regularly attempting to cover 85 per cent of a relatively broad audience for short periods within a year when the majority of brand marketeers would kill for a brand penetration of 20 per cent?

The box highlights how, for the high-penetration brand Polaroid (the UK's highest-selling camera), a focused media approach helped sales in the most profitable sector of the business.

Polaroid is the only company to have successfully created and marketed instant photography around the world. However, with an increasingly competitive photographic marketplace and encroaching newer technologies (video, digital) Polaroid sales were stagnating. Consumer research highlighted that non-Polaroid consumers didn't recognize a role for Polaroid in their lives and that they were making rational comparisons with other photographic options believing that Polaroid didn't appear to stack up in areas such as film quality and price. However, regular users had a fundamentally different perspective. They did not use Polaroid as an alternative to conventional photography. For them the Polaroid experience was something fundamentally different.

Polaroid's role is more of a 'social lubricant'. People act up in front of a Polaroid, its instantness is used to add to social occasions. Polaroid is closer in usage to alcohol and party games than it is conventional photography – therein lies the relevance to the consumer. Over time Polaroid had also suffered an ageing profile as it failed to reinforce this distinctive positioning. The new positioning demanded a refocus towards the most sociable group, 20–30-year-old adults, and was put into place with a focused television media strategy.

Research highlighted that this group, usually at their most sociable at the weekends, used television in a very specific way. Early evening TV on Friday and Saturday was, to them, 'before you go out TV'. Its outwardly trashy, often kitsch, format made it particularly appealing. It was about sociability, excitement, living for the moment. It was watched in anticipation of a night out (for example, *Blind Date*). Focusing on a number of these key programmes and consistently using them to drive Polaroid's association with this environment created an extended campaign presence – the role of which was to deliver a consistent, relevant consumer dialogue. Absolute weekly advertising weights were remarkably low for a relaunch. Following the first two-month phase of activity IM Ltd, the research consultancy tracking the campaign, described the cut-through of the activity as a '1 in 50' result on given weights. This focused, extended presence had the benefit of driving ongoing film consumption; the most profitable area for Polaroid. Film sales increased by 35 per cent.

Strong, well-exploited media territories become part of a brand's fabric. To *Sunday Times* readers, Virgin Atlantic Airlines' consistent use of a colour strip at the bottom of the business page announcing their latest initiative, inevitably in a witty and appealing way, has become part of the regular read. The Gap's successful launch in London using bus sides (a part of the outdoor media landscape largely dismissed by fashion and clothing brands at the time) was so distinctive and differentiating from both a media and creative perspective that they achieved enormously disproportionate payback – the campaign became a discussion point. As with any good idea, it has been copied. Indeed the medium has become overexploited by this type of brand but the followers have failed to recreate the same success.

Guidelines for successful media communication plan development

Just in the way that a successful brand has a well-defined positioning in the minds of its consumers, in the multi-choice media environment a brand requires a clearly defined 'media positioning' to ensure cut-through. Our aim should be to be able to articulate a brand's distinctive media positioning in much the way that you could articulate the brand's consumer positioning and its advertising proposition – clearly and usually in one line.

This media positioning, an expression of how the brand will own a relevant consumer territory in the media, may, of course, involve other forms of media usage beyond advertising, for example sponsorship, programme production, etc. The media discipline is unusual in that it has two equally important elements: strategic development and executional delivery. Increasingly these have to be interrelated. Developing a plan in the absence of media market realities, at best, means you are likely to miss the latest opportunity, at worst, that the plan will be undeliverable cost effectively.

Given that a brand's media architecture increasingly determines communication success it is clear that much of the media thinking needs to be done at the front end of the marketing planning process. For example, the fact that the Whitbread Beer Company had the opportunity to use the 1995 Rugby World Cup as a brand communication vehicle, in the form of a sponsorship, largely defined their approach to marketing the Heineken brand, from their trade marketing approach through to their consumer presence on television.

Figure 11.3 broadly illustrates the sequence of events required to generate effective media communication plans. The process is cyclical and not quite as sequential as the figure suggests. For example, what is achievable in the media impacts upon the setting of realistic marketing objectives, hence the interrelated nature of this process. The following list

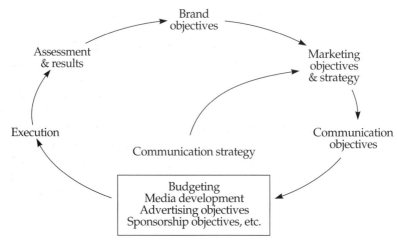

Figure 11.3   *Generating a media communication plan*

gives the major areas of information required when developing a detailed media plan:

1 Market background – describe the brand and the market it functions in
2 What are the brand's business and marketing objectives?
3 What is the marketing strategy?
4 What is the role for advertising?
5 What are your media objectives?
6 Describe the target audience(s)
7 Timing and seasonal considerations
8 Are there any trade considerations?
9 Geographical/regional profiles and objectives
10 What is the budget?

So we now have all the background information, what is the thought process that a good media practitioner goes through in order to find distinctive and brand-focused solutions? The starting place is the consumer, and there are three fundamental areas of interrogation:

1 Who is the most valuable, 'real' brand consumer, how do they behave and how can we best define them?
2 How does this consumer interact with the brand (and its competitors)?
3 How does this consumer really use and relate to the media?

With these insights in place the planner is well positioned to build the most effective connections between a brand and its consumers.

1 Who is the most valuable, 'real' brand consumer?

I say 'real' because many traditional definitions are driven by the capabilities of syndicated media research rather than consumer realities. A description such as ABC1 adults, 20–45, living in London, hardly provides the backcloth of rich insight required to build effective brands. Focus requires prioritization however broad a brand's consumer franchise. For example, at the launch of Boddington's Beer (see box) rather than attempt to broadly target all beer drinkers, a group that was both particularly interested in trying new beers and tended to lead opinion in this area by advising friends, were actively targeted providing disproportionate payback on the media investment (Figures 11.4 and 11.5).

2 How does this consumer interact with the brand?

When does the consumer use the brand? Is there a particular time when the brand is more likely to be at the forefront of the consumer consciousness? As people consider buying petrol when in their car it probably makes sense to attempt to influence them in this environment. In-car radio listening happens to be extremely high.

Is the consumer going to be more susceptible to the brand proposition when in a particular frame of mind? In the Häagen-Dazs case history, talking about a private adult treat during this busy consumer's quiet, self-indulgent moments was an important factor in generating a relevant brand dialogue with the consumer.

What are the key associations that a consumer makes with the brand? Is there a natural link between what the brand stands for and other interest areas? For example, Diesel jeans have a natural link with music.

3 How does this consumer really use and relate to the media?

Media is widely consumed by any consumer type you will ever come across. You may have light and heavy viewers of television but relying on averages to gain an insight into how people are really using the media is very misleading. A light TV viewer may avidly watch *The News At Ten* every night.

What parts of the media does your consumer seek out? Which pages does he or she turn to first? How does your consumer fit their media around their lives? What interest areas does your consumer have and how do they use the media to help fulfil these?

The launch of Boddington's Beer

Conventional media wisdom in the beer market had been that television provides the best advertising opportunity given the need to entertain and capture the imagination of the 'hard to talk to' younger male. However, the problem is that this group are particularly light viewers of TV – they are out and about doing other things. Posters are therefore a natural support medium.

At the launch of Boddington's Beer it was realized that, if the brand were to optimize its chances of success outside of its home territory of Manchester, it would have to be adopted by those most likely to try a new beer, i.e. people specifically interested in beer. This male group were upscale, urban and sophisticated consumers. They were particularly heavy consumers of magazines that reflected their interests as well as weekend newspapers.

The poster creative format (quick, witty, visually strong) remained a potent means of communication with this audience. The opportunity was to create a targeted poster campaign for this group by consistent usage of the outside back covers of magazines and newspaper supplements. Initially eight titles were chosen and with each new edition came a different expression of the same core proposition for Boddingtons – its creamy, smooth delivery. Following launch the brand went from a regional cask ale to take-home leader.

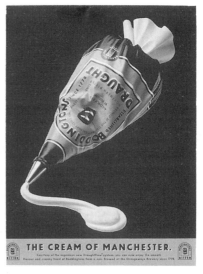

Figure 11.4   **Figure 11.5**

Developing a brand media positioning

With these three areas of insight it becomes possible to identify potential brand-focused media positionings. The recent Club Med relaunch provides a good example. Club Med was the original provider of packaged escape for busy professionals and their families. The Club provides the opportunity for both the physical and spiritual refreshment for this much-pressured group. The package format has since been copied and cheapened. Club Med needed to restate their position, which has become more relevant in our stressed society than ever, separating themselves from the package holiday pack.

Club Med's selected media positioning was the 'ownership of specific hard news environments':

- Their real audience, although broadly ABC1 adults with young families, is a more specific group within this definition. They tend to live in major cities, work long hours, often in service or financial industries. They are extremely work orientated and their interests reflect this (for example, they have an active interest in economic and current affairs).
- They treat their holidays as an oasis to which they flee once or twice a year. They see their holidays as an escape from the stress, a time during which they recuperate and reacquaint themselves with their families.
- They are heavy consumers of news and business media. They actively seek out these environments. Although light viewers of television, they make an effort not to miss specific news programmes to keep themselves informed.

These consumer insights were drawn from a combination of both qualitative research and closer interogation of syndicated research such as TGI. Focusing solely on using news environments within television provided an opportunity to:

- Juxtapose the brand proposition of escape against a harsh real world media environment, a juxtaposition that the consumer would immediately recognize and relate to
- Create stand-out by focusing on a very specific and relevant part of the television landscape, not heavily used by the competition
- Challenge the consumer to reconsider Club Med by appearing in unexpected but relevant environments
- Differentiate the brand

Of course, a brand media positioning is only valuable if it can deliver against the business criteria set for the brand in the brief, and if its success is measurable. Figure 11.6 summarizes the approach to developing a viable brand media positioning. Stage 3 in the figure is of particular importance.

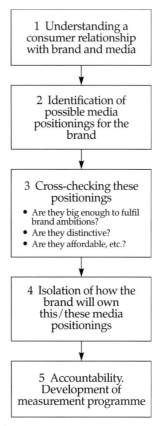

Figure 11.6   *Developing a brand's communication platform – the discipline*

Just as blindly chasing 75 per cent coverage of some arbitrary audience is no longer a recipe for success, nor is defining an area in the media that is relevant to the brand but is so small that it could never lead to the required incremental sales.

As a strong brand has to own a 'position' in the consumer's consciousness, so it does in the commercially overpolluted media environment if it is to stand out. Stage 4 is about developing a programme that ensures that your brand can own the distinctive media positioning. How will you creatively exploit it? Can you focus on it consistently to ensure ownership (see box – The launch of Boddington's Beer)?

Once a positioning has been identified the criteria for detailed planning and buying need to be set, for example:

- Definition of a media-buying audience that provides both a trading and measurement currency usable on the syndicated industry media measurement databases
- Setting of key performance criteria such as optimum frequency and target coverage
- Optimum seasonality and regionality
- Weekly advertising weights

The issue of media buying

Media buying is at the core of a media operation's ability to deliver effective media solutions, not simply in terms of price but also in the ability to isolate precisely the right parts of the media for any given brand. The days of media buying as a one-dimensional negotiation process are fast drawing to a close. Negotiations often include many different aspects of added value to the brand other than simply the trading of time and space.

The individuals who will ultimately be responsible for buying the media must be a core part of the media development team. They bring to the planning process a realistic view of what is actually achievable as well as the best, most up-to-date understanding of how individual media are performing.

Although the buying area appears to be shrouded in mystery and, indeed, the sheer volume of information that needs to be handled only adds to this perception, the broad principles are reasonably clear. The markets are largely influenced by standard principles of supply and demand. In high-demand periods if audiences (supply) remain stable, pricing increases. If the size of the available audience is expanding more quickly than demand then pricing reduces. In the media markets pricing is not fixed so there are always efforts to understand average pricing in the market and an advertiser's position against this.

A fundamental difference between day-to-day trading in television and all the other media is that television is a futures market, that is, you are buying a commodity to be realized in the future and you are estimating a price for your air time against how you believe your air time will perform for your chosen audience. This way of dealing reflects the variable nature of the television audience and the way it is therefore measured.

The complexity, scale and skill required for this task largely explains why it has become a specialist area within media operations. The other media in the main remain more straightforward, trading is typically on the basis of recent audience performance.

In 1995 £2.9 billion was spent on display advertising in the UK, in addition to the millions spent on industry media research and syndicated and privately commissioned research. The majority of this money is spent generating the basic audience currencies of ratings, readership, poster exposure, listenership, etc. against which this money is traded. As research has become more sophisticated so advertisers have attempted to more clearly define which parts of a medium are of the most value to them. Simultaneously, media owners have become increasingly sophisticated in the way that they manage and market particular parts of their inventory.

Over the past ten years as brand companies have examined every cost base behind brand building, media buying has been a major focus. The UK has witnessed the fastest growth of media auditing companies in the world and there is an established base of these businesses whose original primary aim was to provide an objective perspective to clients on their agencies' media price positioning.

As media buying has become an increasingly competitive and measured business and media owners are more accomplished at effective inventory management there has been a flattening out of the price differential between premier division media buying points. This has coincided with the rapid development of new media opportunities where buying 'cheap' media has often become less of a challenge than actually selecting effective media in the first place. You can put your brand on television for less now than ever before!

The development of media specialist companies

In year ending June 1996 (*Register Meal*) 76 per cent of all media buying was done by some form of media specialist company. Why do these companies exist and thrive? Isn't there currently a demand for brand communication integration, not separation? Shouldn't advertising development now be closer to media development than ever before to help ensure effectiveness?

Media separation is an idea that has been around for a long time. To be historically accurate, the first advertising agencies were in fact media broking companies that came to realize that as an additional service they could provide their clients with the advertisements to go in the spaces as well! The first media independents that you would recognize started to appear in the UK in the early 1970s. In the late 1980s a new term was coined with the launch of Zenith, a 'media dependant'. A media dependant is simply a media company that is owned by an advertising agency, an agency group or an agency holding company. The distinction between independents and dependants is becoming largely irrelevant in the eyes of the client community. Both businesses are competing for the same assignments, both businesses are in the main having to run as profitable, effective businesses in their own right.

In brief, three fundamental factors have driven and will continue to drive the growth of these businesses:

1 *Client demand*   Clients continue to look for objective media advice, given in the absence of the need to sell a particular creative solution. Growing demand for accountability in every aspect of the communication mix has also led clients to look for media services that are fully accountable in their own right. Also, of course, under increasing competition and pressure to maintain margins there is an ongoing need to shop around in every aspect of marketing services to ensure that best value is being obtained, particularly within the largest single area of marketing spend. These trends are likely to increase, not reduce, in importance.
2 *Growing availability of all media*   This trend increasingly demands a focused, dedicated media service. Even the specialists find it hard to keep up! This growing availability means higher investment in IT, research and personnel able to operate in the broader brand environment. These costs have increased the price of market entry, leading to prohibitive start-up costs for new full service agencies. The last agency to set up a full service media department was, in fact, Bartle Bogle Hegarty in 1987.
3 *The business opportunity*   Rewards are high for a media service that can genuinely provide effective channels to the consumer in the media environment I have described. In addition, media buying remains a high cash flow business, making it attractive to those companies accomplished at managing money. In fact, the vast majority of larger agency businesses either have or are in the process of setting up media companies with these rewards in mind.

The fact is that the creation of media specialists does not go against the undoubted need for integrated brand planning in today's environment. As media has moved up to the brand strategy table, the opportunity to take a broader view of how a brand can build relationships with its consumer actually has the tendency to pull together various creative disciplines.

Summary

Pretty annoying, isn't it? At a time when media issues seem ever harder to stay in touch with it is becoming increasingly important to do just that. But should our prognosis really be that gloomy?

Media is in fact moving out of the secret hidden world that could justify itself by using a language apparently bearing little relationship to the world of effective brand communication. As media moves from undersupply to oversupply the opportunity to create bigger differences between brands has grown. And the opportunity to get it wrong has grown correspondingly. There will be a bigger difference between winners and losers, and that is good news if you are in the competition business.

And what about the practitioners? Media services operate in an extraordinarily competitive environment. When not competing with each other, an auditor is looking at their work. You are only as good as your last buying result! But again this will ultimately lead to an increasing professionalism within the business and a greater demand from clients that their media thinkers contribute more fully to the business of building brands.

Finally, investment is flowing into the media servicing business, not just in the UK but around the world. This can only increase competition and therefore the quality of the industry's output.

As an individual, take solace: keeping up with every development in media is impossible even if you work full-time at it. If you are involved in helping manage the communication process you don't need to know everything about every medium. You do, however, have to recognize what is achievable in this area, and when a brand is not making full use of the media armoury available to it. In short, you have to be more demanding.

If you ask the right question, the type of question that you would ask of any other element of the marketing mix, you will have started on the track to a successful media solution. The question? How exactly does your media solution add brand value?

Overview: Chapter 12

This chapter from Paul Feldwick examines one of the less glamorous but most important roles of advertising: to defend share for an established brand. Paul is one of the industry's leading thinkers on advertising effects and evaluation – and his chapter is both provocative and stimulating. Specifically, Paul argues:

- The purpose of advertising need not always be growth or conquest. Most big advertisers are using it primarily to defend the business they already have.
- Much 'conventional' advertising thinking, starting from early theories based on direct response, has been based on the idea of *conversion*. But for defensive advertising the concepts of *nudging*, *reinforcement* and *enhancement* are more relevant.
- Understanding the way defensive advertising works has implications for budget setting, for creative strategies, and for campaign evaluation and pre-testing.

Paul Feldwick designed and chaired the IPA's Training and Development workshop on 'Evaluating Advertising' in 1994, from which this chapter is in part drawn.

12 The defensive role of advertising

Paul Feldwick

Introduction

Perhaps some older British lager drinkers remember George, the Hofmeister bear, a cockney jack-the-lad in a pork-pie hat who featured in the 1983 TV campaign to relaunch Hofmeister lager in the UK (Figure 12.1). This campaign produced impressive sales results, subsequently described in a paper which took a first prize in the 1984 IPA Advertising Effectiveness Awards (Channon, 1985). The analysis argued, fairly convincingly, that advertising expenditure of £1.7 million had been responsible, within the same year, for additional profit to the client of £1.9 million.

So what? you might say. Isn't this what all successful advertising is supposed to do? The client spent a pound, and got over a pound back. Why else would they bother? Claude Hopkins, back in 1922, wrote 'The only purpose of advertising is to make sales. It is profitable or unprofitable according to its actual sales. Treat it as a salesman. Force it to justify itself'. The Hofmeister campaign was a salesman who had earned his wage.

But in reality, as most people who work in advertising come to realize, cases like Hofmeister are very rare. I'm not talking here about the large number of campaigns that simply don't work, though we shouldn't forget about how many of these there probably are (estimates range from 50 per cent and well upwards) (Jones, 1995). But it's unusual to find this type of short-term payback, even among successful campaigns.

The advertising payback

Consider the arithmetic. An advertiser might spend £1 million on advertising. If the profit margin on sales is 33 per cent, the company will need to see an increase of around £3 million in net revenue before they even get their money back. On a £15 million brand this is an extra 20 per cent, and not just for a month or two but sustained across a whole year.

Figure 12.1

This might just happen in a growing market – but then that growth could not entirely be attributed to advertising. In a mature market (and more and more markets today are mature) it means that growth must come at a competitor's expense. And to sustain a modest budget of £1 million per annum (this might just about buy one national TV burst of 300 TVRs), this rate of growth would have to take place every year.

Of course, for a much larger brand – say £100 million a year – the percentage increase needed to pay back the advertising is that much smaller (3 per cent, in the example given). But the larger the brand, the more likely it is to be an established brand in a well-developed category, and therefore the chances of achieving substantial growth rates year on year are reduced.

Hofmeister was a large brand already, worth over £100 million. It had been launched by the Courage brewery some three years previously and achieved its size by having guaranteed distribution in most Courage pubs. The new campaign was not its first advertising, but two previous campaigns had been ineffective, so this was effectively a launch campaign which suddenly stepped up the brand's rate of sale by 13 per cent. A large brand, plus a dramatic movement in sales due to advertising – the combination of these two events is very unusual. (In fact it is unlikely that it ever happened again for Hofmeister, although the brand was successful for some years.)

So if advertisers are spending their money in the expectation of a short-term sales increase big enough to return their investment with interest, the vast majority are almost bound to be disappointed. Extensive analyses of advertising elasticities (Jones, 1992) show that they average around 0.2 – that is, a 1 per cent increase in advertising will create an increase in revenue of 0.2 per cent. For most brands with established budgets, this calculation will show that they would be more profitable in the short term if they reduced their ad spending, and less profitable if they increased it.

Yet most of the really big advertising budgets are spent on behalf of established brands in mature markets which cannot realistically expect to see dramatic sales growth every time they advertise. Either major advertisers such as Mars Pedigree and Unilever are sadly misled, or there must be some other reason why they continue to advertise established brands at the weights they do.

'Long-term' and 'defensive' effects

One way of explaining the benefits of advertising in these circumstances is to talk about 'long-term effects'. What people usually seem to mean by this is to suggest that the advertising cost not covered by immediate revenue increases will be paid for out of future revenue increases in years to come. This is partially correct. We now have some very good evidence, from IRI in the United States, that a successful advertising campaign in one year continues to boost sales in years two and three, even if the advertising has been stopped (Lodish and Lubetkin, 1992). But the effects in years two and three are not as great as in year one. And it is not really an argument to convince a finance director, because the expectation is that similar advertising budgets will also be spent in years to come, with similar modest sales effects – so that even if the longer-term effects materialize, they will never result in a payback from incremental revenue.

A much better explanation involves focusing on what we mean by the word 'incremental'. A financial appraisal of a business investment should be based on comparing two scenarios: what we expect to happen if we make the investment, and what we expect to happen if we don't (the latter usually known as the 'base case scenario'). The assumption made in the preceding paragraphs is that the base case (for sales without advertising) would be a straight line. But is this realistic?

It is tempting to assume, as some people do, that once advertising has 'built' a brand, its sales will continue at the same rate almost indefinitely. We do know that purchasing patterns are strongly driven by habit and inertia (one reason why even heavyweight advertising is unlikely, on its own, to change brand shares very quickly for an established brand). In fact, if nothing ever occurred to disturb the forces of habit and inertia, this picture of a 'steady-state' market might even approximate to the truth. In reality, however, other things *do* happen. Competitors advertise. New brands are launched. Products are reformulated. Prices are cut, permanently or on promotion. And the consumers themselves change over time, looking for variety, quality or reassurance. All these things suggest that the 'natural' state for a brand is not stable, but a long-term decline.

It therefore makes sense to talk of the major justification for advertising of established products as *defensive*. Although advertising may continue to build volume and revenue over time, and although, in particular circumstances, it may achieve startling and dramatic results, the majority of the money is being spent, as Tom Corlett (1976) said, to protect the 90 per cent of sales which the brand already has, rather than to gain a possible extra 10 per cent.

But in any given case it is difficult to prove that revenue will decline without advertising. A year or two without advertising often has little clear effect on sales, giving encouragement to those who think sustained advertising is unnecessary. In the short term the brand's sales are held up by the forces of habit and inertia. Also, it is possible that during this time the brand is living off a reservoir of goodwill built up with the help of advertising over the years, and which will be difficult to replenish once it is empty. The only way to test the hypothesis is to withdraw advertising until the brand visibly suffers, by which time it is often too late.

Simon Broadbent (1989) has a telling image of a brand's sales as an aeroplane cruising along at a fixed altitude. If its engines (i.e. advertising support) are cut, it will continue for a while at the same height. After a while, however, it begins to descend – and at an ever-increasing rate. If the pilot leaves it too late before restoring the power, it may be in an unstoppable downward spin.

Another metaphor for advertising an established brand is of routine maintenance, say, repairing tiles on an old roof. If the tiles are not repaired there may be no immediate effect on the people in the house. But they will certainly find out about it, too late, when it rains. Similarly, the effects of not advertising may only become apparent on a brand's sales when competitive activity becomes more intense.

To justify further the importance of advertising's defensive role we can point to the fact that large, successful brands, almost without exception, do continue to advertise heavily. Analyses published by PIMS (Biel, 1990) show correlations between advertising/sales ratios, perceived quality, and profitability. Specific cases of the 'longer and broader' effects of advertising, such as PG Tips and Andrex, have been published in the *Advertising Works* series from the IPA (Baker, 1993; Feldwick, 1991). What is less often understood, however, is the process by which these so-called 'long-term' effects occur.

Advertising agencies have not always been their own best advocates in this matter. 'Long-term effects' or 'brand effects' are talked about as if they work in a mysterious way which has little connection with short-term sales effects. At worst, agencies can use the rhetoric of 'long-term effects' or 'brand imagery' as an attempt to justify any piece of advertising which is failing to show any results in the marketplace. But 'long-term effects' is rather a misleading expression to describe the defensive effects of advertising on a brand. There are genuine longer-term effects of advertising, as demonstrated by the evidence from IRI quoted above. These can come about because advertising memories lodge in people's minds for a long time, or because a purchasing habit, once started, is likely to continue (or a combination of the two). This is different from the *long-term business consequences* of advertising (or not advertising) which may well have more to do with some very *short-term effects* of advertising. The following is an attempt to build a picture of how, and why, defensive advertising works.

How defensive advertising works

The first thing to say is that defensive advertising makes little sense if we try to explain it using the traditional 'persuasion' model of how advertising works. By the 'persuasion' model I mean something like this:

Prospect sees/hears advertisement

↓

prospect is convinced

↓

prospect buys product

This sequence of events is elaborated in well known 'linear-sequential' models such as AIDA (Awareness – Interest – Desire – Action) and Russell Colley's 'Communication Spectrum' in his 1961 book, DAGMAR. It sounds rather obvious; in fact Colley felt he only needed to justify his hierarchical model by saying it was 'applied common sense'.

This is what the public, on the whole, *think* advertising is meant to do. The interesting thing, though, is that none of them think it does it to them. They say, 'advertising doesn't make *me* buy the product'.

This model is highly pervasive and often unconsciously colours our thinking. It derives from the earliest advertising theorists, Daniel Starch and Claude Hopkins. Like most advertising theories it is not so much entirely wrong as only partially right. It applies reasonably well, for instance, to what Hopkins was writing about, what we should today call Direct Response advertising. A Direct Response ad (look at any 'infomercial') *is* like a salesman; it is designed to take the prospect from ignorance, to conviction, and then to a sale, which is the end of the sequence.

But this is very different from what we expect a TV commercial to do for an established packaged goods brand like Ariel or PG Tips.

- Here there is very little ignorance. Most of our potential customers have bought our product many times before.
- They have formed their own opinions about it from experience. They are unlikely to take seriously anything we say that conflicts at all with that experience.
- And the sale, as far as they and we are concerned, is far from being the *end* of the process. We want them to go on buying the brand, again and again.

In this repeat-purchase situation, it is far harder to change people's minds about things (which is why major changes in behaviour are hard to achieve). However, we have evidence that advertising *can* influence their behaviour in a number of ways;

1 Memories and associations created by advertising are accessed *during* the purchase decision.
2 Behaviour is reinforced *after* the purchase.
3 Experience of the *product itself* is 'transformed' or 'enhanced' by advertising.

1 Memories and associations accessed during the purchase decision

First, it is important to remember that most people are not loyal to one brand; they buy within a repertoire of brands; and the decision which of the repertoire to choose on a particular occasion is often a trivial one, driven by habit, a desire for a change, a penny or two price difference (or, of course, availability, a particular need, etc.). Given the essential triviality of the choice, memories or associations created by advertising, and in many cases, probably, the fact of advertising itself, can be enough to *nudge* the shopper towards one brand or another. It is important to stress that ideas or images created in this way need not amount to conviction on the part of the consumer in order to affect behaviour, in contrast to models like DAGMAR, where conviction is supposed to be a necessary stage before purchase.

Colin McDonald (1970) demonstrated that advertising has immediate effects on the probability of buying the advertised brand at the next purchase occasion. These findings have since been replicated by John Philip Jones (1995) and others. These immediate effects, because small, have often been disregarded by ad agencies as of little importance. It seems very likely, though, that these small influences on behaviour have a powerful cumulative effect on both the brand's performance and the consumer's relationship with the brand over time.

Although it is possible to find examples of genuine 'long-term effects' – in the sense of advertising memories which persist over a number of months or years and continue to affect behaviour – we also know that most advertising memories decay in a more or less predictable manner. And McDonald's most recent work suggests that these short-term sales effects can be more marked the closer the advertising exposure is in time to the point of purchase (personal communication). The majority of advertising's primary effects on the individual consumer should therefore be apparent relatively soon after exposure. (What we are probably seeing here, however, is the effect of a memory which is accessed, not always very consciously, *at the point of purchase*. This is different from the notion of a 'conversion' taking place *at the time of seeing the ad*.) These short-term effects are likely to constitute the building blocks of how long-term effects on brand performance are built up. A further important observation, coming from McDonald's (1995) work particularly, is that if the consumer sees ads for competing brands shortly before the purchase, neither brand gains an advantage over the other. Share of voice is therefore as important as the absolute number of exposures.

2 Reinforcement of existing behaviour

It is difficult (though by no means impossible) to change people's minds with advertising. What advertising does very well, however, is reinforce their existing beliefs and patterns of behaviour. A consumer will not only be inclined to believe an advertisement for a product that they have bought and found satisfactory; they will be positively encouraged that they made the right decision, and their judgement endorsed, all of which leads to an increased probability of them buying it again in the future. This notion of reinforcement has been much talked about in connection with the so-called 'weak' theory of advertising – giving rise, perhaps, to the belief that reinforcement is itself a weak force. But as anyone who has been involved in behaviour modification knows (training dogs to obey commands, or children to pick up their clothes) regular positive reinforcement of the desired behaviour is often more effective than threats or punishment. Reinforcement is a powerful way of affecting, and indeed modifying, behaviour. In fact, behaviourists argue that reinforcement (positive or negative) is virtually the only psychological principle that is necessary to explain all human behaviour (Skinner, 1972).

3 Transformation or enhancement of the experience of the product itself

There is, however, a third mechanism by which advertising can affect consumer behaviour. Bill Wells (1992) calls this *transformation*, Millward

Brown (Farr and Brown, 1994) have called it *enhancement*, Deighton and Schindler (1988) have called it *framing*. I believe they are all talking about the same thing. Very simply, people are suggestible. They experience what they expect to experience. As a result, when their expectations are modified (or 'framed') by advertising they can experience technically identical (or indistinguishable) products as very different. This can be a major enhancement of the satisfaction they get from it.

This human suggestibility is most powerfully demonstrated by considering the effects of placebos in medicine; an inert pill containing only sugar can have a surprisingly powerful effect on a number of ailments *if* the patient believes it is a drug. The parallel with advertised brands was underlined some years ago by an experiment conducted by Alan Branthwaite and Peter Cooper (1981) where they found that people's headaches were cured faster if they knew they were given their preferred brand of analgesic than if they were given a chemically identical own-label product. The same result occurs regularly in 'blind versus branded' product tests.

Millward Brown's experiment (Farr and Brown, 1994) showed that exposure to advertising had no positive effect on people's intention to buy a new product, but that among those who had tried the product, exposure to advertising substantially increased their satisfaction with the product and their intention to subsequently repurchase. Deighton and Schindler (1988) exposed a group of American students to an ad claiming that a particular Boston radio station 'played more new music'. In fact different subgroups heard the same ad but for four different stations. After four weeks they were asked to rate a number of stations on how much new music they played, and in each case the station respondents rated most highly on this dimension was the one featured in the advertising they had heard.

This is not a new idea. As long ago as the 1950s, Philip Morris used to test advertising by showing different ads for a brand of cigarette, then asking respondents to smoke one of that brand and rate it on various product dimensions. The ads that led to the best perceptions of the product quality were preferred.

It can therefore be argued that advertising actually creates a part of the satisfaction which the user derives from the brand. In terms of creating consumer-perceived quality or value, advertising cost may be as important as the cost of ingredients, processes, or packaging.

Summary

In place of the traditional 'persuasion' model, then, which depicts advertising creating conviction which leads to a sale, the consumer should be imagined buying repeatedly from a repertoire of brands. At a number of stages in this continuous process – at the time of purchase, after purchase, and while using the product – advertising can increase the probability that the consumer will choose the advertised brand either at that time or on a future occasion.

Advertising influences both consumer behaviour – by 'nudging', and by reinforcement – and consumer perceptions of the product – by 'transformation'. Repeated over time, these processes will build up a strongly reinforced pattern of purchasing behaviour, which will resist competitive activity or price dealing – and so create the phenomenon which we refer to as 'a strong brand'.

Implications

If we understand how often the role of advertising is fundamentally defensive, and something about the likely processes by which this works, it has a number of implications for

- Budget setting
- Creative strategy
- Campaign evaluation

Budget setting (and media scheduling)

The object of advertising in its defensive role is the long-term protection of the brand's profit stream rather than the maximizing of short-term profit. Justifying advertising by reference to one year (or even two or three year) profit projections is therefore largely irrelevant – except in-so-far as short-term profit targets, of course, exist and have to be addressed!

What sometimes happens is that utterly unrealistic growth targets are written into the plan in order to justify the advertising budget. When these are not met, it is easy – once or twice – to blame it on the executions, perhaps fire the ad agency, and start again. This has a number of undesirable consequences (not just for the unfortunate ad agency). It means that no continuity is built up in the advertising for the brand; and we can observe that many large brands maintain continuity in their advertising over a number of years (the PG Chimps have been running since 1956 – see Figure 12.2). It also means that advertising develops a bad reputation within the company, because it consistently fails to deliver what it promises. And as the brand suffers from a lack of consistent support, it becomes progressively harder to justify the advertising budget while the demands for advertising to work a miracle become ever more unrealistic.

Figure 12.2

For an established brand, the cost of advertising has to be evaluated like any other cost; as an ingredient in creating value to the consumer, or part of the value chain. A value chain might look like this:

Ingredients
+ manufacturing
+ R&D
+ packaging
+ distribution
+ service
+ advertising   →   Consumer Value

If the sum of the left-hand side of this equation is less than the right-hand side, the brand is viable; if the value of the right-hand side is better than competitors, the brand is a success. It makes sense to scrutinize all the costs on the left-hand side and reduce them if possible. But any reduction risks creating a disproportionate effect on the right-hand side. Reducing advertising is potentially as dangerous as cutting back on quality of ingredients or service – for some brands, perhaps more so. The question is determining which costs represent key factors for success for that particular business.

Advertising then becomes a strategic decision, rather than a tactical one. Paul Freeman of Kraft Jacob Suchard once said in a speech,

'Advertising for us is a cost of doing business, like the cost of cocoa beans'. No-one wants to spend more than they have to on cocoa beans or advertising. But if you don't spend enough, the business will suffer.

One important factor affecting how much is enough to spend on advertising is what competitors are spending. There *are* differences between advertising executions, probably quite significant ones, ranging from ads which create no link to the brand at all to extremely powerful communications which transform the way customers feel about it. But what we know about the importance of advertising's short-term effects on sales suggests that both a continuous presence and a weight which matches or exceeds competition can be crucial, and having a better execution can only compensate for lack of weight up to a point. (This, naturally, gives the biggest brand an advantage. It should be able to afford to spend more, but if the brand leader fails to deliver on this and is outspent it becomes vulnerable. Brands that spend above their market share tend to grow; those that spend less, tend to decline (Biel, 1990).)

Creative strategy

The 'persuasion' model referred to earlier carries a strong implication that advertising addresses non-users. In fact, Claude Hopkins (1968) was quite explicit about this:

> *In every ad consider only new customers. People using your product are not going to read your ads ... Bear in mind always that you address an unconverted person.*

Much advertising thinking unconsciously starts from this assumption – advertising is about growing the brand, converting non-users, over-coming barriers to use, etc. Now this is one possible strategic route, and in many cases the appropriate one. But for an established brand in a mature market the chances of getting significant growth from converting new users are generally remote, while the chances of losing heavy and loyal current users, over time, to competitors are much greater (Hallberg, 1995). It makes sense, therefore, to regard existing users, especially heavy users, as a very important target market. This means that advertising should understand who these people are and why they use the product and the brand. It should reflect their beliefs and concerns. It should avoid alienating them in a wild-goose chase for some hypothetical new user group. They should form a key part of any research sample, qualitative or quantitative.

There is a counter-argument to this, which I have heard particularly from creative people. This is that simply recycling existing attitudes back to current users makes for boring advertising, and in time leads to the brand itself becoming dull and stale in their perceptions. It is said, after all, that the best means of defence is attack. I think this is a sound point. I have no easy answer to it, except to suggest that advertising for an established brand – especially a brand leader – continually has to strike the right balance between keeping fresh and challenging, and understanding and meeting the expectations of its loyal users. No-one said it had to be easy.

Campaign evaluation research

Measuring the effects of any type of advertising is fraught with difficulties. But where the object of the advertising is a sales increase, or any other kind of definite *change*, it is at least conceptually straightforward – we would start by looking to see whether the desired change took place or not. (If it did, there remains a question as to whether it was advertising or something else that caused it; if it did not, a question as to whether the advertising failed, or other factors counteracted it.) But when the object is not so much to change things as to maintain the current position, the start point is more problematic. What, in this case, constitutes 'success'? How can we distinguish (except over the very long term) between effective and ineffective advertising?

One obvious implication of understanding advertising's defensive role is that we should not look for sales increases where none was intended. But what should we look for instead?

In evaluating advertising there are three main types of quantified evidence we can base our conclusions on: sales performance (and attempts to model it); survey measures (often in the form of 'tracking studies'); and single-source panels, although at present these are not widely available. Here are some brief thoughts about how each of these can be used to monitor 'defensive' advertising.

1 Sales performance

Sales may not go up. But judgementally, we may say that holding sales level is an achievement in a competitive market, particularly if other things are changing. For example, if there is increasing competition from private label with a widening price gap, and brand A maintains its relative price and volume share while brand B loses share, we need to explain why this is so – the answer may be brand A's advertising.

The key question is – What do we think would have happened to the brand without the advertising? The answer may be based on looking at what happened to competitors, or simply on informed judgement. Alternatively, it could be based on an experimental area test where advertising is reduced or withdrawn. The results of such a test may take more than a year to come through; it has its risks, but it is less risky than a national 'test to destruction'.

Modelling, although it can be valuable, needs to be approached with caution in this context. Econometric modelling looks at statistical relationships between different series of data. Although we talk of sales for established brands as 'stable', looked at more closely they move up and down and vary by area or outlet type. Econometricans can relate these ups and downs and variations in sales to possible 'explanatory variables' (providing they have the data for these), such as price, advertising, distribution, and the economy.

For a long time econometric modelling of sales was criticized because it explained the short-term 'blips' in sales but did not explain longer-term movements – therefore failing to detect the effect of 'defensive' advertising on maintaining a brand's share. Such models could prove misleading (see Simon Broadbent's chapter, 'Death of a Brand' (Broadbent, 1989)). This is still a difficult area, but in recent years there have been serious attempts made to relate advertising to the longer term, underlying movements in brand shares, by increasing the lag effect or 'half-life' of the advertising (Broadbent, 1993). Modelling can also be used in a less direct way; for example, if a model shows a brand is less sensitive to price changes than a competitor, or becomes less sensitive over time, this might be an advertising effect – even if share has not increased.

2 Tracking study research

Tracking studies give a lot of potential information about two things; consumers' awareness and perception of the advertising itself, and their awareness and perceptions of the various brands in the market. Where sales movements are hard to read, such measures may take on relatively greater importance.

Good recall and positive perceptions of advertising do not necessarily prove effectiveness, but for a large established brand advertising that is not remembered or actively alienates brand users would usually be a danger signal. Tracking studies can also tell us whether the desired communication of the advertising is coming across.

Depending on market circumstances, awareness, perceptions of, and degrees of 'attachment' to a brand may be relevant measures to evaluate defensive advertising. (Such measures are among those that have been associated with the rather ambiguous expression, 'Brand Equity' (Feldwick, 1996).) It is true that in general all these may tend to correlate with brand size or share; but they are not identical with it. If a brand's top-of-mind awareness or 'loyalty' declines this might well be an early warning of a trend which will only show up later in sales. In some markets where purchasing is infrequent and strongly influenced by other factors – such as holidays, or motor cars – such attitudinal data may represent the best indication of a brand's relative demand. It is also important in a defensive context (as logic would suggest), to monitor competitors' positions as closely as your own. The effect of transformation or enhancement can be measured by using blind versus branded product tests.

3 Single-source panel data

A brief comment on this is included although at present it is not easily available commercially. A single-source panel collects data on the same consumers' purchases and advertising exposure. This is expensive and difficult to do, which is why such panels have struggled to become commercially viable. One mode of analysis which might be applied to defensive advertising is described in John Philip Jones' book, *When Ads Work* (1995). The brand's share among panel members who have seen its advertising in the previous seven-day period is compared with its brand share among those who have not; this difference, which can be quite marked, is called 'Short-Term Advertising Strength' or STAS for short. Jones claims this as a 'pure' measure of advertising effect, independent of price, distribution, etc. which are assumed to be equal between the two sub-samples.

A brand can have a positive STAS without necessarily enjoying any short-term increase in its total sales because the effects have been countered by other factors, which include competitive advertising, or because it has not spent enough relative to competition. It therefore suggests itself as a useful immediate measure of advertising effectiveness for non-dynamic situations.

However, while the STAS seems clearly to show the existence of one type of advertising effect – what we referred to above as *nudging* – it is more questionable whether it shows the total effects of all types of advertising. Does it reflect, for example, the transformation or enhancement mechanism?

It remains to be seen whether single-source panels used in this way offer a serious commercial contribution to advertising evaluation. They may well do – research is active at the moment in Germany, and data fusion offers an alternative means of conducting similar conclusions. I do not expect, however, that it will provide the complete answer.

Pre-testing

Finally, a section on evaluation should include a comment on the controversial area of pre-testing. As was said above, the principle of defensive advertising is that existing users form a key part of the target market. They should therefore form a key part of any research sample, whether this is qualitative or quantitative, and the desired response should be imagined as reinforcement, rather than as conversion. In particular, I find it hard to see how Persuasion Test (or attitude shift) methods give meaningful information about defensive advertising, being designed around the idea of converting non-users. For advertising to existing brand users, a model of advertising based on involvement seems more appropriate than one based on persuasion; this suggests that qualitative research may be particularly valuable in developing and evaluating creative work.

Conclusions

Does it pay to advertise? It depends on the corporate objective. If this is to maximize this year's profit, it may be hard to justify advertising. But if the business is to be flourishing in ten years' time, advertising may be a valuable and even a necessary investment.

If the role of advertising is more defence than conquest, a number of implications follow for the planning and evaluation of the campaign which may run counter to some 'conventional' thinking:

- The cost of advertising should be treated as a strategic part of the process of creating value as perceived by the consumer.
- Advertising sales effects should be evaluated in comparison with an estimate of what would happen over the longer term without advertising, not with a straight-line projection. Sales modelling should look for long-term trends influenced by advertising, not just 'blips'.
- Creative executions and research should recognize the importance of existing brand users.

Larry Light, President of the American Coalition for Brand Equity, defines a brand's objective as 'enduring profitable growth'. There are no guarantees for achieving this, but if advertising both continues to stimulate and reinforce buying of the brand, and enhance customers' perceptions of the brand, it will make an important contribution; if not to enduring profitable *growth*, at least to *enduring profit*.

References

Baker, C. (ed.) (1993), *Advertising Works 7*, NTC Publications Ltd, Henley-on-Thames, pp.53–74.

Biel, A. (1990), 'Strong brand, high spend: Tracking relationships between the marketing mix and brand values', *Admap*, **26.11**, November, 35–40.

Branthwaite, A. and Cooper, P. (1981), 'Analgesic effects of branding in treatment of headaches', *British Medical Journal*, 282.

Broadbent, S. (1989), *The Advertising Budget*, NTC Publications, Henley-on-Thames, p.28.

Broadbent, S. (1993), 'Advertising effects: more than short term, *Journal of the Market Research Society*, **35**, (1), January, 379.

Channon, C. (ed.) (1985), 'Hofmeister lager', in *Advertising Works 3*, Holt Rinehart and Winston, London, 1985, pp.70–83.

Colley, R. (1961), *Defining Advertising Goals for Measured Advertising Results*, Association of National Advertisers, New York, p.53.

Corlett, T. (1976), 'How we should measure the longer-term effects of advertising on purchasing', *Admap*, **12.9**, September, 422–433.

Deighton, J. and Schindler, R.M. (1988), 'Can advertising influence experience?' *Psychology and Marketing*, **5**, (2), 103–115.

Farr, A. and Brown, G. (1994), 'Persuasion or enhancement? An experiment', MRS Conference, p.69.

Feldwick, P. (ed.) (1991), *Advertising Works 6*, NTC Publications Ltd, Henley-on-Thames, 3–24.

Feldwick, P. (1996), 'Do we need "brand equity"?', *Journal of Brand Management*, **4**, (1), August, 9–28.

Hallberg, G. (1995), *All Consumers Are Not Created Equal*, John Wiley, New York.

Hopkins, C. (1968), *Scientific Advertising*, MacGibbon and Kee, London.

Jones, J.P. (1992), *How Much is Enough?* Lexington Books, New York, 1992, p.110 for references.

Jones, J.P. (1995), *When Ads Work*, Lexington Books, New York, p.28.

Lodish, L.M. and Lubetkin B. (1992), 'General truths? Nine key findings from IRI test data', *Admap*, **27**, 2, 9–15, February.

McDonald, C. (1970), 'What is the short term effect of advertising?' ESOMAR Congress, Barcelona, 1970; reprinted in *Market Researchers Look at Advertising*, edited by Simon Broadbent, Sigmatext for ESOMAR, 1980, pp.39–50.

McDonald, C. (1995), *Advertising Reach and Frequency*. NTC Business Books, Lincolnwood, Illinois, Chapter 4.

Skinner, B.F. (1972), *Beyond Reason and Dignity*, Jonathan Cape, London.

Wells, W., Burnett J. and Moriarty, S. (1992), *Advertising Principles and Practice*, Prentice Hall, Englewood Cliffs, NJ, p.258.

Index